Tennessee at the Crossroads

Tennessee at the Crossroads

The State Debt Controversy 1870-1883

Robert B. Jones

KNOXVILLE ⅃ᗡ THE UNIVERSITY OF TENNESSEE PRESS

Library of Congress Cataloging in Publication Data

Jones, Robert B   1942-
    Tennessee at the crossroads.

    Bibliography: p.
    Includes index.
    1. Debts, Public—Tennessee—History. 2. Tennessee—Politics and government—1865-1950. I. Title.
HJ8463.J65   336.3'4'09768   76-18820
ISBN 0-87049-198-9

to my Parents

Preface

Tennessee, like many other states, borrowed sizable amounts of money for internal improvements during the years between 1830 and 1860; the Civil War and Reconstruction, however, greatly altered the state's ability to repay these obligations. Wartime devastation, the enlargement of the debt by Republican administrations, and resentment of Republican policies during Reconstruction charged the debt issue with emotion and threw the problem into the political arena. Resurgent Democrats captured the legislature and the governor's mansion in 1869 and 1870, and thus began more than a dozen years of party struggle over how to retire the outstanding securities. Before the acceptance of a compromise settlement in 1883, the debt question managed to divide the party into two factions, soon appropriately called "state credit" and "low tax" Democrats.

The party leadership, attempting to establish a policy of payment in full, gained the support of city interests and some farmers. Many of the leading state credit Democrats were socially prominent and well-to-do with interests in railroads and large businesses, and of these many of the most influential were former Whigs. They maintained that only a dollar-for-dollar payment or a compromise settlement freely accepted by the creditors would be a just solution. Following the economic tenets of the New South, they argued that good credit was essential to attract the outside capital and immigrants so badly needed for economic growth and diversification. Republicans also supported the aims of the Democratic leadership, but even with this help, the debt remained a dilemma.

The other faction—residents of the economically depressed

agricultural areas of Democratic Middle and West Tennessee—
rejected what they felt was the excessively pro-business orientation of party leaders. These insurgents favored a massive
discounting of the debt, saying that the state had contracted
it illegally and that payment would require taxation which
would impoverish the average Tennessean. The cost of the
New South was too high; apparently only urban capitalists
and business interests would share in its boons.

Increasingly alienated by attempts of the state credit Democrats to settle the debt on their own terms, low tax men
eventually left the party. In 1880 they ran their own candidate for governor, so dividing the Democratic vote that a Republican was elected for the first time since Reconstruction.
Desire to regain the governor's chair, however, and the ac-
companying return of prosperity caused the Democrats to
unite in 1883 behind a compromise settlement that substantially scaled the outstanding indebtedness. The price of harmony was the state credit wing's abandonment of the New
South orientation and the redirection of party concerns toward the traditional Jacksonian emphasis—improving the
plight of the average farmer and laborer.

Assistance from a number of persons and organizations
made completion of this study possible. I am deeply indebted
to Professor V. Jacque Voegeli of Vanderbilt University, who
has provided constant advice and encouragement. Professor
Donald L. Winters of Vanderbilt improved these pages with
his criticisms, and my prose has benefited from the editorial
scrutiny of Miss Mary Lee Tipton. Mr. David Starnes and the
Learning Resources Center of Middle Tennessee State University aided in the preparation of the maps. Professor Robert E.
Corlew of Middle Tennessee State University gave me his
continued support.

I am most appreciative of the cooperation given me by the
staffs of the following libraries: Joint University Libraries
and Tennessee State Library and Archives, Nashville; Lawson
McGhee Library and University of Tennessee Library, Knoxville; Chattanooga Public Library; and Southern Historical
Collection, University of North Carolina, Chapel Hill. Grants

from the Tennessee Historical Commission, the American Council of Learned Societies from funds provided by the Andrew W. Mellon Foundation, and Middle Tennessee State University aided with publication. I wish to thank the Tennessee Historical Society for permission to reprint parts of my article, "1800–The Collapse of the Democratic Party," *Tennessee Historical Quarterly* (Spring 1974).

Finally, I cannot adequately express my gratitude to my wife, Roberta, whose typing and editorial help have been invaluable. Without her support this book would not have been completed.

Contents

TABLE AND MAPS

                 Crops, 1870-1879   *Page* 69

    Map 1.   Low Tax Vote in 1880   *116*

    Map 2.   Election of 1882   *141*

Tennessee at the Crossroads

Origins of the Debt

The state debt question—the dominant and most turbulent issue in Tennessee politics in the late 1870s and early 1880s—had roots stretching back five decades. In the 1820s and 1830s many states, including Tennessee, began programs of assistance to projects for internal improvements. To those Americans who were intent on rapidly developing and exploiting the resources of their country, governmental aid for the construction of canals, turnpikes, and railroads appeared essential. A shortage of capital, lack of experience in large-scale corporate enterprises, and the frequently slender or remote prospects of financial profit for investors deterred many private businesses from entering into such ventures and often hampered the efforts of those that did. To overcome these obstacles, state, federal, and local governments gave help in such forms as loans, stock purchases, land grants, and tax exemptions to underwrite the endeavors of private companies.[1]

Tennessee participated to some extent in this movement. The constitution of 1834 contained a clause that urged the General Assembly to assist transportation projects that would benefit the state. In response, the legislature in 1836 authorized the governor to purchase one-third of the stock of turnpike and railroad companies, and the next General Assembly allowed him to subscribe to as much as one-half of the stock of such companies. Results were discouraging; the Panic of 1837 and a combination of poor management and planning caused many of these companies to fold, and more than a decade elapsed before the state again ventured to support such enterprises. In 1848 the legislature purchased a portion of the

stock of the Nashville and Chattanooga Railroad and the East
Tennessee and Georgia Railroad with state bonds.[2]

Compared with other states, Tennessee's initial investment
of $1,162,167 in transportation projects was small. By 1841
state governments had allocated over $200 million in bonds
for canals, railroads, and turnpikes. The Panic of 1837 and
the depression that followed imposed severe financial problems on several states with large bonded debts. Pennsylvania,
Illinois, Maryland, Indiana, Mississippi, and Michigan, for instance, were unable to pay interest on their securities, although eventually all but Mississippi and Michigan discharged
their obligations. Tennessee avoided similar financial embar-
rassment because its debt was small. Benefits did accrue to
states that invested heavily, however; Pennsylvania, which
had the largest public debt of any state in 1841, could boast
of a network of 793 miles of canals and railroads, while Tennessee as late as 1850 had not one mile of operating railroad
track within its borders.[3]

The return of economic prosperity in the mid-1840s renewed demands for public support of transportation. In this
second surge of aid during the antebellum years, railroads received the most substantial help. States that had defaulted
earlier shunned further extension of public credit. In the late
1840s and 1850s it was the states of the South and West,
along with New York, that began to borrow heavily. Virginia
borrowed the largest sum, followed by Missouri and Tennessee. By 1860, Tennessee, with a debt of almost $21 million,
ranked fifth among the indebted states. Only Pennsylvania
with $38 million, New York with $33.5 million, Virginia
with $33 million, and Missouri with $26 million surpassed it.
Ten years later Tennessee advanced to second behind Virginia;
as late as 1902 it still stood third.[4] There was little wonder
that this indebtedness became an important issue in state politics for more than twenty years after 1860.

In 1852, Tennessee began to provide liberal support for
railroads. In that year the General Assembly passed an act
calling for the issuance of bonds to the railroads; in return,
Tennessee would receive a first lien on the company's proper-

ty. To be eligible for assistance, companies had to meet certain requirements. Each company must have graded and bridged a thirty-mile section of its line at either terminus, have no prior liens on its property, and have sufficient stock subscription to finance all the preparatory work for laying rails for the main trunk line planned for the state. Companies meeting these qualifications were to receive bonds not exceeding $8,000 per mile. The state was to issue these bonds in lots as the work progressed, and the railroads were to pay the interest on all bonds issued in their behalf. Five years after the line was completed, the company was to set aside annually for the state 1 percent of the sum borrowed; these monies were to be used as a sinking fund for the retirement of the bonds when they matured. Under no circumstances could the railroads sell the state bonds at below their par value, and officials of the lines were required to guarantee that the bonds would be used only for the purpose intended. If a railroad failed to make its interest payments, the governor could appoint a receiver to administer the line. Subsequent legislative acts raised the amount required for the sinking fund to 2 percent and then to 4 percent of the company's debt, allowed railroads to receive up to $10,000 in bonds per mile, and reaffirmed the right of the state to sell roads that defaulted.[5]

Until the Civil War, the system appeared to be working well. Railroad construction in Tennessee rose sharply, and the 1850s saw the completion of such valuable lines as the Memphis and Charleston, the East Tennessee and Virginia, and the East Tennessee and Georgia. The Louisville and Nashville, the Mobile and Ohio, the Nashville and Chattanooga, the Memphis and Ohio, and a number of other railroads received aid under the provisions of the new law. In 1860, Tennessee contained just 1,197 of the nation's 30,635 miles of railroad track, but among Southern states only Georgia and Virginia had larger rail systems.[6]

The state's debt in 1860 stood at $20,898,606. Assistance to railroads since 1852 accounted for the largest portion of the debt. The remainder, $3,894,606, had resulted from

earlier aid to railroads and turnpike companies, investments
in several banks, bonds issued in 1847 to cover the cost of
constructing the Capitol, bonds issued to purchase Andrew
Jackson's home, the Hermitage, and securities sold to enable
the Agricultural Bureau to erect a building on the State Fair
Grounds. Tennessee would not be liable for the railroad debt
unless the companies defaulted, and the prospects appeared
good for their expansion and profitable operation.[7]

The Civil War and Reconstruction era drastically altered
the nature and size of the debt, turning it into a burdensome
public obligation, and set the stage for it to become a burn-
ing political issue. The South suffered a tremendous financial loss in the Civil War. In 1860 the assessed valuation of
property in the region was $4,363,030,347 (including
$1,634,105,341 for slaves); in 1865 it had declined by 33
percent to $2,917,105,731. In 1860 the Southern states
owed debts of about $90 million and held around $70 million
in trust funds and other accounts that represented assets. But
by 1865 their debts had reached approximately $112 million,
while assets had declined to an estimated $33 million. Ten-
nessee's experience was typical. Its residents lost slave property alone worth $114,976,374. In 1870 the state produced
181,842 bales of cotton as compared to 296,464 bales in
1860, and the corn crop failed to meet the 1860 total of
52,089,926 bushels by more than 10.5 million bushels. The
tobacco harvest in 1870 was 50 percent lower than that of
1860, and the value of all livestock was approximately $5
million less than the 1860 figure of $60,211,425. All taxable
property in Tennessee was valued at $389,047,352 in 1860,
and the average value per acre of land was $8.13; in 1865 tax-
able property valuation had fallen drastically to a total of
$194,849,387, and the average value per acre for land was
$6.09. Two years later the assessed value of taxable property
was still more than $130 million below the 1860 level. Not
until 1892 did the total assessed value of all taxable property
in the state exceed the 1860 figure.[8]

The war years also gave rise to the major political organizations that would attempt to deal with the debt problem for

nearly two decades after 1865. East Tennessee, a Whig party stronghold before the war, opposed secession and harbored Unionist sentiments throughout the struggle. Middle and West Tennessee, where the Democratic party was most powerful, supported secession and the Confederacy. The defeat of General John B. Hood's Confederate forces near Nashville in December 1864 opened the way for formal organization of a Unionist government under the direction of the military governor, Andrew Johnson. Johnson called on loyalists, the majority of whom were East Tennesseans and prewar Whigs, to establish a civil government and assume control of state offices. In early 1865, Unionists approved amendments to the state constitution that abolished slavery, annulled the state's secession ordinance, and nullified the actions of its Confederate government. William G. Brownlow, an East Tennessee newspaper editor and prewar Whig, was elected governor in March, and a Unionist legislature took power at the same time.[9]

The political and financial policies of the Brownlow administration in the late 1860s set the stage for the struggles over the debt in the following ten years. Under Brownlow's leadership, the legislature enfranchised blacks, disfranchised ex-Confederates, and ratified the Fourteenth Amendment to the United States Constitution, assuring all citizens equal protection under the law. Congress rewarded this zeal by readmitting Tennessee to the Union in 1866. Negro suffrage and the disfranchisement of ex-Confederates and their supporters insured Brownlow's election to a second term in 1867 and also Unionist control of the legislature. Increasing dissent in Unionist ranks, however, was evident throughout Brownlow's administration. The terms "Radical" and "Conservative," already in use in 1865, designated the two poles of Unionist attitudes. The Radical faction had endorsed the wartime actions of the federal government and supported the Brownlow administration after the war. The Conservative Unionists, on the other hand, had been less enthusiastic about the policies of the Lincoln administration, and the faction became increasingly dissatisfied with the activities of the Radicals led

by Brownlow. Conservatives, whose leaders were mostly former Whigs, generally opposed the disfranchisement of ex-
Confederates, the ratification of the Fourteenth Amendment,
enfranchisement of the Negro, and Brownlow's use of the
state militia to suppress disorders and maintain his ascendancy. In April 1867 at a Nashville convention the Conservatives formally organized as a political party on the state level.
Their ranks were further increased by those who disapproved
of the Radicals' merger with and endorsement of the national
Republican party. Approval of the impeachment of President
Johnson by Brownlow and his followers also caused many of
Johnson's followers to join the Conservatives.[10]

Brownlow's fiscal policy, especially his handling of the
state debt, became very controversial in the Reconstruction
period. When Brownlow took office, he confronted an array
of pressing financial problems. Tennessee had been a battlefield for four years during the Civil War, and the armies of
both sides had inflicted a heavy toll in property destruction
and loss of life. At the war's end, returning Union and Confederate soldiers frequently found their homes and barns
burned, their fences down, their livestock missing, and much
of the railroad system damaged or destroyed. Many Tennesseans faced a desperate struggle for existence. Return to normality was slow because thousands had lost their businesses
and slaves and had little more than worthless Confederate
currency to show for their prewar labors. A lack of credit and
monetary resources, the onset of guerrilla activity in some
areas, and problems that accompanied the transition of slaves
to freedom hampered recovery. A postwar crime wave in certain locales and Unionist harassment of ex-Confederates in
East Tennessee delayed the restoration of order.[11]

Against this gloomy background, however, Governor
Brownlow struck a note of optimism. In 1865 he predicted
that in three years the state would be able to meet its operating expenses and pay interest on its bonded debt. While in
office, Brownlow supported the creation of a bureau of immigration to attract new settlers and called for the diversification of Tennessee's economy through the development of

mining and manufacturing enterprises.[12]

But despite Brownlow's hopes and plans, Tennessee's financial situation was not destined for speedy improvement. A defective and inefficient revenue structure handicapped efforts to restore the state's solvency. Property assessments were often unequal and far below market value, revenue officers were frequently irresponsible, and penalties for nonpayment of taxes were not stringent enough to encourage promptness. In 1867 the comptroller described some of the flaws in the system. The process of assessing property, he wrote in significant hyperbole, was "a farce" because revenue officials "wholly disregarded" the requirement to assess property at its true value. Many assessors determined property value from lists twenty to thirty years old and never personally inspected the property. The system of selling land for unpaid taxes in many cases cost the state large sums in sales fees to revenue officials. No state, the comptroller concluded, had or would "attain to a healthy and prosperous financial condition that was trammelled [sic], clogged and cursed with such a system of revenue laws . . . as have for years, and still affect our State."[13] The total amount of delinquent taxes in January 1868 was $996,022 and, despite at least one attempt to stiffen penalties for nonpayment, was more than $1.2 million by 1871.[14] In 1869 the treasurer of the state lamented that "little money [was] being received, while warrants [were] being constantly issued upon the treasury." At the time, the treasury contained $28,649.93, while warrants against the state totaled $297,815.71.[15]

Inadequacies in the tax assessment and collection structure, coupled with the increased expenditures required to implement the programs of the Radicals, aggravated Tennessee's desperate financial situation. Under the Brownlow government, the property tax rose from twenty-five cents per $100 of assessed valuation in 1865 to sixty cents on $100 in 1869. In addition, the total value of property for taxes grew under the Republicans from $214,446,241 in 1866 to $223,936,687 in 1869. The General Assembly set records for the length of its sessions, and the taxpayers bore the cost of these meet-

ings. In the 1867 election campaign, the state paid $100,000
to finance militia activities. Popular resentment of rising
taxes and public expenditures was exceeded by an even
stronger dislike for the Brownlow administration's handling
of an inherited problem—the bonded debt of Tennessee.[16]

At the end of the war, the state's railroad system was di-
lapidated. Much of the rolling stock, track, and other capital
of the companies had been destroyed. Governor Brownlow
called for extension of aid to Tennessee railroads on the
grounds that a prosperous rail network was vital to general
economic recovery. Also, in his first message to the legislature in 1865, he warned that Tennessee would ultimately be
liable for over $16 million of railroad debt if the companies
were unable to honor their obligations, and he urged the legislature to take steps to pay interest on bonds still unpaid
from the war years. In October the comptroller reported that
because of the war, all of the railroads had defaulted on their
interest payments; as of January 1866 this overdue interest
would amount to $4,320,187. Contending that neither the
state nor the railroads could meet this debt, the comptroller
advised the legislature to permit new bonds to be issued for
the unpaid interest. He warned that placing the delinquent
lines in receivership would further diminish their value, thus
jeopardizing Tennessee's investment in them.[17]

Responding to the administration's prodding, the legislature passed a funding act that allowed the governor to issue
new bonds for any amount needed to pay all bonds and interest due and overdue as of January 1, 1866, and any bonds
that might fall due during 1867. The new securities, bearing
an annual interest rate of 6 percent and dated January 1,
1866, would mature on January 1, 1892.[18] Early in 1866 the
commissioner of railroads recommended that the legislature
take action to "protect the interests of the State, giving them
[railroads] timely aid, as will enable them to meet the requirements of business and travel in the country, and thus regain a prosperous condition."[19] Subsequently, the legislature
authorized the governor to issue more bonds to nearly all the
state's railroads under the requirements and conditions of the

1852 law. The provisions of these laws allowed Tennessee to
issue approximately $9 million in new securities.[20]

If the Radicals had gone no further with their financial
support of railroad companies, the course of Tennessee politics in the 1870s might have been quite different; but the law
that extended aid in the spring of 1866 was just the beginning of a chain of acts giving assistance to these lines. In December of that year a bill passed the legislature granting aid
to ten railroads in the form of state bonds in the amount of
$2,550,000. A year later the "Omnibus Bill" allocated about
$3.7 million in securities to more than a dozen railroads. Sub-
sequent measures increased the state's financial commitment
to railroads and turnpikes. All too often the lines that received assistance did not prosper and were unable either to
pay the interest on the new bonds or to contribute to the
sinking fund. At the same time, Tennessee could not redeem
maturing bonds and pay the interest on the outstanding securities. To satisfy these obligations, the state issued new bonds
to exchange for old securities now maturing and to meet interest payments on previous issues. In December 1868 the
concerned comptroller, noting that there was a bill in the
legislature calling for a further increase in the bonded debt,
urged the house of representatives to halt the expansion of
indebtedness, declaring that it would seriously damage Tennessee's standing in New York financial circles. The railroad debt,
including interest, he estimated, was now $34,441,873.44.[21]

Under the Brownlow administrations and that of his Republican successor, DeWitt C. Senter, railroads received approximately $14,393,000 and turnpikes $113,000 between
1865 and 1870. Bonds were issued by the General Assembly
to assist these companies in repairing war damage and under-
taking new construction that the lawmakers deemed benefi-
cial. Furthermore, all of the railroads supposedly met the requirements and guidelines set forth in the internal improvements act of 1852 and its subsequent amendments. In actual
fact, however, the legislature sometimes violated this statute.
Apparently, greed as well as concern for economic recovery
and the public welfare contributed to the state's largess and

overrode strict adherence to the letter of the law. These actions led Democratic legislatures in 1870 and 1879 to conduct probes of the origin of the debt. Although the investigations were incomplete and failed to reveal the exact extent of fraud and bribery connected with the bonds, they did uncover enough evidence of such activities to cause many Tennesseans to question the validity of the debt. The investigations revealed that railroad officials and their agents and lobbyists had used a variety of inducements such as money, new clothes, and alcohol to persuade the legislators to assist them and to disregard the antebellum legal requirements applicable to aid. Insolvent railroads received bonds and sold them at below par value, using the proceeds for purposes other than those for which they were intended. Joseph A. Mabry, head of the Knoxville and Kentucky Railroad, told a legislative investigative committee that Brownlow received $5,000 to insure his support for the railroads' demands for aid. Among other leading railroad lobbyists trying to influence lawmakers in this period were Mabry's close associate, C. M. McGhee, M. D. Bearden of the Knoxville and Charleston, and Thomas H. Calloway of the East Tennessee and Georgia.[22]

The most flagrant case of fraud against the state involved the Mineral Home Railroad. Although this road received $100,000 in bonds, it never laid a mile of track. Indeed, the route was not even surveyed. The line was to have begun on Stone Mountain on the North Carolina border, about fifty miles from the nearest railroad connection, and run through a sparsely settled part of Johnson County to the Virginia boundary, ending at a point some twenty miles from any other railroad. While railroads were supposed to receive no more than $10,000 in bonds per mile, Mabry's Knoxville and Kentucky line was awarded $60,000 for each mile of its track. Moreover, his company obtained $2,350,000 in bonds, while its capital from other sources amounted to only $378,911.55. Eventually, even Brownlow became concerned about the state's policy toward railroads. In 1868 he charged that there was a conspiracy to depress the value of the bonds for specu-

lative gain. Declaring his opposition to further aid except in
cases where Tennessee had a vital interest in the completion
of the line, he recommended the sale of delinquent roads. He
placed several lines in the hands of receivers, but these failed
to prosper.[23]

Brownlow's belated efforts to alter state policy did not
halt mounting public and political opposition to his administration's actions in extending aid to railroads. In August 1868,
Captain J. H. Raht of Ducktown, Tennessee, received a letter
advising him to press for organization of the Cleveland and
Duck Town Rail Road Company as soon as possible so that it
might apply for aid. The letter implied that the legislature at
its fall session might yield to pressures to stop further increase of the debt.[24] But decisive action did not come until
December 1869, when a Conservative-controlled legislature
passed an act repealing all laws granting aid to internal improvements and declaring that "no further or additional State
aid [should] be granted or issued to any railroad or turnpike
company in this State."[25] In October 1869 the comptroller
placed the total bonded indebtedness at $39,212,211.55. He
estimated that the turnpike and railroad debt of the 1850s
and 1860s constituted $34,639,084.89 of this sum, while
those portions of the debt contracted before the railroad
boom of the 1850s and for purposes other than transportation accounted for the remaining $4,573,159.66.[26]

The large debt was not a home-owned obligation. While
exact information on the owners of Tennessee's securities is
apparently not extant, it seems clear that most of the bonds
were held by nonresidents. In 1866 the Brownlow administration revealed that of 3,862 bonds for which they had the
owners' addresses, only 966 were held by Tennesseans, while
New York investors held 2,045. Educational and charitable
institutions in Tennessee did own $619,000 worth of bonds,
however, and the correspondence of the governors' and
comptrollers' offices from 1865 to 1883 contains a few letters from Tennessee bondholders. Former President James K.
Polk's wife owned twenty-nine securities. The amount of the
debt owned abroad is uncertain, but one very large British

investor, represented by a New York agent, held $1.1 million in bonds in 1882. It was, in fact, to New York creditors and brokers that the state turned when attempting to settle the debt in the 1870s and 1880s. In 1882 a New York association of Tennessee creditors claimed to represent owners of more than half the outstanding debt, and the state did not challenge this claim. The fact that outsiders owned much of the debt weakened the influence of the creditors on politicians and public opinion in Tennessee in the years after Reconstruction and aroused the hostility of many natives toward the bondholders.[27]

In February 1869, Brownlow resigned the governorship to accept a seat in the United States Senate, and DeWitt C. Senter, speaker of the state senate, assumed the duties of chief executive. A native of McMinn County and a prewar Whig, Senter desired election in his own right in the fall of 1869. William B. Stokes, former Whig congressman and well-known Union general in the war and currently a Republican congressman, sought the Republican nomination as well. Personal ambition rather than ideological differences kept both men in the field, with the result that, despite attempts by Brownlow and others to preserve harmony, the Republican state convention split. A portion of the divided meeting nominated each man, and both Senter and Stokes claimed to be the legitimate candidate of the party. Worried about the strength of his opponent, Senter adopted a policy designed to win him the support of Conservatives and appreciative ex-rebels—he called for the removal of suffrage restrictions on former Confederate soldiers and their supporters. To implement this policy, he began to replace all county commissioners of registration who desired the continued enforcement of franchise restrictions. Instead of running their own candidate for governor as they had in 1867, Conservatives backed Senter. Ex-Confederates, who had long favored the Conservative cause, could now vote, and their support enabled the governor to win easily by a vote of 120,333 to 55,036. In the legislature, only eight Stokes Republicans were elected to thirteen Senter Republicans and seventy-nine Conservatives.[28]

The Conservative-controlled General Assembly soon began to repeal Radical laws it considered objectionable. In addition to ending further aid to railroads, the legislature in January 1870 amended a Radical measure passed nearly a year before that allowed railroad companies to discharge any part of their obligations by presenting to the state bonds issued for their benefit. The Conservative law authorized the indebted lines to present the bonds of *any* series issued by the state to discharge all or part of their obligations. This act permitted the companies to buy up the most depreciated securities available and to receive full face value credit for these in reducing their indebtedness. The measure was designed to offer the railroads a means by which they could reduce the amount they owed and at the same time trim the debt by decreasing the amount of bonds outstanding. It proved to be a great boon to solvent railroads, which often purchased depreciated issues at far below their face value to utilize in discharging their obligations. Tennessee benefited in that this procedure appreciably lowered its bonded indebtedness. Under the provisions of this measure, the state received and retired some $11 million in bonds. Investors, however, apparently had little faith in Tennessee's willingness to honor securities of the Brownlow era because these bonds consistently brought lower prices than prewar issues. Railroads generally bought these cheaper postwar bonds to turn in to the state.[29]

Following the election of Senter and the legislature, the voters approved a call for a constitutional convention in December 1869. The Conservative-dominated convention, which assembled in January 1870, drafted a new constitution which was ratified by the people in March. It removed Radical restrictions on suffrage for adult males, while the Negro's right to vote, despite some debate, was not taken from him. The new provision for a poll tax, however, proved to be an indirect limitation on poor voters, both black and white. Other changes in the constitution were designed to prevent the re-emergence of many of Brownlow's detested policies.[30] In the area of finances, the proposed constitution explicitly prohibited the further extension of aid to private or public enterprises, declaring, "The credit of this State shall not be hereafter loaned or given to or in aid of any person, association, company, corporation, or municipality . . . ." Tennessee was also banned from becoming a stockholder or owner, singly or with others, in any company or municipality.[31]

Reflecting the convention's desire to reverse the state's internal improvements policies, the legislature took steps to sell railroads delinquent in their interest payments. Governor Senter had recommended such action in the fall of 1869, and in July 1870 the legislature designated the governor, the secretary of state, the comptroller, and three other citizens—Robert J. McKinney of Knox County, Francis B. Fogg of Davidson County, and Archibald Wright of Shelby County—to serve as railroad commissioners. It became the duty of these men to sell those lines that had failed for two consecutive years to pay the interest on their bonds. Despite some legal complications and a failure to get bidders for some of the roads, by 1872 Tennessee had sold eleven railroads for $6,698,000. The sales figure represented a loss of about $7,950,000, compared with the state's original investment in these lines.[32]

In summary, the years 1865 to 1869 were unsettling ones for Tennesseans. Political dissension was widespread, as Brownlow and his Unionist followers developed and applied their policies. Each step in the construction of the postwar government seemed to generate division in the Unionist ranks, and the result was the development of a Conservative Unionist party opposed to the actions of the Radical Republicans. In the background were the ex-Confederates, disfranchised by the Brownlow government, but continually working in closer harmony with the Conservative Unionists and supporting the latter's efforts to overthrow the Brownlow administration. Senter's removal of Radical voting restrictions on the former rebels won him the grateful support of these men and the endorsement of the Conservative Unionists; the backing of these groups and his own Republican followers enabled him to defeat Stokes. But enfranchised Confederates greatly enlarged the ranks of the Conservative party, and this party now held the majority of Tennessee voters. It would not again support a Republican candidate for governor.

Brownlow's policy of extending liberal state aid to transportation companies was to have a tremendous impact on Tennessee finances and politics: no single aspect of his administration, except for his actions in disfranchising former Confederates, would provoke more angry controversies in the years to come. The new constitution offered franchise provisions that were satisfactory to those who opposed Brownlow's suffrage restrictions, but the debt problem was not so easily solved. It became an albatross around the neck of each successive Democratic administration.

CHAPTER II

The Funding Act

Although signs of its importance emerged earlier, the debt question first became a significant political issue in 1870. In preparation for the upcoming gubernatorial election, both the Conservative and the Republican parties held state conventions in September in Nashville. Former Confederate General John C. Brown was the unanimous nominee of Conservative delegates, who drew up a platform that did not mention the bonded debt. The platform did, however, denounce the Republican administration in Washington and support the Northern Democratic party in its opposition to Radical policies. Because of this alliance and the increasing prominence of prewar Democrats in the ranks, the term "Democratic" rapidly replaced the party name "Conservative" in the early 1870s.[1] Unlike their Democratic counterparts, delegates to the Republican convention took a firm stand on the debt question. Their platform pledged their party to the "payment of every dollar of state and national indebtedness." Their nominee for governor, William H. Wisener of Bedford County, echoed this sentiment, emphatically endorsing full payment of the state debt.[2]

In these two candidates, the governor's race pitted two prewar Whigs against one another. Wisener had served four terms in the General Assembly before the war and was a member of both Brownlow legislatures. Brown, a native of Giles County and the brother of former Whig Governor Neil S. Brown, was a successful lawyer before the war. He became active in politics in 1860 when he served as an elector for the Bell-Everett presidential ticket. Although Brown at first opposed secession, he enlisted in the Confederate army as a private and, by the end of the war, had risen to the rank of major general. An early member of the Ku Klux Klan, Brown opposed Governor Brownlow's Reconstruction policies and became an active supporter of the Democratic party. In 1875, after serving two terms as governor, he became a director of the Memphis and Knoxville Railroad and vice president of the Texas and Pacific Railroad. In the 1880s he served as general solicitor for all of Jay Gould's lines west of the Mississippi and headed the powerful Tennessee Coal, Iron, and Railroad Company. This business-minded politician had definite ideas about the debt problem and how the state should solve it.[3]

Although the Democratic platform for 1870 did not mention the question of the state's bonded indebtedness, Arthur S. Colyar, a member of Brown's own party, forced the nominee to face the problem. The day after the convention, Colyar announced that Brown had failed to address himself to the issues of the state debt, Tennessee's need for immigrants, reconciliation with the North, and the employment of convicts; therefore, Colyar would continue his candidacy for governor as an independent. This action was characteristic of the man. A native of Washington County, he was a prewar Whig who had opposed secession but supported his state's Confederate government and represented Tennessee in the Confederate congress at Richmond. During the Brownlow era, he disapproved of Radical policies and led the opposition to Nashville's Radical mayor, A. E. Alden. By 1870, Colyar was well known politically, and his Nashville-based legal practice was thriving. His influence, however, did not rest solely on his political and legal activities. Soon after the Civil War, he reorganized the Tennessee Coal, Iron, and Railroad Company and assumed its presidency. Under his leadership this corporation became the largest industrial concern in the state. In addition, he was a major stockholder in the Nashville and Chattanooga Railroad and served for a time as vice president of the Tennessee Manufacturing Company, a Nashville cotton mill. His wealth, legal skill, and business acumen, coupled with his seemingly boundless energy, made him a formidable force in business and political circles.[4]

Wisener made repudiation a campaign issue by warning of its dangers, but Brown gave the Republicans no grounds for charges that the Democrats opposed paying the debt.[5] Debating with Colyar in early October, Brown rejected repudiation, saying that the state was "bound to pay all bonds issued according to law with interest" and that he was willing to allow the railroads to continue presenting bonds to the state to retire their debt. Appealing to state pride, he declared opposition to the sale of railroads to "foreign monopolies and speculators."[6] Colyar retired from the race after this debate, saying that he and Brown agreed on the state's need for immigrants and the advantages of the convict lease system. In addition, Colyar expressed approval of Brown's indication that he would not resurrect the old states' rights doctrine on secession. Colyar failed to mention, however, that he differed with Brown on the idea of full debt payment; in Colyar's view the oppressive taxes required by such a policy would hinder the flow of capital and immigrants into Tennessee and depress the state's economy.[7]

Colyar's withdrawal assured Democratic unity, and the party won easily. Brown gathered 78,979 votes to Wisener's 41,500. The main issue was the Republican record under the administrations of governors Brownlow and Senter. Civil War animosities also contributed to the outcome, as most of Brown's supporters had been Confederates while former Unionists made up Wisener's party. Pride in the Lost Cause, distaste for the actions of the Radicals in Washington and Tennessee after the war, and a determination to prevent the Republicans from regaining power in the state all combined to unite the majority of Tennesseans behind Brown. In this election, the main outline of the political divisions in the state emerged—divisions that were to dominate Tennessee political behavior until the mid-twentieth century. Middle and West Tennessee, where Confederate sympathies had predominated, became the stronghold of the Democrats while East Tennessee, a bastion of Unionism, remained the center of Republican influence. The Democrats not only gained the governor's mansion in 1870; they also secured solid majorities in both houses of the legislature.[8]

Democrats were elated at the results of the election, for the returns seemed to indicate that most Tennesseans were loyal Democrats and that the Republicans would never be more than a minority party. But the Democratic party contained many different elements: prewar Democrats and Whigs, including those who had backed secession and a number of persons who had supported the federal government in the Civil War but had broken with the Republicans during Reconstruction (former President Andrew Johnson was the most prominent Unionist Democrat); large and small farmers; businessmen and industrialists; men who yearned for a return of the Old South; others who faced toward the New. Thus beneath the unity of their oppostion to Radical Republicanism lay the potential for division. Colyar had threatened the cohesion of the ranks in the midst of the party's effort to unseat the Republicans and had pointed out a basic difference between his views on the debt and those of Brown. This difference still remained essentially unresolved.[9]

Although victorious, Brown and the Democratic coalition, under the terms of the new constitution, would not begin administration of state affairs until October 1871. In the meantime, the legislature that met from May to mid-July 1870 and from December 1870 to early February 1871 cut the property tax rate—only to have to raise it later to meet expenses—and investigated Brownlow's bond policy. The lawmakers continued to sell delinquent railroads but did little else to deal with the debt problem, while the passage of time worsened the state's financial condition.[10] In December 1870 the comptroller reported that Tennessee was living beyond its income and was "relying upon the ruinous policy of borrowing to supply the deficit."[11] Eleven months later the treasurer declared that only by borrowing had the state been able to keep its three eleemosynary institutions in operation.[12]

Brown faced serious fiscal problems when he assumed the governorship in 1871, but he was determined to uphold the integrity of the state by retiring the matured bonds and paying past-due interest with a new series of bonds. The legisla-

ture took no action during his first term, although it still continued selling delinquent railroads and provided for the can-
cellation of bonds presented by railroad lines.[13] In January
1872 the governor wrote a Maryland bondholder that, in
spite of the General Assembly's having failed to provide for
debt payment, he was sure that the legislature to assemble in
January 1873 would adopt a plan funding all matured bonds
and coupons in new 6 percent securities and providing for interest coming due after 1873. He went on to explain that
"Carpet Baggers and adventures [*sic*], whose object was plun-
der" had created the debt problem, but that Tennessee would
not repudiate a penny of its obligation. Be patient, he advised,
"and you will not loose [*sic*] a dollar."[14]

In the 1872 gubernatorial race, Republican candidate A. A.
Freeman and Colyar, again an independent candidate, both
charged that Tennessee had avoided facing the debt problem.
Brown, however, in his bid for reelection, defended the fiscal
record of his administration and called for action on the
debt. He declared that while he was in office government expenses had been significantly reduced and the penitentiary
put on a paying basis. He criticized the bond-issuing policy of
the Republicans during Reconstruction, saying that millions
of bond dollars had produced only 100 miles of railroad
track.[15] Brown insisted that all of the matured debt and interest must be funded in a new series of state bonds. Convinced that Tennessee ought to pay every cent it owed, he
condemned those who might embrace the "odious doctrine
of repudiation" to gain political power. They would fully de-
serve "all the infamy that it would heap upon them."[16]

Brown withstood a strong Republican effort to unseat
him, gaining a second term by 97,700 votes to Freeman's
89,089.[17] Soon after the election, newspapers began speculating about the next legislature's response to the governor's
plan. The Democratic Nashville *Union and American* in December 1872 interpreted a rise in the value of Tennessee securities on the New York market to mean that holders of
these bonds were confident that the state would soon pay its
debt. The editor stated that he knew of no legislator or legis-

lative candidate in the last election who opposed improved
state credit. In fact, he knew of "no state in the Union more
able or more willing to pay than Tennessee."[18] On New
Year's Day 1873 another Democratic paper, the Nashville
Republican Banner, echoed the same sentiment when the
editor predicted that the coming legislature would act on the
matter because that body had a "business sense" and realized
that "the commercial future of the State" depended upon
payment of the debt.[19]

The governor officially brought the debt problem to the
attention of the legislators in his January message to the General
Assembly. He placed the amount of the bonded debt,
including unpaid interest, at $30,732,200.76 as of the first
of the year; the amount due from solvent railroads plus proceeds
from the sale of delinquent lines would reduce this figure
to an estimated $21,362,654.31. Past-due interest constituted
$4 million and would probably increase by $1 million
per year so long as Tennessee failed to pay interest. A number
of bonds had matured, and more would soon come due.
Brown told the lawmakers that the problem of debt payment
could not "upon any pretext, justifiable either before the
world or before the enlightened public sentiment of Tennessee,
be longer postponed."[20]

Declaring that Tennessee could not pay the entire debt immediately
without burdening the people unduly, Brown again
proposed to fund the matured debt and the past-due interest
coupons in a new series of bonds to mature in forty years at
a 6 percent annual interest rate. This plan of exchanging old
bonds for new, he hoped, would allow a check against state
records of bonds presented for funding, thus enabling state
officials to detect any securities that had been issued illegally.
Consolidating the matured bonded debt in a single new series
of bonds would also help to remove some of the confusion
caused by frequent legislative acts. The governor asked the
General Assembly to decide whether to pay interest on matured
bonds for the interval between their date of maturity
and that of the new funding by the legislature. He urged reform
of the laws on tax assessment and revenue collection,

asserting that such measures would enable the state to meet current expenses and pay the interest on the debt.[21]

Nearly a month later, the legislature had not acted, but Governor Brown was still optimistic. He privately assured "Messrs. Bohn & Brother" of Philadelphia that he had recommended funding in the "strongest terms" to the current General Assembly and he trusted that a finance bill would pass.[22] Impatient, the Nashville *Union and American* asked the legislature to face its responsibilities and provide for payment. It also charged that legislative procrastination on the matter endangered the state's credit and that, if the General Assembly should refuse "to pass a plain, practical, emphatic funding bill, or should they pass one ambiguous in its terms, filled with ifs and buts, and hedged with doubts, it [would] be regarded as the first step toward repudiation."[23] On February 13 someone writing anonymously to the Memphis *Daily Avalanche* expressed disgust that the legislature had used up half its session and still had accomplished little. In this correspondent's opinion, the people wanted "less demagoging" and "more legislating."[24] Signs of resistance surfaced, however, as some legislators expressed doubts that the state should be responsible for paying the railroad bonds.[25] A pessimistic Nashville observer reported on February 15 that, although few in the General Assembly favored repudiation of the debt, the funding proposal was "finding little favor" with the "intelligent, thinking classes" and concluded that no funding bill would pass.[26]

As if to prove this prophet wrong, the senate soon began debate on a debt settlement bill. Democratic Senator E. A. James, representing Hamilton and seven other southeastern counties, introduced a measure that called for funding the matured bonds and interest through June 1874 in a new series of securities that would mature in forty years and bear 6 percent interest. On February 25 the senate Committee on Finance, Ways, and Means reported the James bill favorably with an amendment that specifically excluded from the provisions of the measure any securities or interest coupons from bonds issued to assist the state's Confederate government. In late February and early March debate in the upper house centered on the wisdom of funding and on the James bill.[27]

Opposition to the administration's funding plan came from the governor's own party, as two Democratic senators contended that the proposal would impose too great a financial burden on Tennessee. J. C. McCall, representing four West Tennessee counties, argued that the state had been devastated by the war and was not able to pay the debt and meet the other financial demands of government operation. He insisted that the proposed measure would necessitate a property tax rate of more than $1.00 per $100 valuation, which the people could not afford.[28] McCall believed that the state should delay attempts to pay and that creditors should wait until "we become a prosperous people in the sense of the term as used by the people of the North, who suffered nothing by the war—then, and not till then, will we meet these liabilities . . . ." His Democratic colleague, Middle Tennessee Senator Noble Smithson, also charged that Tennessee was financially unable to fund. He proposed that the state establish a special account for the purposes of making payments on interest that would come due in the future and of retiring overdue bonds and coupons as rapidly as possible.[29]

Members of the upper house who favored the measure asserted that funding was necessary and that the state could assume the cost. Senator J. M. Coulter of West Tennessee, who had earlier proposed a funding bill of his own, contended that the James bill would not require higher taxes. Middle Tennessee Democrat James D. Richardson agreed and informed his colleagues that passage of the bill was vital to ensure the development of Tennessee's natural resources and to attract immigrants. On the final day of debate, James defended his bill, denying that it was designed to benefit the state's creditors. The senate passed the measure by a vote of fourteen—nine Democrats, four Republicans, and one independent—to ten. Seven of the advocates of funding were from Middle Tennessee. Democrats cast five of the ten opposing votes, along with three Republicans and two independents. Half of the dissenting legislators were from West Tennessee, four from Middle Tennessee, and one from East Tennessee.[30]

On March 10 the house Committee on Ways and Means, chaired by Republican L. C. Houk, representing Knox and Anderson counties in East Tennessee, reported the recently passed senate bill and with but one dissenting vote recommended passage.[31] Three days later, Democratic Representative J. F. Brown of Shelby County filed a minority committee report, asserting that the "already tax-ridden people" of the state could not assume the additional burden that funding would entail. The measure would make their children "hewers of wood and drawers of water" for capitalists and bondholders, he declared, and it would only temporarily silence the "cry of shylark [sic], at our heals [sic], for the last pound of flesh."[32] In the ensuing debates, other opponents of funding expressed opposition to the James bill in similar terms.[33] Democrat J. H. Jamison of Rutherford County warned that passage would create a "bonded monopoly reared here in our midst that [would] hold in its iron grasp and chain down the true interests of the people."[34]

Like their senate counterparts, opponents of funding in the house also objected to the proposal because they feared it would make legal and binding those portions of the debt that they regarded as improperly, fraudulently, and illegally contracted. Representative J. F. Brown estimated that Tennessee legitimately owed less than one-third of the outstanding debt, while Jamison cited violations of the internal improvements law of 1852 and insisted that the state avoid payment of a fraudulent debt.[35] West Tennessee Democrat Holmes Cummins declared that state aid had been dispensed with a "lavish hand" and "squandered" on certain parts of the state, and insisted that the state attorney-general be empowered to examine each bond to determine its legality.[36]

Nevertheless, opponents of the measure were outnumbered. Houk, originally opposed to the bill, spoke for it on the final day of debate.[37] Those against it, he charged, had mentioned rings and speculators so often that it frequently seemed that they objected more to the ownership of property and the right of a government to tax its citizens than to the legislation under consideration. He reviewed the history of the debt and argued that the money of the much-maligned bondholder had enabled Tennessee to grow, develop, and prosper. The Capitol, the railroad system, the schools and asylums, and other improvements were made possible by people now being denounced as "sharks and thieves" and " 'bloated bondholders.' " He referred to Britain's struggle to remain solvent and reminded his listeners that British securities were now among the most prized in the world. The real question was one of "right and justice"; he called on all, regardless of party, to do the fair thing and leave an honorable heritage to their children.[38] His views were representative of those who supported the bill, and, significantly, the state's leading Democratic journal, the Nashville *Union and American,* pronounced his speech the finest of the whole legislative session.[39]

At its third reading, the bill passed the house forty-four to twenty-four, nearly a two-to-one margin. The party affiliation of all but one of the lawmakers who voted affirmatively can be determined. Twenty-three Democrats, seventeen Republicans, and three independents supported the debt plan. Twenty-one represented Middle Tennessee constituencies; seventeen were from East Tennessee and five from West Tennessee. Fourteen Democrats, seven Republicans, and three independents opposed the bill. Five of the opponents were from Middle Tennessee, four from East Tennessee, and fourteen from West Tennessee; one came from a district that straddled the boundary between Middle and West Tennessee.[40]

The statute called for the funding of all legally issued bonds of the state now due or to be due before January 1, 1874, as well as all overdue coupons and coupons to be due on or before January 1, 1874. The new bonds would carry 6 percent interest, payable semiannually, and would mature in forty years, although the state had the option of redeeming them at any time after July 1, 1884. The act excluded Confederate bonds. To provide some regular income for the struggling public school system in the state, the law authorized a single bond in the amount of $2,512,500, which would be held by the state, with the interest distributed to the schools. Provisions were made for keeping a strict account of bonds issued, and coupons on bonds that matured after July 1, 1874, were not to be paid until these bonds had been examined for legality and registered. In order to inspire the confidence of Tennessee's creditors, the new law pledged the "faith, honor and credit" of the state to the payment of these securities and required the treasurer to set aside for this exclusive purpose as much revenue as needed to meet the interest payments that would begin in July 1874.[41]

The passage of the bill was a major victory for the Brown administration. With the help of Republican lawmakers, most of whom stood by their party's platform pledge to support full debt payment, the governor and his supporters were able to enact a program designed to honor the outstanding bonds. Republicans and Democrats who favored the bill regarded it as vital to the encouragement of economic growth and development in Tennessee. In addition, many Democrats saw the measure as an honest fiscal policy that would further their goal of administering the state frugally and forthrightly, in sharp contrast to the actions of the preceding Republican administrations. In the legislature, most Democrats followed the lead of their governor; opponents of funding were mainly Middle and West Tennessee Democrats who contended that the cost of refinancing the debt was too great for impoverished Tennessee. Moreover, they objected to the payment of bonds that they believed were fraudulently issued in the Brownlow era. Although the Republican minority had established a working coalition with the independents and a group of Democrats who looked to Andrew Johnson for leadership on such matters as poll tax repeal, redistricting, and speaker elections, voting records of this group show no unity on the debt bill.[42]

Newspaper reaction to the law was generally favorable. The Nashville *Union and American,* the Chattanooga *Daily Times,* and the Memphis *Daily Appeal* supported the measure, defending its provisions.[43] The Gallatin *Examiner* declared joyously that the law meant the end of seven years of "floundering along in an Egyptian darkness that could almost be felt with the hands."[44] The editor of the Nashville *Republican Banner* reported that news of the passage of the act had caused the price of Tennessee securities to advance on the New York market.[45] Complimenting Tennessee on its debt action, the New York *Evening Post* expressed the opinion that too often capitalists desiring to invest in the South had been "driven away by the unfortunate manner in which public finances have been managed and the disregard to [sic] public obligations, faith and honor in several of the States of the South."[46] Offering one of the few dissenting opinions, the Democratic Memphis *Daily Avalanche,* which had opposed the governor on the debt issue, concluded that funding "from its first appearance to its exit—is the boldest exhibition of legislative folly *and* rascality ever made to the people of Tennessee, not exceeding the worst days of political fanaticism which cursed the State on the heels of the late war."[47]

Within the General Assembly, one observer reported, opponents of funding were "very bitter" and strongly denounced "lobbists [sic] and suddenly converted members [of the legislature]."[48] They expressed their continuing displeasure by attempting to delay the passage of revenue and assessment bills considered vital to the success of the new law. Supporters of funding accused them of absenting themselves from the legislature purposely to avoid the necessary quorum and of introducing less important topics to prevent the lawmakers from taking up critical fiscal matters.[49]

On March 22 the governor informed the legislature that its appropriation bills for eleemosynary institutions and other programs could not be honored if the state paid the current operating costs of the government and interest on the debt. Brown made it clear that Tennessee needed improvements in its revenue laws to meet its fiscal responsibilities and that his administration regarded the interest payments as the foremost obligation. Letters from both the comptroller and the treasurer concurred.[50] Comptroller W. W. Hobbs observed that the recent funding act constituted "a primary charge upon all the revenue of the State, to the exclusion of any and all the demands upon the Treasury for other purposes." The treasurer said that he had to set apart state revenues to pay the interest, "even if it [should] take every dollar therf [sic]."[51]

Brown's message did little to encourage cooperation. A new law dealing with revenue collection passed, but a desired assessment measure failed. Two days after the legislature adjourned on March 25, a Nashville paper published a protest to the passage of the funding act, signed by nineteen house members. The protesters charged that proper debate had not occurred and that revenue and assessment laws should have preceded consideration of funding. The measure constituted a "renewal of our State obligations," they continued, but there were no "means, either in hand or in sight" to carry out the commitments.[52] Debate had not revealed the actual amount needed to carry out the law, which would largely benefit the bondholders and railroad men. A portion of the old bonds to be funded carried 5½ percent interest, and the dissenting representatives objected to replacing these securities with new ones bearing 6 percent. They also found unjust the requirement that the bondholder must pay a fee for converting his securities. Denying that they were repudiators, the lawmakers called for repeal of the bond law, passage of a sound revenue and assessment bill, and establishment of a sinking fund to begin paying the debt.[53]

Meantime, Brown's administration prepared to carry out the law. The governor asked a Philadelphia company about the cost of printing new bonds, and on April 30 he released a public letter to answer inquiries concerning funding and his efforts to obtain a new assessment law. The state had ordered the new bonds, Brown wrote, and registering and converting would probably begin July 1 or sooner. Because they had found evidence of illegal issuance of bonds of the Mineral Home Railroad and those of the Insurance Company of the Valley of Virginia, state officials would not accept them; the only others excluded would be Confederate war bonds. No fraudulent securities had appeared in the $13 million in bonds presented to the state since 1870; but, even though the "presumption [was] very strong that none such [were] in existence," all bonds would be examined upon presentation.[54] Brown concluded by saying that he believed the existing assessment statute would provide sufficient monies to meet the July 1, 1874, interest payment from 1873 revenues; therefore he would not call an extra session of the legislature unless he later found that revenues were insufficient to meet operating expenses and debt interest.[55]

The next day the governor accepted the resignation of Comptroller W. W. Hobbs, who pleaded ill health. Brown named to the comptrollership John C. Burch, his own son-in-law and editor of the Nashville *Union and American.* The paper had favored funding and backed Brown in the last election, and now its editor would be the financial officer most involved in implementing the funding program. In late July the American Banknote Company sent the last part of the state's order of new bonds, and on July 31, nearly a month later than planned, Comptroller Burch announced that old issues could now be presented for funding and registration at his office.[56]

If the advocates of funding expected unanimous approval from the bondholders, they were doomed to disappointment. Some bondholders were irritated because the law did not recognize and provide for interest on matured bonds from the date of their maturity to the date of their exchange for new bonds. In a published letter to the Philadelphia *Public Record,* Comptroller Burch explained that the original bill had contained a clause calling for payment of interest on matured bonds, but the legislature had struck it out before the measure passed; the attorney general had ruled that the act precluded payment of interest on matured bonds.[57] An eastern bondholder reported that friends who owned Tennessee bonds hesitated to exchange them because the law failed to provide for this interest, and he asked Nashville banker Dempsey Weaver if there existed "even a remote probability" that the next legislature might approve payment.[58]

In early September, in a letter to the governor, the secretary of the London-based Council of Foreign Bondholders protested that the fee of $1 per bond charged to the holder to exchange his securities violated the "general principle and practice" that the debtor assumed all charges. In addition, the state's failure to issue certificates for fractions of bonds or coupons amounting to less than the standard denomination of $1,000 disregarded accepted practice.[59] Brown dismissed most of these complaints as minor and gave little hope that the next legislature would alter the controversial provisions. The dissatisfaction of some of the creditors with the new law was disappointing to supporters of the bill, he said, and he reminded the secretary that railroads had sold most of the bonds illegally at below par value. The recent law was a compromise measure, and "the non-acquiesance [*sic*] of the creditors in the result [was] not calculated to inspire any sympathy in their behalf." Nor could he, in candor, recommend any changes in the law. Creditors should accept the act "most cheerfully" and be thankful the state would meet its obligations.[60] A month later the governor wrote that the "political caldron" was "comparatively quiet" and that funding was proceeding. Yet his closing statement was tinged with doubt: "We can & will pay the interest as it matures, I think."[61]

For two years the Republicans had attacked the Democrats for failing to deal with the debt problem, and Brown had struggled to commit his party to a policy of full debt payment. He had attained this goal in the spring of 1873 and pledged his party to a policy designed to insure the maintenance of public credit by honoring past state obligations. Not all of those within the ranks of the Democratic coalition shared the governor's views on the debt problem, however. Colyar, for one, was convinced that the debt had to be scaled, and a group of Democratic legislators had defied the wishes of their governor and voted against the funding bill. The debt law of 1873 might, nevertheless, have proved a permanent solution if the state and its people had prospered during the ensuing years. The statute was based, to an extent, on an optimistic view of the state's future; yet only a few months after its passage the nation's economy turned sharply downward and dashed the hopes of many Tennesseans for growing prosperity.

CHAPTER III

Collapse of the Debt Measure

In the spring of 1874 the state continued to receive matured bonds and interest coupons and to issue new securities under the provisions of the 1873 debt law. The New York Stock Exchange Committee on Securities recognized the new bonds, and in February the comptroller announced that the state would pay the interest due July 1, 1874. As a result of this assurance, Tennessee bonds became some of the most active of all state and railroad securities on the market.[1] A confident Governor Brown told an inquirer that the state's bonds were a "safe investment" and offered the opinion that no particular issue was more secure than another.[2]

Throughout the year the governor received and answered queries and complaints about the new debt measure and its provisions. By the end of June, Tennessee had funded or registered securities to the amount of approximately $20,249,000. The comptroller was able to pay the July debt interest on schedule, and in January 1875 Brown reported that over $6.2 million in new bonds had been issued.[3] The state had rejected the securities of three companies because of their questionable legality, he said, but with these exceptions no bonds had been presented "that were not authorized by some act of the Legislature, however improvident and reckless may have been the subsequent disposition of them."[4] The comptroller's report of the preceding month placed the total bonded debt at $22,908,400.[5]

While Tennessee was carrying out its funding program in 1874, the state and the nation were feeling the impact of the major economic depression that had begun in late 1873. As hard times set in, opposition to full debt payment grew. In the spring of 1874 newspapers debated the debt settlement. The Democratic Memphis *Daily Avalanche* continued to attack the funding law, and the Nashville *Republican Banner*, a Democratic paper which had supported the law, now began to publish letters of dissent. These papers reported growing public discontent over existing taxes and mounting fears that the funding law would require even greater burdens. In March a Shelbyville correspondent wrote that farmers in his area were greatly concerned about taxes and were determined to support only proponents of low taxes.[6] The editor of the *Republican Banner* asserted that some Bedford County farmers were prepared to leave Tennessee to escape high levies and land prices and warned of increasing animosity toward taxes and tax collectors. No other issue, he claimed, would "overtop or obscure" that of taxes in the next state race.[7]

Some newspapers repeated charges that the legislature passed the funding bill for the benefit of a few. The *Daily Avalanche* declared that it was common knowledge that the funding act was backed by a "moneyed, speculating Ring whose headquarters are in Wall street."[8] But three influential Democratic papers—the Nashville *Union and American*, the Memphis *Daily Appeal*, and the Chattanooga *Daily Times*—staunchly defended the funding policy and full debt payment, saying that Tennessee could not hope to lure immigrants and capital and prosper if it failed to honor its debts.[9] The editor of the *Daily Appeal* rhapsodized as he contemplated the value of a good credit rating: "What an inestimable jewel is public honor. How it helps private credit; how it facilitates the prosperity of a State; how proud, and bright, and happy it makes her people! "[10]

Backers of the governor's policy pointed out that Tennessee's tax rate was one of the lowest in the Union and that to honor the state's obligations would ease the tax burden by stimulating economic growth, which would lessen the load on the individual taxpayer. In the long run, repudiation would constitute greater economic hardship than the current tax rate. The editor of the *Union and American* was particularly concerned that the issue of debt payment might be injected into the coming gubernatorial contest and endanger Democratic control of the state. In May, Arthur S. Colyar and Andrew Johnson seemed to substantiate this fear as they began to formalize plans for the coming election.[11]

Former President Andrew Johnson had not sought a quiet retirement upon leaving the White House in 1869, having lost a close election for the United States Senate later that same year. Driven by personal ambition, a desire to vindicate his past actions during the Civil War and Reconstruction, and his resentment at the dominant position ex-Confederate Democrats were assuming in his party, Johnson was determined to play an active role in state politics and secure election to Congress. In 1872 he ran unsuccessfully as an independent for a specially created statewide seat in the federal House of Representatives against the Democratic candidate, former Confederate General B. F. Cheatham, and Republican Horace Maynard. His candidacy divided the Democratic vote and made possible Maynard's election. Johnson shared with Colyar not only that industrialist's dislike of the growing political influence of prominent Confederate officers, but also his conviction that full debt payment would impoverish Tennessee. Like Thomas Jefferson, Johnson believed that no people have a right to create a debt that would be binding on the next generation.[12]

Colyar, chairman of the Johnson state executive committee, called a meeting in Nashville in early May 1874 to discuss both the state's financial policy and Johnson's coming campaign for the United States Senate seat to be vacated upon Brownlow's retirement. At an organizational meeting at the Maxwell House, Jesse Brown of Shelby County delivered an address calling for a twenty-cent property tax rate and repeal of the clause in the funding law that required payment of debt interest to be made before payment of current expenses of government. He maintained that West Tennesseans would defeat at the polls by a ten-to-one margin anyone backing the present Democratic debt policy.[13]

The following day the participants engaged in an extensive debate on the funding program. Colyar wanted the meeting to adopt a clear statement favoring a twenty-cent rate, saying that the poor should not be "stripped of all property" to pay a debt "transmitted to them from a former generation." The people were unable to fund the debt because of current economic conditions, he said. Although others expressed similar views, the convention rejected Colyar's resolutions. One delegate warned that to adopt a set of low-tax, anti-funding declarations would be to light a "fire-brand in the ranks of the Democratic party."[14] Colonel Thomas Boyer of the Gallatin *Examiner* urged the group to adopt no platform, and eventually the meeting disbanded without acting on the matters of taxes and the debt.[15]

Democratic newspapers generally criticized Colyar's meeting, although the Memphis *Daily Avalanche* did defend his right to call it.[16] The Chattanooga *Daily Times* characterized it as a gathering of a "little crowd of malcontents" for which the Democratic party was in no way responsible.[17] Expressing relief that the assembly was small, the Nashville *Union and American* depicted the participants as men whose activities might jeopardize the interests of the "people at large." It carried an angry letter from Thomas Boyer, who charged that he had been tricked into attending the meeting and was shocked to find that the sponsors had gathered the committee to "comit [sic] the party to opposition of the Funding and Assessment laws, and make this the test of Democratic principle." They were going to cut the "throat of the Democratic party," and a new party would be "born and baptized."[18]

Although the conference of Johnson supporters failed to produce either a platform or a set of principles, it confirmed that the ex-president was running for the federal Senate. But the changed economic situation, growing criticism of the funding law, and the influence of Colyar led Johnson to alter the thrust of his speeches and public statements. Devoting less attention to a defense of his actions in the Civil War and as president, he emphasized the debt and taxes. In Nashville and Memphis in May he called for lower taxes and insisted that the people could not now pay the state's bonded debt.[19] Repudiation was not an accurate term to use when "a man fails to pay his debts every time they are due for the want of ability to pay."[20] Johnson defended the Colyar meeting and proposed a tax rate of twenty cents rather than forty cents per $100 of assessed value and a reduction of interest on the bonded debt from 6 to 3 percent. In an interview with a Nashville newspaper reporter in the same month, he predicted that even with the current tax rate the Brown administration would not be able to continue paying interest beyond January 1875.[21]

Sporadic discussion of taxes and the debt continued into the summer as Democrats and Republicans prepared for the governor's race. If Democratic opponents of the debt law had any hope of influencing party policy at the state convention, they were sorely disappointed. Assembling in Nashville on August 20, the delegates selected Gustavus A. Henry as permanent chairman of the convention. The selection of Henry, a famous antebellum Whig orator and politician, is indicative of the influential roles many old Whigs played in the post-Reconstruction Democratic party. A friend and supporter of Governor Brown, the chairman strongly endorsed the funding law.[22] Reflecting this point of view, the platform called for the payment of the state's "just debt and obligations" to preserve its "credit and honor untarnished." In an attempt to placate those who wanted tax cuts, it favored no more taxes than were absolutely necessary to run the state government economically and pay the debt.[23] The party nominated Henry County's James D. Porter for governor. The Republicans met nearly a month later and nominated Congressman Horace Maynard. Their platform called for debt payment but condemned the funding and the tax assessment laws passed under Governor Brown.[24]

The nominees of both political parties were well-known figures from the state's past political and military history. Porter, the Democratic candidate, was a prewar Whig and a former Confederate general who had also been a delegate to the constitutional convention of 1870. A businessman and a lawyer, he was a friend and business partner of Arthur S. Col-

yar. In 1880 he became president of the Nashville, Chattanooga, and St. Louis Railway. Like Brown, he represented
the dominant business-oriented wing of the party. In complete agreement with his predecessor, he opposed any sugges-
tion to scale the debt. Maynard, Porter's Republican opponent, was an experienced East Tennessee politician who had
come to Knoxville in 1838 from his native Massachusetts. He
served in the national House of Representatives as a Whig before the war and as a Republican from 1866 to 1875. An accomplished orator with quick wit and a gift for sarcasm, Maynard was probably the most talented public speaker in the
Tennessee Republican party.[25]

Porter and Maynard were not the only men on the campaign trail. The legislature selected in November would name
Senator Brownlow's successor when it assembled in January
1875, and two hopefuls for his seat, Andrew Johnson and incumbent Governor John C. Brown, sought public exposure
that fall. The preceding June, when the governor had in-
quired concerning possible public response to his active contention for the Senate seat, C. M. McGhee of the East Tennessee and Georgia Railroad reported that he was unable as
yet to measure the impact of Johnson's speeches and that
Brown would have "time enough to enter the field after the
state of funding is more fully developed."[26] Following the
Democratic convention, Brown embarked on an active speaking tour, using the fiscal policy of his administration as his
main theme.

Besides Brown's fiscal record, the other major campaign
issue was the federal civil rights bill. Aware that his party's
support of the civil rights measure in Congress might weaken
his appeal to white Tennesseans, Republican Maynard denied
that he favored the bill and attempted to focus attention on
the policies of the Democratic state administration. Maintain-
ing the ambiguity of the Republican platform, which favored
debt payment but denounced the 1873 law, Maynard asserted that Republicans now opposed the funding bill even
though they had originally backed it. Thus he hoped to appeal to those who normally supported his party and perhaps

attract some Democrats who were unhappy with their party's action on the debt question. Maynard did not offer, however, any alternative program or solution to the debt dilemma. He cited Democratic irresponsibility in granting the state printing contract and in leasing convicts, charged corruption in the appointment of Governor Brown's son-in-law, John C. Burch, to the comptrollership, and denounced the tax rate established during the Brown administration.[27] At Lebanon in mid-October, Maynard waved the state tax schedule before the crowd and described it as a "Democratic love letter to the people of Tennessee."[28]

Assaults on the administration's debt policies also came from Andrew Johnson, who, now back in the party fold, made the funding bill a major point of his speeches in the weeks before the election. Before the Civil War, he maintained, he had opposed the state's assistance to internal improvements. Corruption had surrounded the issuance of antebellum securities, which railroad and turnpike companies had illegally sold below their par value.[29] Funding had made the debt permanent—one that would be "inflicted upon your children and children's children,"[30] Johnson declaimed. "Once make a permanent debt, and . . . people are no longer free."[31] Johnson opposed the state's efforts to pay its debt when such action caused the citizen to be "crushed to the earth with a burden of taxation." In this situation, he said, "I would have the bondholder wait a little or do the best he can."[32] Nor should Tennesseans be alarmed at the cry of repudiation; no public debt had ever been erased without some degree of repudiation.[33]

Johnson made the issues of hard times, high taxes, and funding the cornerstones of his campaign. Speaking before the Sumner County Agricultural and Mechanical Association in the latter part of September, he mentioned Russian serfdom, warning his listeners that, "if the present state of things continues in this country, you too, will soon be reduced to the condition of serfs."[34] He favored suspension of debt payment until economic conditions improved, and payment of interest on the actual cost of the bonds, not on their face

value. Since he believed that many bondholders had purchased securities at half their face value, this would mean
that the state owed only half of the present annual interest
payments.[35] Early in October, he announced that he would
go beyond his party's call for maintenance of the present rate
and declared for a tax reduction.[36]

Porter and Brown carried the campaign battle to Maynard,
and the governor also crossed lances with Johnson. Brown defended the funding act by pointing out that Republicans had
taken similar action regarding the bonded obligation when
they controlled state government and had backed the recently
enacted debt and revenue laws. In fact, a majority of Republicans in the legislature had voted for the funding bill, and
Maynard had even written a letter to legislator L. C. Houk
urging its passage. The governor ridiculed Johnson, charging
that he had condoned, both as governor and as president, the
creation of public debts he now talked of repudiating. Indeed, Brown said, most of the Johnson men in the last legislature had voted for passage of the funding bill, and Johnson
had personally favored the measure. According to Brown, the
former president owned state bonds and had willingly exchanged them under the terms of the funding law; Johnson
had come out against the law only after the Republicans had
done so.[37]

In the opening speech of his campaign, Porter made it clear
that he was in complete agreement with Governor Brown's
funding policy. The "credit and good name of the State must
be maintained, and all of its obligations paid," he stated,
going on to warn that the "Democratic party cannot afford
to imperil its good name by the adoption of any policy that
looks to repudiation."[38] Both Porter and Brown said that under Democratic management Tennessee had reduced its debt
from a figure in excess of $43 million to an estimated
$20,980,000 and that officials had found that only a few of
the bonds were improperly issued. They pointed to a reduction in the floating debt of Tennessee as additional proof of
the Democrats' excellent management. Optimistically pre-
dicting a steady rise in property values over the next twenty

years, Brown informed his audiences that this increase would yield more revenues and allow the state not only to pay the debt interest regularly, but also to build a sinking fund to retire a major portion of the debt principal.[39]

Confident of a Democratic victory, the Nashville *Union and American* predicted on election day a 60,000-vote majority for Porter. The prediction, as it turned out, was quite accurate; the vote was 105,061 to 55,847; Porter even carried Republican East Tennessee. Democratic supremacy was almost complete; only eight Republicans captured seats in the legislature. The weak Republican showing was primarily a result of the effective exploitation by Democrats of Tennesseans' antipathy toward the federal civil rights bill. Maynard's attempt to blunt this issue by denouncing the funding act and other Democratic policies had proved singularly unsuccessful.[40]

Following the election, dissatisfaction with the financial policy of the Brown administration appeared in the General Assembly. When the new legislature convened early in January 1875, Democratic Senator John Overton of Shelby County introduced a bill to repeal the section of the funding law that required the treasurer to set aside sufficient state revenue to meet interest payments. Governor Brown and his staff had interpreted this section to mean that the interest payments constituted a primary claim on revenues of the state, one that they had to pay before meeting other expenses. The Overton bill met no resistance: it passed the senate without a dissenting vote and the house seventy-two to one.[41]

Not content with repealing a section of the debt law, the legislature also initiated investigations of charges that lawmakers had accepted bribes to vote for passage of the funding bill and that John C. Burch had purchased the office of state comptroller. After Burch was appointed in the spring of 1873 to serve the remainder of W. W. Hobbs's term as comptroller, the Republican Nashville *Bulletin* announced that it had evidence of Hobbs's having sold his post for $12,000 to Burch or his friends. Republican papers charged that a funding ring of Wall Street interests had bought the post from Hobbs.

Governor Brown and Hobbs denied these allegations, but the stories would not die. In June 1874, C. M. McGhee informed Brown that Hobbs's stepping down had "some how or other had the effect of creating . . . a suspicion of bargain and sale [which seemed] hard to get over."[42] In his campaign for governor, Maynard had cited the persistent rumors, and they were more widespread than ever now that Burch was seeking a full term as comptroller.[43]

Perhaps because of the embarrassing nature of the evidence, the major Democratic journals did not give extensive coverage to the proceedings of the investigative committee. At first little turned up except rumor and hearsay evidence, but on January 13, 1875, Hobbs admitted having received $10,000 from William R. Duncan of Nashville to resign his office. Yet he swore that neither Burch nor the governor had had any knowledge of the affair. Duncan, a banker and broker, had been cashier of the Mechanics Bank of Nashville when the funding act was passed. He appeared before the committee and testified that in 1873 he had $250,000 invested in Tennessee bonds on margin and had advised a number of friends to make similar investments.[44] He had realized that only a comptroller of "first class capacity" could meet the interest payments on the debt promptly, and he regarded Hobbs as "incompetent." If the state had failed to meet the interest, Duncan would have suffered, as he said, a "loss that would have utterly bankrupted me and injured severely the friends who had aided me in raising the funds for my margins."[45]

Eager to protect his investment, Duncan testified, he had talked to Hobbs and found the comptroller willing to retire if he could do so without personal loss. Admitting that he had been motivated primarily by a "regard for [his] own interests," Duncan had then paid Hobbs $10,000 to resign. He insisted that he had acted alone and had had no dealings with either Governor Brown or Burch regarding the matter. Duncan, convinced that the state had greatly benefited from Hobbs's resignation, had been confident that the governor was "so pledged to funding" that he would name a "capable man" to replace Hobbs. Later, Brown and Burch appeared before the committee and denied any knowledge of the sale of Hobbs' office.[46]

The investigation damaged the prestige of the Brown administration. In addition to the evidence concerning his sale of the post, the committee also heard testimony that Hobbs had made a pact with an opponent when both were seeking election to the comptrollership. By the terms of this agreement the man who got the job would supposedly pay the loser's expenses in lobbying for it. The lawmakers exonerated the governor and Comptroller Burch; but as for Hobbs, the committee firmly concluded that "a high official deliberately sold a public trust in violation of every principle of morality, duty, and decency . . . " and expressed some doubt that Duncan had acted completely alone in purchasing Hobbs's retirement.[47] Pleased with the committee's report, Burch announced that personal vindication had been the main purpose for his seeking another term as comptroller; since this had been accomplished, he was withdrawing from the race.[48]

Meantime, a joint legislative committee began to look into charges that some legislators had taken bribes to support the funding bill. Members of the preceding legislature, newspapermen, state officials, and others testified before the committee. They usually either denied knowledge of any improper influence on legislators or repeated rumors and snatches of conversations that they had heard when the measure was pending before the General Assembly. There were, they agreed, a great many rumors that a legislator could enrich himself by agreeing to back funding.[49] On the other hand, one witness testified that he had heard that "a man walked into the Senate Chamber and offered a $100,000 [payment] for seven votes against the funding bill."[50]

Witnesses were unwilling or unable to support with facts their charges of undue influence being used to pass the 1873 debt law. James W. White of Hawkins County, an independent member of the legislature that passed the funding measure, acknowledged to the committee that he believed that a "large amount of money was brought to bear" to purchase support for the bill. But when shown a legislative journal and asked to name the members of the General Assembly con-

nected with the rumors of undue influence, he weakly replied,
"I find I am not able to designate parties who made those allegations."[51] Witnesses told of rumors of bribes that impli-
cated several legislators, some declaring that they had heard
of New York lobbyists' being present during the funding debates. One charged that he had overheard editor J. M. Keating
of the Memphis *Daily Appeal* say that he, fellow-editor W.
Galloway, and another man would receive payment for their
newspaper's support of the measure.[52] Galloway, however,
denied that he had had any such contact with bondholders.
Rather, his newspaper had supported funding because Governor Brown had called for it and because he "presumed it was
the policy of the Democratic party . . . ."[53]

Several who met with the committee testified to rumors
that supporters of funding had offered money to Republican
legislator L. C. Houk to change his stand on the bill. Houk
had initially opposed the measure but later became a forceful
advocate of its passage. Republican Representative L. T.
Hyder of Carter County declared that Houk was staunchly
opposed to the measure but that proponents of the bill promised him $20,000 to shift his position. According to Hyder,
when Houk returned to Nashville after a weekend trip to
Knoxville, he had changed his stand and supported funding.
William Rule, Republican rival of Houk and editor of the
Knoxville *Daily Chronicle,* had used charges of this sort to
help defeat Houk in the latter's bid for the congressional
nomination in the Second District in 1874. He repeated the
story that Houk had said he could receive a large sum of
money for backing funding but admitted to the committee
that he had no evidence that Houk had accepted a bribe.[54]

Houk, appearing before the committee, maintained that he
supported funding but had objected to some of the provisions
of the bills introduced in the legislature. When Representative
E. A. James of Chattanooga altered his bill to exclude the
possibility of recognition of the Confederate debt and to include the school fund, Houk said, he dropped his opposition
and supported the bill. Although he admitted that he might
have spoken in a general way about the possibility of a legis-

lator making money if he backed funding, he swore that he had not "in any manner, way, shape, nor form, nor under any pretense whatever received any consideration in any shape . . . ."[55] James, the author of the funding law, told the committee that he had, indeed, changed his bill to get the support of Houk and improve the chances for its passage.[56]

Upon completion of their probe in March, the majority of the legislative committee stated that the evidence was "wholly insufficient" to support the charge of wrongdoing on the part of members of the last legislature. But four members of the investigating committee submitted a separate report concluding that the evidence, although conflicting, cast "grave and serious suspicions" on the actions of several lawmakers.[57] This investigation and the one surrounding the sale of the comptrollership were serious embarrassments to the Democratic leadership. The revelation that a stock market speculator had purchased the retirement of the state's most important fiscal officer to insure the success of the new law and to protect his own investment seriously tarnished the image of the funders, who talked a great deal about public honesty and the need for Tennessee to deal fairly with its creditors. Although investigators unearthed no concrete proof of bribery, the hint of such acts tended to erode support for dollar-for-dollar debt payment. In addition, both of these legislative probes influenced the outcome of the federal Senate election in January.[58]

On January 19, 1875, while charges and rumors surrounding the Hobbs affair and the passage of the funding act circulated through the halls of the Capitol, the legislature began balloting to select a United States senator. The press mentioned a number of men for the post. An East Tennessee Republican journal sarcastically described the maneuvering for the office as a "dog fight" between "ambitions [sic] Generals, Colonels, Captains and [the] Ex-President of the Democratic party."[59] The Memphis *Daily Avalanche* endorsed Andrew Johnson, but the Democratic press was not unified on the subject.[60] The Columbia *Herald and Mail* called for the election of a man who was "sound to the core" on the "financial question."[61] The Chattanooga *Daily Times* revealed a preference for Governor Brown and declared it would use "any and every weapon at hand" to oppose Johnson.[62] It soon became obvious that the contest was among Democrats Johnson, Brown, and Confederate General William B. Bate of Nashville. Johnson had the lead on the first ballot, and a dedicated group of thirty-five legislators backed him throughout the numerous ballots cast over the next few days. Neither Brown nor Bate could muster the majority needed for election; finally, on January 26, on the fifty-fifth ballot, Johnson won by two votes.[63] The Republican Jonesboro *Herald and Tribune* cheered the Johnson victory, claiming that the "noble little band of eight" Republicans in the General Assembly had stood firmly behind Johnson. His election, it concluded, was a victory for Republicans and the people and a defeat for the "Bourbon rings of Middle and West Tennessee."[64]

Johnson's election was a setback for the regular party leadership, and it indicated growing dissatisfaction among Democrats with the fiscal policy of their state administration. The former president had centered his campaign on criticism of the debt program and tax rate established by his own party. His drive to capture the federal Senate seat received a boost when the legislature began to probe the appointment of Burch to the comptrollership and the passage of the funding law. These investigations seriously weakened the appeal of John C. Brown, Johnson's most powerful opponent in the race. Any hopes that Colyar and others might have held of building a political organization around the newly elected senator and the debt issue were shattered, however, when Johnson died in July 1875.[65]

Following the senatorial election, Porter made his first address to the legislature, in which he acknowledged that economic conditions were such that "the people of Tennessee never possessed so little ability to bear the burdens of government as at present." For this condition he blamed crop failures and an industrial depression caused by "financial disorders" in the nation. Admonishing the General Assembly to pursue a policy of strict economy, he called for reform of the state criminal code, continued support for public education, sponsorship of a geological survey of the state to foster the development of manufacturing, and passage of laws to attract immigrants to Tennessee. Regarding the debt, Porter argued that it was too late to debate the wisdom of creating the debt, but that now the issue was "how to preserve the public faith and credit without an increase in public burdens." He prescribed a familiar panacea: economy in government would enable the state to maintain its credit without raising taxes.[66]

The legislature's actions were not all that the governor desired. The lawmakers did repeal an act to build two additional insane asylums and imposed a tax of 1½ percent on the gross earnings of railroad companies operating in Tennessee. They also attempted to increase the efficiency of the revenue system by enacting a law to reform and improve collection of county taxes. Responding to the desperate financial conditions of the depression, the legislature passed a taxpayers' relief law exempting from legal penalties those who were delinquent in the payment of their 1873 and 1874 taxes if they paid their obligations before October 1, 1875. This last measure, while undoubtedly popular with many hard-pressed citizens, stripped Porter's administration of the legal remedies it could use to collect badly needed overdue taxes.[67]

Worsening economic conditions fed opposition to the funding law. Lawmakers proposed a variety of actions such as an investigation of the origins of the debt, the purchase of the bonds by the state at the going market price, the reduction or elimination of the payment of interest, and the funding of the debt at less than 100 cents on the dollar. A bill to repeal the funding act passed the house but failed in the senate. Democratic Representative Lee Head of Wilson County and Republican H. R. Gibson, representing the East Tennessee counties of Union, Campbell, and Scott, both introduced measures that called for the state, after meeting current expenses, to secure periodic offers from bondholders for the amount they would be willing to accept for their securities and to make the best deal it could with the creditors.[68]

The funding law withstood attempts to change or replace

it, but proposals to do so worried its backers. In late February and early March the legislature held heated debates on a bill offered by Representative Head to cut the property tax rate from forty cents to twenty-five cents per $100 of assessed valuation. Supporters of the 1873 debt law saw this as an attempt to reduce state revenues to a level that would make impossible the required semiannual interest payments. The Head bill did not pass the legislature, but discussion of the tax rate impelled the Democratic members to call a caucus to restore unity to their ranks. Instead, in an atmosphere of disharmony, members offered resolutions endorsing a sixty-cent tax rate, the existing forty-cent rate, and a twenty-five-cent levy. Concerned about the amount of dissension and low tax feeling at the meeting, Senator William A. Quarles, Clarksville lawyer and former Confederate general, rallied the supporters of the funding law and managed to get the bickering Democrats to agree to the adoption of a harmonizing resolution that proclaimed the members' faith in the party and the platform of 1874.[69] Another lawmaker, who attended the meeting and shared Quarles's concern about the calls for tax cuts, said that "if the way to the lower regions were paved with bad, instead of good resolutions, they were laying a double track in that direction at a quick-time schedule."[70]

Even with the existing tax rate, the state was hard pressed to meet the interest on the debt. In January 1875 a $600,000 loan made payment possible, and the treasurer predicted that slow tax collections would make another loan necessary if Tennessee were to meet the obligation coming due in July. Senator Quarles attempted to persuade the General Assembly to provide for additional revenue that would clearly allow the state to meet expenses and carry out the funding law, but he failed. Indeed, he and others who stood with the governor in support of the 1873 debt law had to work diligently to fight off efforts to slash the tax rate. The General Assembly adjourned without altering the existing rate, leaving the Porter administration with the task of trying to carry out the provisions of the funding law amid increasing signs of revolt within the party and mounting evidence of hard times.[71]

As the date for the July interest payments drew nearer, bondholders expressed concern about the state's ability to meet its obligations. A bondowner who was an acquaintance of Comptroller James L. Gaines wrote, "There never was a time in my life when I needed more to make money than now," and he entreated Gaines to tell him whether the state would pay the July interest so that he could "operate with some certanty [sic]."[72] C. B. Harger, a banker from Watertown, New York, bluntly asked the comptroller if he had "any idea that there [would] be funds in the Treasury for any parties of this account coming due!"[73] On June 21, J. R. Hills of New York City wrote Gaines that the Third National Bank of New York had advised him that it had no Tennessee funds to pay the July interest; he asked if the state intended to announce whether it would pay. Most "intelligent persons," said this writer, "appreciate the difficulties existing in the Southern portion of our country and are willing to wait patiently for what is due them, but would like a *definite time fixed for payment.*"[74]

Hoping to influence Gaines, W. H. Kent of New York City sent a newspaper clipping telling of South Carolina's decision to pay its debt interest and asked Gaines to imagine "how many widows and orphans hearts [sic]" would be made happy by South Carolina's decision. Tennessee should "do likewise."[75] Closer to home, the Knoxville *Daily Chronicle* expressed grave doubt that the state would meet its interest obligation, and in mid-June an editorial in the Nashville *Union and American* indicated that officials had failed to obtain a loan which would enable the state to redeem coupons for the July interest.[76] The first of the month passed, and the New York *Commercial and Financial Chronicle* reported that the "coupons were not paid," adding, "Nothing further is known of the prospects of payment . . . ."[77]

In mid-July the governor revealed the reason for the default. The state, wrote Porter in a public letter to General M. J. Wright of Columbia, had sought to secure a loan of $60,000 to meet the July interest payment, but the best terms the comptroller could obtain called for a 7¼ percent

interest rate and for $850,000 in state bonds as collateral.
Tennessee could not meet such terms and thus did not secure
the loan.[78] Porter continued that he did not believe the current legislature would provide the means to pay the interest
or "enlarge the power of the Comptroller of the Treasury to
borrow money, and [he could not] therefore see any good
result from an extra session of the legislature."[79]

Characteristic of Republican newspaper reaction to the default were the.comments of the Knoxville *Daily Chronicle*
and the Chattanooga *Daily Commercial,* which blamed the
Democrats' control of state government for the action.[80]
Democratic papers expressed a variety of views. The Nashville
Union and American labeled the loan terms those that "Shy-
lock gives a beggar." It said that the financial plight of Tennessee had resulted from too much talk of repudiation in the
state and from the General Assembly's action in allowing
those who still owed taxes for 1873 and 1874 to pay without
penalty until October 1875.[81] The Woodbury *Press* declared
that members of the last legislature were not to blame, as
many persons in the state had believed that the debt could be
paid without difficulty. The Columbia *Herald and Mail* also
defended the legislature and attributed the default to the
treasurer's overconfidence in the state's ability to borrow to
meet its needs.[82] The Franklin *Review* called for calm and
for the election of the best "financial men" in the state for
the next "session or so" and predicted that this would result
in the payment of debt interest and a reduction of the principal.[83]

As the year drew to a close, worried creditors again wrote
to the comptroller, asking if Tennessee was going to meet its
debt obligations and if it would pay the January 1876 interest. But financial conditions failed to improve in the months
immediately following July 1, and the state announced in December that it could not meet the January payment. When
money did accumulate in the treasury, the governor said, it
would first go toward repaying money borrowed to meet the
interest in January 1875.[84] Thus the attempt to discharge the
state's obligations on a dollar-for-dollar basis collapsed.

The failure of the funding program marked a turning point in Tennessee's attempt to solve the burdensome problem of its bonded debt. In 1874 and 1875 opposition to the funding act of 1873 had grown considerably. Andrew Johnson and Horace Maynard attempted to capitalize on the growing popular dislike for full payment, and legislative investigations in the spring of 1875 seriously compromised the image of the funders as men who were concerned only with following an honest fiscal policy. Economic reality and political expediency dictated that the Democratic leadership must change its tactics.

CHAPTER IV

The State Credit Rationale

Tennesseans divided into two camps on the debt question. "Low taxers" were the opponents of the funding act of 1873, the proponents of delaying debt settlement, and those who favored sizable scaling of the debt. Their adversaries often referred to them as "repudiators," but they preferred to be known as opponents of the oppressive taxation that they felt full or near-total debt payment would require. Those who supported funding the debt were known as advocates of state credit: they contended that payment was vital to the preservation of the state's credit rating and thus its economic progress and development. Their foes often labeled them "high taxers," an obvious effort to link the stand for debt payment with the need for additional taxes.

The state credit faction was not completely unified. Members of this group originally supported the attempts of governors Brown and Porter to pay every cent of the debt, but after the mid-1870s the pressures of their opponents and the reality of an empty state treasury forced them to support a series of compromises that called for paying less than the full amount. The thrust of their efforts shifted from insistence on full payment to fighting the sentiment for massive scaling and for delaying settlement until Tennessee became more prosperous. Despite their agreement about what should not be done, however, they sometimes disagreed among themselves about the merits of the various plans that were considered after 1875.

Advocates of state credit were prominent in both of Tennessee's major political parties. Within the ranks of the Democrats, state credit spokesmen held the reins of party power and monopolized the federal and major state elective offices controlled by the Democrats. Frugality and honesty were the watchwords of their political philosophy, which was partly rooted in their perception of the historic role of the Democratic party, in their commitment to a largely inactive government with limited powers, in their determination to avoid the extravagance and corruption they associated with the Brownlow era, and in their view of the financial straits of the state and most of its citizens. Yet they knew that principles alone would not lift Tennessee from the slough of economic adversity and stagnation, and believed that future prosperity also depended on the state's ability to abandon its overwhelming dependence on agriculture and diversify its economy. In short, they wanted the state to participate fully in the business and industrial expansion that, in good times at least, characterized American development in the Gilded Age. If, they reasoned, Tennessee made every effort to pay its debt, welcomed newcomers, and publicized its natural resources, it would attract the immigrants and Northern businessmen, investors, and industry necessary for diversification. With these attitudes, it is little wonder that state credit Democrats viewed the movement to repudiate or scale down the debt radically not only as a menace to party unity and their position of dominance in it, but also as a threat to orderly economic progress.

The Republican party, with some aberrations and exceptions, adhered to the state credit position even more strongly than the Democrats. It attempted to court low tax sentiment in the gubernatorial races of 1874 and 1876 and included in its ranks some individuals who held low tax views, but, for the most part, the vast majority of Republicans subscribed to the state credit doctrine. Republican East Tennessee had traditionally supported programs extending federal and state aid to transportation projects. As early as the 1820s and 1830s, this mountainous section had pressed for public financing of endeavors that would improve its communication with the rest of the state and the nation. After the Civil War, similar concerns and the desire to exploit their abundant natural re-

sources also spurred East Tennesseans to press for debt payment in the hope that such a policy would lead to economic
development. Party loyalty reinforced their state credit pro-
pensities; an important element of their dislike of proposals
for radical scaling of the debt was their abhorrence of charges
that the Republicans had grossly mismanaged the debt problem in the Reconstruction period.[1]

After the Civil War former Whigs were quite prominent in
the Democratic party in a number of Southern states, as several historians have emphasized. Before its demise prior to
the war, the Whig party had been known for its probusiness
philosophy and Unionist views; Tennessee men who had been
members of this party now played key roles in shaping state
and party policy on the debt. Indeed, old-line Whigs held positions of leadership in both major political parties and were
usually ardent exponents of the state credit view. Former
followers of Henry Clay, Hugh Lawson White, and John Bell
took the lead in developing and defending the funding act of
1873 and in the struggle to obtain a compromise debt settlement after this law proved inoperable. John C. Brown, James
D. Porter, Gustavus A. Henry, Neil S. Brown, and James E.
Bailey, all staunch state credit Democrats, had been prewar
Whigs. In addition, such high tax Republicans as William G.
Brownlow, L. C. Houk, and W. H. Wisener, like the vast majority of white Republicans, had been Whigs.[2]

Many of the most vocal and strident Democratic supporters of debt payment were ex-Whigs, but the state credit leadership was not exclusively Whig in origin. Numerous antebellum Democrats such as Confederate Governor Isham G.
Harris and Confederate Generals William B. Bate and William
A. Quarles backed the state credit position. It was, however,
old Whigs who largely shaped the Democratic policy toward
the debt in the early 1870s; with the support of Whig Republicans they committed Tennessee to a policy of dollar-for-
dollar debt payment. Working in harmony with conservative,
business-minded prewar Democrats, they dominated party
councils without serious challenge until the late 1870s and
greatly influenced party policy from 1870 to 1883.

A number of leading state credit men had close ties with railroads, corporations, and businesses within and outside the state. Governors Brown and Porter had railroad interests and were business partners of industrialist Arthur S. Colyar. Republican Alvin Hawkins, elected governor in 1880, was a railroad president. Jacob McGavock Dickinson of Nashville, a well-to-do backer of debt payment, was a successful corporation lawyer. State credit Republican Congressman William R. Moore of Shelby County was the leading wholesale drygoods merchant in Memphis. James L. Gaines, who served as state comptroller under two Democratic governors in the 1870s, had worked in New York and Knoxville business firms before becoming the state's most important fiscal officer. William J. Sykes, a Democratic proponent of debt payment who spoke on this question frequently in the 1870s and early 1880s, was vice president of the Mayfield, Kentucky, Narrow Gauge Railroad and a tireless booster of railroad projects such as the Alabama and Chattanooga Railroad and the Memphis and Knoxville Railroad. E. A. James, who wrote the funding act of 1873, was an officer of the Chattanooga Gas Light Company, an iron dealer, and a prominent figure at national commercial and river improvement conventions, and was associated with the Cincinnati Railway.[3]

Not all were businessmen, however, nor did the state credit position appeal to only one segment of society. Isham G. Harris of Memphis and William B. Bate of Nashville were two very popular public figures who seem not to have been directly connected with business enterprises. Yet as well-known city attorneys, they undoubtedly included many of Tennessee's more influential businesses among their clientele. Although state credit leaders were often from the most prosperous and socially prominent class of Tennesseans, they attracted far more than just the financial and social elite. Farmers who believed that state aid to railroads had helped them by providing better transportation facilities, and lawyers, merchants, newspaper editors, and other Tennesseans who regarded debt payment as vital to a good credit rating and future prosperity swelled their ranks. Many voters probably supported state credit policy simply because the proponents of this view frequently were among the best known, most admired and respected men in Tennessee. Democratic leaders who espoused this policy were typically men who had been high-ranking Confederate military or civil officials in the war, and party members had a natural inclination to support the policies of men who had led them in the war. Republicans felt the same bond of allegiance toward their chieftains who had supported the Union and reconstructed the state when the conflict was over.[4]

In spite of their defense of the Confederacy, state credit Democrats had no desire to recreate the Old South. In his important *Origins of the New South, 1877-1913*, C. Vann Woodward argues that the term "Bourbon," used by some historians to characterize the Democratic party in the post-Reconstruction South, is inaccurate. Instead of Bourbons, who looked to the past and refused to face the realities of a changing post-Civil War America, Woodward visualizes these Southerners as Redeemers—men who were ardent exponents of the New South idea and who hoped to adjust or adapt their states to place them in step with the industrial and commercial North. Despite their homage to the Lost Cause and the civilization of the antebellum South, they did not wish to rebuild the economy along the agricultural lines of the prewar years.[5] With respect to Tennessee, Woodward's interpretation seems to be basically correct; the state credit Democrats, with some exceptions, appear to have been more akin to Redeemers than to Bourbons. State credit men, even those who were not in business or closely connected with corporations, saw a need to adapt to the rapidly industrializing world around them. They desired the development of industry to complement the state's agricultural economic base. If this end could be achieved, they argued, all Tennesseans, farmers and non-farmers alike, would enjoy a greater degree of prosperity.

Recurring themes unified the rationale of state credit men of both parties. The various arguments at times merged, overlapped, and even contradicted one another, but the force and aggressiveness with which the state credit leaders articulated their views more than overcame any shortcomings in clarity and consistency. To defend their position, these men drew on their understanding of past history, present conditions, and future prospects of Tennessee.

The most often-voiced contention of high tax men equated debt payment with economic progress and diversification. Refusal to pay or delayed payment bespoke poverty and economic stagnation. This idea was an integral part of an attitude toward industry and manufacturing that grew to maturity in the years after 1865. Defeat in the Civil War had shaken the faith of many Tennesseans in an agricultural economy, and the arrival of Northern industrialists, bent on developing and exploiting the natural resources of Tennessee in the years after the war, augmented the ranks of those who advocated industrialization. Governor Brownlow, for example, believed that the old antebellum cotton and slave economy was gone with the war and endorsed industrialization as the key to recovery in Reconstruction. Those who vocally and enthusiastically reiterated this view between the end of the war and 1883 were, almost without exception, supporters of the state credit position.[6]

Governors Brown and Porter backed efforts to develop the state's natural resources and attract new residents. The resulting economic expansion, they said, would bring prosperity and the revenues necessary to pay the debt. A few legislators made proposals to extend state assistance to manufacturers and industrialists in the form of tax exemptions for their enterprises in the 1870s, but the General Assembly rebuffed them. Apparently, popular espousal of the New South creed did not include special tax concessions or financial inducements for industry. The legislature did, however, take a number of significant steps to encourage economic growth and industrialization. Tennessee created an immigration agency in 1867, and the biennial message to the legislature of every governor from 1865 to 1881 stressed the need for new settlers. In 1875 the legislature authorized the post of commissioner of immigration, and in the same decade the General

Assembly simplified procedures for the incorporation of business concerns. The Bureau of Agriculture, Statistics and Mines, created in 1875 and directed by the energetic Joseph B. Killebrew, made a strong effort to publicize data on the state's valuable resources and the condition of its agriculture and industry.[7]

State credit men and most of the large city papers saw debt settlement as a necessity if Tennessee were to lure new settlers. Immigrants would farm idle lands and provide the manpower for industrial development.[8] "We need more landowners who will be cultivators of the soil, more laborers of every description," the Memphis *Daily Appeal* said, and "all of these repudiation will drive from us."[9] The immigrant, according to the Nashville *Union and American,* desired to live where he could prosper, and he would not select a state that defaulted.[10] The Knoxville *Daily Chronicle* said that "communities where the people are honest" attract settlers and that if Tennessee did not resolve its debt honestly, it would be "regarded as a community of robbers."[11] In 1881 the Chattanooga *Daily Times* conjectured that immigrants considering settling in the state were scared away by Tennesseans' continually bragging about the wealth of their soil and mineral resources and yet at the same time complaining that they were too poor to pay their public debt.[12]

Not only would new settlement be discouraged, said the state credit forces; they warned that a reputation for repudiation would also frighten away Northern and foreign capital and thus forever impair Tennessee's economic future. This admonition, first developed in defense of a full debt payment in the funding act of 1873, was later used to muster support for proposals that provided for scaling of the original indebtedness.[13] A legislator pointed out in the General Assembly that loss of credit because of repudiation would cause "our fields [to] go to waste, our wheels [to] cease their motion and business circles to stagnate."[14] In 1876, William G. Brownlow reminded his fellow Republicans that Mississippi had repudiated its debt before the Civil War and urged them to prevent Tennessee from being led through "the same pu-

trid slough, from the slime and stink of which that unfortunate State has never yet escaped . . . ."[15] United States Senator Isham G. Harris reported in 1877 that he had heard of an
English company that had abandoned a plan to invest in mineral lands in Tennessee because it feared repudiation.[16] The
Nashville *Daily American* stated a few years later that it knew
of several capitalists, including the largest mine and railroad
owner in Pennsylvania, who were waiting to see if the state
would honorably settle its debt before investing in Tennessee.[17]

In contrast to their gloomy predictions concerning the impact of repudiation, however, advocates of debt payment
were almost ecstatic when they considered the potential effect of their policy on Tennessee. They were confident that a
reasonable solution would allow the state to flourish.[18] One
editor predicted, "New enterprises and industries will spring
up and the State will enter upon a new and unknown era of
prosperity."[19] An honorable answer to the problem, another
prophesied, would result in "such a burst of prosperity as
[would] gladden the heart of every Tennessean."[20] Factories
would appear on every hand, and the state would become a
"hive of busy workers."[21] Republican Governor Alvin Hawkins foresaw "a new life . . . infused in every department of
business [with] unparalleled prosperity [spreading] its happy
influences throughout all our borders."[22] When a settlement
bill passed the legislature in 1882, Republican Commissioner
of Agriculture, Statistics, and Mines Ashton W. Hawkins said,
"Every indication now points to an era of prosperity such as
our State has not enjoyed for many years."[23]

The supporters of debt payment had definite ideas concerning the origin and legality of the public debt. Generally
they accepted the debt as legal and asserted that the majority
of Tennesseans had endorsed prewar aid to transportation
projects. In 1880, Colonel J. J. Turner told an audience that
the policy had been so popular that no one who was against
aiding internal improvements could have been elected to the
legislature prior to 1861. State credit speakers repeatedly reinforced their arguments by asserting that many of the bonds

of the state bore the signatures of such honored Tennessee politicians as James K. Polk, James C. Jones, Andrew Johnson, and Isham G. Harris.[24] One high tax Democrat, noting that Democratic rather than Whig governors had issued most of the antebellum railroad bonds, concluded that to deny the legality of this debt was to "say that the Democratic party has all the time been a fraud and still remains so . . . ."[25]

Legislative investigations in 1870 and 1879 uncovered considerable evidence that legislators in the Reconstruction era had not followed the guidelines first laid down by the 1852 internal improvements law and by subsequent amendments to it, but in the face of these revelations state credit forces usually continued to reject charges that the debt had been illegally contracted. Even though railroads used bribery to get aid and a number of lines before and after the war had unlawfully sold their bonds at less than par value, yet many state credit men simply ignored the information unearthed by these studies, others belittled the value of the evidence, and some stubbornly refused to believe the sworn testimony.[26] R. R. Butler, an influential East Tennessee Republican, insisted that "all the talk about corruption was the weak cry of demagogues."[27] In 1880 the editor of the Memphis *Daily Avalanche* characterized the charge that some of the debt had been improperly contracted as "merely loose talk, without facts to support it."[28]

Many who acknowledged possible fraud or impropriety in some of the bond issues contended that this had no bearing on Tennessee's liability for the debt. The state, as the duly constituted agent of the people, had issued these securities and was bound to honor them.[29] The bonds, said the prominent Rutherford County barrister Edwin H. Ewing, represented a binding contract made by the agents of the people, and there was "no mode of relief from such contracts except revolution."[30] A West Tennessee correspondent expressed substantially the same view when he wrote that, if the people's representatives betrayed them, the people "must visit their wrath upon the faithless public servant, and not upon an innocent third person [the bondholder] who has been led into the toils."[31]

High tax spokesmen frequently pointed out that the state had taken no action since the end of Reconstruction to renounce allegedly fraudulent portions of the debt and that on several occasions Democratic-controlled legislatures had tacitly recognized the validity of the debt. For example, they said, the Conservative-dominated legislature of 1869-70 had not repudiated any of the bonds issued by the Brownlow regime and had, in fact, permitted railroads to present bonds of any series to discharge their obligations. By the same token, the Democratic-controlled constitutional convention of 1870 had failed to renounce these securities, the funding act of 1873 encompassed all but a few bonds, and the state had made several interest payments on the debt. In brief, they maintained that it was too late to close the barn door because the horse had gone; the legality of the debt had been accepted by practice and lack of prompt challenge.[32]

No evidence has been found to indicate that the high tax leaders were bondholders and thus had a direct personal interest in debt payment. They were, nevertheless, clearly sympathetic to the creditors' position. Bondholders were innocent of any attempt to defraud Tennessee, state credit advocates said, and they should not be dealt with unjustly. Any settlement that would involve less than the full payment of the debt could not be enacted, in fairness, without the voluntary consent of the creditors. State credit men praised the contribution of the bondholders to Tennessee. Without their investments the state would have lacked benefits that it now took for granted. The "widow and orphan" and the "quiet investor," said the Chattanooga *Daily Times*, "who has put his earnings in stock, which he hoped would some time be a small bonanza for his children—these are the sufferers by such jayhawking financial raids as our repudiators are conducting."[33] State credit spokesmen argued that possession of most of the bonds by Northerners and foreigners should have no bearing on whether or not the debt should be paid. Outsiders were not enemies; many had even sympathized with the struggle of Tennessee and the Confederacy in the Civil

War.[34] Former Whig Governor Neil S. Brown cited widows' and orphans' investments in the bonds and rejected the argument that a debt to foreigners was different from any other debt. "It is as sacred to me as if it were held in the town I live in [because it] bears the seal of the State—it is the note of the State, and that is enough for me."[35]

State credit arguments involving a concern for the good name and reputation of Tennessee were in part a heritage of the pride and tradition of personal honor that had characterized the Old South. According to this view, rejection of the bondholders' claims would tarnish the proud name and integrity of the state. The Columbia *Herald* compared the struggle over the debt to that of the Tennessee Confederate soldier for his home state's honor, and the Chattanooga *Daily Times* reminded its readers that many of these men had lost all but honor in the Civil War.[36] The editor of the Nashville *Republican Banner* emphasized the vulnerable nature of Tennessee's good name when it warned, "A State's financial honor is like a woman's virtue—not a matter for the trivial gossip of curb-stone circles to be bandied about in the interests of factions or politics or rings . . . ."[37] A legislator reminded his audience that, if the state repudiated, "a stigma would be cast on Tennessee for generations unborn."[38]

These adversaries of repudiation saw world history as bearing out their contention that debtors must deal honestly with their creditors.[39] The editor of the Memphis *Daily Avalanche* called the policy of honoring financial obligations the "taproot of civilization" and asserted that from it came "all individual and social prosperity."[40] Such a policy, he said, was what separated the "most flourishing" nations such as England, France, and the United States from Egypt, Turkey, and Spain. Who wanted to see Tennessee sink as low as Spain?[41] The editor of the Nashville *Daily American* characterized nonpayment of obligations as being "worthy only of Turkey or the Barbay [*sic*] States of Africa."[42] David M. Key warned that history showed that "without exception liberty, life and property have less security in those countries or States which repudiate their obligations than in those who regard their honor as pledged to redeem their promises and therefore do redeem them."[43]

There was a direct relationship, state credit advocates said, between public honesty and private morality; if government set a low standard, the people would follow its example.[44] A prominent Presbyterian minister, concerned about debt repudiation, told his Nashville congregation that people would be no more righteous than their government. "The foundation of corruption opened in the seat of authority will," he continued, "through a thousand channels, infest the whole population."[45] The Athens *Post* repeated this sentiment when it commented that people would not pay their private obligations if the state did not honor its debts. Failure to settle in a just fashion, said the Nashville *Daily American,* would result in a "wild carnival of wrong-doing" and produce a "society honeycombed and eaten up with corruption."[46] And Tennesseans were not alone in establishing a link between repudiation and social degradation. When the legislature discovered in January 1883 that Tennessee's treasurer had misappropriated nearly $400,000, several newspapers outside the state characterized the theft as the natural product of a repudiating society.[47]

Time and again, state credit men stressed the benefits that the bonds had provided. They reminded the public that Tennessee securities built the Capitol and a railroad network.[48] Tennesseans should blush with shame, one politician said, to look at the Capitol and remember that "the money which reared it was obtained from other people by assurances which we are every day falsifying and which is in imminent danger of being utterly lost."[49] L. C. Houk, in Congress after 1878, praised the bondowners for providing the money that built turnpikes and railroads, and newspaper editors and politicians repeatedly cited the prosperity brought by the railroads. In 1879 the Memphis *Daily Appeal* asserted that the value of Tennessee land had risen from four dollars per acre in 1836 to more than six dollars in 1878 because of the development of a statewide railroad network.[50] Major William J. Sykes of Shelby County told his listeners in Union

City in 1880 that they saved a substantial sum in the sale of their wheat, cotton, and other farm products because railroad transportation was cheaper than any other. Rail rates also meant that products came into Tennessee at a lower cost. "You experience the benefits of these railroads built by this state debt in every cup of coffee or tea you drink, in all the clothes you wear, in every pound of salt you use, in all the farming tools with which you make your crops," he said.[51] Two years earlier, Sykes had estimated that railroads saved Tennesseans more in a single year in transportation rates than the taxes required to pay the state debt.[52]

On the question of Tennessee's ability to pay, the state credit forces strove to combat a variety of arguments. They repeatedly stressed that Tennesseans were not burdened with excessive taxes and that the state could pay its debt without oppressive new tax levies. Nor in their opinion did Civil War destruction and the loss of slave property release them from their obligations. Postmaster General David M. Key of Chattanooga reminded his fellow citizens that the state had willingly entered the war and accordingly must accept its consequences, while Sykes challenged an audience to name a single bondholder who had freed a slave in Tennessee.[53] "In nearly every instance," the editor of the Memphis *Daily Appeal* said, those who use the loss of slave property as an excuse for nonpayment "never owned a slave," and the "largest slaveowners are generally the advocates of State credit."[54] The argument that the loss of slave property and wartime destruction constituted grounds for repudiation had dangerous implications, said one state credit spokesman: "Upon this theory, every debtor might scale or repudiate his debt when it becomes due, should he be possessed of fewer goods than when his debt was created."[55]

As representatives of the political and economic elite, state credit leaders were quick to denounce low tax arguments as attacks on property rights and appeals to class antagonism. In 1879 and 1880 they charged low tax Democrats, who desired a massive scaling of the debt, with fostering communism in Tennessee. The low taxers resembled communists in their use

of demagogic appeals to arouse the passions of the people
and in their lack of respect for established political leaders,
past and present, who supported bond issuance or debt payment. But above all, they branded as communistic the low
taxers' portrayal of the debt as the creation of the rich for
which the poor were being forced to pay.[56] The Nashville
Daily American called it an attack on "accumulation" and on
"prudence and industry in every branch of society."[57] The
Knoxville *Daily Chronicle* warned that low tax men desired
to "array one class against another" and "baptize the country
in fraternal blood" to achieve their goal.[58] Speaking for the
high tax camp, the editors of the Nashville *Daily American*
and the *Banner* expressed a view of society reminiscent of
Adam Smith and the school of classical economy. Society
was made up not of classes but of individuals; each person
contributed to the good of the whole by accumulating property. Those who had achieved success and those who were
striving for material prosperity should beware of doctrines
that threatened to divide society and array rich against poor.[59]

Far more effective, however, than attempts to tar the low
tax movement with a communistic brush were the frequent
warnings of state credit Democrats that division of the party
over the debt question might allow the Radicals to regain
power. Party unity insured Democratic control of state government; division would bring Republican rule and the return
of policies similar to those of Reconstruction. In utilizing this
argument, state credit Democrats did not make blatant and
pointed appeals to white fears that a Republican-controlled
state government would give increased political and social
status to Negroes. Nevertheless, references to the Brownlow
era undoubtedly reminded Democrats of the disfranchisement
of white Confederates and the extension of the vote and of
civil liberties to former slaves. Forthright calls for the preservation of white solidarity, however, used effectively by the
Democratic leadership in some other Southern states, were
largely absent from the rhetoric of high tax Democrats in
Tennessee. Perhaps this was because blacks constituted less
than a third of the population and white Republicans had

never given strong support to concerns of blacks.[60]

The ideals of the New South failed to become reality in Tennessee, in spite of the efforts and promises of state credit Democrats and Republicans. Between 1870 and 1880 the amount of capitalization in manufacturing enterprises did rise from $15.5 million to $20 million, but the impact of this growth was confined almost exclusively to the four major urban centers—Nashville, Memphis, Chattanooga, and Knoxville.[61] Tennessee shared in the prolonged national depression that occurred from 1873 to 1879; by 1880, however, the nation was recovering, and expansion and prosperity increased during the early years of the decade. Farm prices improved, and the state's business and industry began to grow significantly. In retrospect, it seems clear that the leaders of the state credit faction failed to understand the slow pace of economic change and, even more important, failed to grasp the compelling influence of national trends on the state's economy. On the other hand, the campaign to forestall repudiation might have favorably impressed the out-of-state financial community during the depression years, thereby helping to encourage the flow of capital and industry into Tennessee in the more prosperous 1880s.

Widely admired and respected by their followers for their roles in the Civil War and in the redemption of the state from Republican control, state credit Democrats seemed in firm control of their party as the 1870s began. They were not backward-looking reactionaries who yearned for the old and feared contemporary trends; instead, they hoped to foster the economic development of the state in ways that would unite it with the industrial Middle West and Northeast. Convinced that debt payment was vital to this goal, they struggled throughout the decade, with the assistance of state credit Republicans, to enact a permanent settlement. They might have resolved the debt problem on their terms if it had not been for the depression. As events turned out, economic hardship spawned a revolt within Democratic ranks that threatened state credit leadership of the party and destroyed Democratic control of state government.

CHAPTER V

Hard Times and
the Low Tax Argument

On September 18, 1873, Jay Cooke and Company of Philadelphia and New York, one of the leading banks in the nation, closed its doors because of shaky investments in the Northern Pacific Railroad and a run on the bank by worried depositors. The collapse of the House of Cooke triggered a financial crisis that quickly developed into a nationwide depression which lasted more than five years. It was the worst such episode in the late nineteenth century and one of the longest periods of economic stagnation in American history.[1]

From 1873 to 1878 more than forty national banks collapsed, and ten thousand businesses failed in 1878 alone. Railroad construction, which had set a postwar record with 7,379 miles of new track laid in 1871, declined to only 2,281 miles in 1877. The American Iron and Steel Association journal reported in 1878 that more than half the industry's furnaces and a number of rolling mills had been closed for a year. Pig iron production fell some eight hundred thousand tons between 1873 and 1876. Hundreds of thousands of men lost their jobs, bread lines appeared in cities, and farmers suffered as agricultural prices fell.[2]

The depressed economy dealt a stunning blow to the high taxers' visions of progress. From 1865 through 1873 railroad mileage in Tennessee grew by 324 miles, but only 81 additional miles of track were laid between 1873 and 1879. Not a single mile of new track went down in 1875. In late November 1873 an East Tennessean wrote that economic conditions had forced coal mines in nearby counties to curb their production and that the Roane Iron Company at Chattanooga had closed its rolling mill, putting 200 men out of work. The state commissioner of agriculture, statistics, and mines reported that low prices had forced more than half the iron furnaces to close and that only seven of the sixteen furnaces in Tennessee were in blast in December 1878. Industrial and business activity in such cities as Chattanooga and Nashville fell off markedly.[3]

Farm and other property values decreased. In 1874 the total assessed worth of all taxable property in Tennessee stood at more than $289.5 million; this figure was around $228.3 million in 1880. The average assessed value per acre of East Tennessee land fell from $5.46 in 1871 to $4.67 in 1880. The drop was appreciably more in Middle and West Tennessee, where commercial farming was practiced on a larger scale. Middle Tennessee, where low tax sentiment was strongest, experienced the greatest decline—from $10.25 per acre in 1871 to $6.17 in 1880. Simultaneously, the assessed value of West Tennessee land fell from $8.39 to $6.00 per acre. Farmers and businessmen complained of falling prices and values, scarcity of currency, unemployment, and general economic stagnation.[4]

More than 72 percent of Tennessee's work force farmed in 1870, and the depression hit the farmer very hard. Corn, the leading cash crop, fell from its decade high of 64 cents per bushel in 1874 to a decade low of 31 cents in 1878. Cotton was a major cash crop in Middle and West Tennessee, where the best quality fiber grew. Cotton that sold for 17.9 cents per pound in 1871 declined 54 percent to 8.16 cents in 1878. The state ranked third in the nation in production of tobacco in 1870. The finest tobacco was grown in a tier of northern Middle Tennessee counties bordering Kentucky, but numerous other Middle and West Tennessee counties cultivated the crop commercially. From a decade high of 13.7 cents per pound in 1874, the price of tobacco fell 61 percent to the decade low of 5.4 cents in 1877. Farm livestock decreased in value from $55,084,075 in 1870 to $43,651,470 in 1880. Certainly the plight of the farmer had a direct effect on the

TABLE I. PRICES OF MAJOR TENNESSEE CROPS, 1870-1879

Crops	1870	1871	1872	1873	1874	1875	1876	1877	1878	1879
Prices in Cents Per Pound										
Cotton	12.1	17.9	16.5	14.1	13.0	11.1	9.71	8.53	8.16	10.28
Tobacco	9.7	10.2	10.7	8.6	13.7	7.7	7.3	5.4	5.8	6.1
Prices in Dollars Per Bushel										
Corn	.521	.464	.383	.483	.641	.419	.361	.357	.313	.364
Wheat	1.042	1.247	1.239	1.168	.948	1.010	1.036	1.085	.772	1.107
Oats	.426	.385	.322	.374	.520	.367	.349	.288	.240	.326

Source: U.S., Department of Commerce, Bureau of the Census, *Historical Statistics of the United States, Colonial Times to 1957: A Statistical Abstract Supplement* (Prepared with the cooperation of the Social Science Research Council [Washington: Government Printing Office, 196C]), 297-98, 302.

state treasury and on the debt question.[5]

The leadership of both the Democratic and Republican parties had desired early in the 1870s to pay the debt at its face value, but the hard times later in the decade and the inadequacies of the revenue system made such action unpalatable and difficult. The inability of many taxpayers to pay, inefficient assessment and collection machinery, and reductions in the tax rate caused a decline in state revenues. In 1877, in response to demands from taxpayers, the legislature cut the tax rate from forty cents per $100 of assessed value to ten cents. Even so, tax delinquency was a major problem, and large amounts of property were sold for taxes. Though complaints by the public and elected officials led the legislature to take some steps to remedy the inequities and inadequacies in the revenue system, the state still lacked an adequate system of raising and collecting public monies.[6]

Cries for tax relief weakened the position of the high taxers. Newspapers reported growing opposition to higher levies and considerable sentiment for tax cuts.[7] "A scarcity of money and a decline of prices," the Memphis *Daily Avalanche* stated, when coupled with an increased public debt and taxes, places the people between the "upper and nether millstone."[8] In September 1876 another correspondent wrote to the *Avalanche* that the cry for tax relief was coming from "every direction" and that "too much cannot be said in its favor."[9] In his race for a United States Senate seat, Andrew Johnson appealed to rising sentiment against high taxes when he informed an audience, "all we eat, drink and wear, and even the last sad act that is performed when clods are heard to rumble on the coffin, is taxed."[10] The people of West Tennessee, declared the Jackson *Whig and Tribune,* "cursed under morgages [sic]," were in no condition to be "gutted by tax gatherers."[11]

Complaints by farmers and reports from rural counties revealed the extent of hard times and opposition to tax collection. A revenue officer from Bolivar reported to the comptroller in August 1876 that he would do his best to collect the taxes but that there was "no money in the Country & Property brings nothing scarcely when sold."[12] "I sometimes feel sorry I was ever elected Tax Col[lector]," said R. J. Turner of Franklin County, who advised Comptroller James L. Gaines that "the people have but little money in circulation and how the taxes is [sic] to be col[lected], I cant [sic] tell."[13] Arguing that the state was taxing farmers excessively and that revenue officers were relentless, a correspondent in the Nashville *Rural Sun* wrote that these "ministers of the law must have their pay [even] if it takes the bread from our childrens [sic] mouths."[14]

The experience of Memphis in the 1870s clearly illustrates the link between economic misfortune and popular support for debt scaling. By 1870, Memphis had regained its prewar level of commercial and business activity, but prosperity did not last. The municipal government was poorly administered, and in 1870 its indebtedness stood at over $4.5 million. During the next few years, the city's financial condition worsened, and by 1878 Memphis was $5 million in debt and unable to meet its obligations. It was a major cotton exchange, where factors, commission merchants, grocers, hardware dealers, and many other businessmen catered to the needs of cotton planters in Tennessee and neighboring states; so the fall of cotton prices in the 1870s shattered the city's economy. In 1870-72, Memphis cotton factors received 380,924 bales worth $36,550,617; 386,129 bales of cotton in 1878-79 brought only $17,456,892. In addition, property values were declining and taxes mounting. Chronic tax delinquency of long duration, the editor of the Memphis *Daily Avalanche* said in 1879, had created a situation in which city tax collectors were able to collect only 70 percent of the total assessment.[15]

Along with the burdens of an inefficient government and a decline in the price of cotton, the "Bluff City" suffered two devastating yellow fever epidemics. One, in 1873, took the lives of 2,000 residents, and a more severe visitation in 1878 killed more than 5,000. Hundreds fled the city, and property values fell as Memphis gained a reputation of being an unhealthy place to live. Between 1870 and 1880 the population of this river town decreased by more than 16 percent. In 1879, answering the pleas of the Memphis Chamber of Commerce and other groups for state financial assistance, the governor signed a law that revoked the charter of the city and placed the Taxing District of Shelby County under the administration of three commissioners named by the governor.[16]

From 1879 to 1893, when the state restored self-government to Memphis, the General Assembly set its tax rate and controlled expenditures. For several years following the creation of the taxing district, legislative committees struggled to settle the city's bonded debt at less than its original face value, and in 1885 the state funded the last portion of the debt at seventy cents on the dollar. It is hardly surprising that low tax arguments appealed to many Shelby County residents and that advocates of tax relief and debt scaling often found warm support in this economically distressed area.[17]

In contrast to the state credit spokesmen, advocates of low taxes did not find their leaders among the prestigious and well-known public figures of the day. Instead, their spokesmen were, for the most part, farmers and small-town attorneys and businessmen with close ties to the soil. Low taxers appeared within the ranks of the Democratic party and the small Greenback party in Middle and West Tennessee, especially the economically distressed rural areas; few seem to have been old Whigs, and their support came from traditionally Democratic counties. They did not demonstrate glamorous Civil War records or high military offices. The ranks of eleven of the twenty-one Democratic legislators who met in 1879 to form the low tax party are ascertainable: they show one colonel, one major, two captains, one lieutenant, two sergeants, and four privates, one of whom later became a chaplain. Their occupations also mirror the orientation of the movement. Among the eighteen whose occupations can be determined were two farmers, one farmer and cattle man, one farmer and miller, one farmer and nurseryman, six lawyers, one lawyer and minister, and one lawyer and journalist. Business occupations represented were a tanyard operator, a newspaper editor, a flour miller, and a surveyor. Only one man in the group, A. L. Landis of Bedford County, was engaged in banking and manufacturing and was associated for a time with a railroad. Deriving their livelihood directly from farming or from an agricultural clientele, these low tax men felt severely the impact of the depression on agriculture. They were convinced that state credit debt policies would only exacerbate their plight and that of most Tennesseans.[18]

The low tax forces drew their main support from the rural areas. When the group of low tax legislators organized in 1879, they passed a set of resolutions identifying their followers as primarily country residents, whereas they saw the cities as the main citadels of state officials, capitalists, and businessmen who voiced state credit views. In the gubernatorial election of 1880, rural Democratic voters gave the low tax Democratic candidate proportionately more support than did Democrats residing in towns and cities. The Grange, whose membership was dwindling rapidly in the last half of the 1870s, apparently took no official position on the debt question. But when the 1873 funding bill was before the house, Amos B. Haynes of Shelby County, a former president of the Shelby County Agricultural Association who would be selected master of the Tennessee Grange in 1876, voted against it. In addition, low tax legislator John M. Head was a state official of the Grange, and low tax Representative John J. Boon of Madison County was a member of the organization. Low tax sentiment was not confined exclusively to farming areas. Memphis, for example, demonstrated considerable support of low tax views, and the Greenback party, which favored substantial debt scaling, drew much of its support from city workers and mechanics.[19]

Although low tax supporters could be found in all of the Democratic counties, the areas where the movement was strongest exhibited significant common characteristics. This was especially true in eastern Middle Tennessee, the center of dissident strength. Democratic counties with predominantly white populations tended to vote heavily low tax. In 1880 the low tax candidate for governor won 50 percent or more of the vote in 11 of the 18 Democratic counties across the state whose population was 90 percent or more white. This pattern was even more pronounced in Middle Tennessee, where the low tax nominee carried 10 of 13 such counties. Low tax victories frequently occurred in counties where most voters owned their farms. Of the 11 Middle and West Tennessee counties which showed the least farm tenancy and share-cropping—25 percent and under—the low tax candidate carried 8. In East Tennessee, where tenancy and sharecropping were rarer, the 3 Democratic counties with the fewest tenants and sharecroppers voted low tax by 29 to 41 percent. State credit influence predominated, on the other hand, in counties with a high rate—40 percent or more. S. F. Wilson, low tax gubernatorial candidate, carried only 2 of 14 such counties; in 8 of these he garnered only 19 percent of the vote or less.[20]

While low tax sentiment was not restricted to counties with relatively poor land, it does appear that the most enthusiastic support for defiance of the state credit position came from such counties. All but 1 of the 19 counties that the low tax group carried with 50 percent or more of the vote in 1880 were in Middle Tennessee, most of them in the eastern part, where the average value per acre of land was 15 percent below the regional average. Democratic counties in this section with land valued at less than $4.00 an acre showed a strong preference for the low tax stand. Wilson carried 8 of 12 such counties with 40 percent or more of the vote, while his state credit opponent won but 4.[21]

Lack of the continuous leadership of a capable and widely admired spokesman was a real hardship to the low tax movement. Andrew Johnson and Arthur S. Colyar were familiar to many citizens across Tennessee; neither man, however, provided long-term leadership. Johnson, an early proponent of debt scaling, died in 1875, just as opposition to payment was beginning to grow. Colyar, who at one time seemed eager to become the spokesman for the low tax forces, joined the ranks of the state credit forces when the issue reached crisis proportions in 1879.

Colyar's political activities in the 1870s have confused some historians. He has been described as the leader of a powerful, old-line, Whig-industrialist faction of the Democratic party.[22] The state credit wing of the party was, to be sure, a New South-oriented group that attracted many former Whigs. From 1870 to 1879, however, Colyar, in his advocacy of scaling the debt, continually differed with this group of business-minded Democrats and allied himself with the low tax dissenters, who were generally cool toward the New South philosophy and who were not typically Whigs and businessmen. Colyar was an ardent spokesman for industrialization and economic diversification, but until 1879 he did not represent the wing of the Democratic party that embraced such views. Indeed, prior to that time it was the state credit, business-oriented group that blocked his efforts to gain political office.[23]

Following Johnson's death and Colyar's defection, John H. Savage of Warren County emerged as leader of the dissidents from 1879 to 1883. Like Colyar, he was an established political figure, having served four terms as a Democratic United States congressman before the Civil War. In 1859 he lost his bid for reelection when his opponent successfully used Savage's opposition to state aid to railroads to defeat him. Before the Civil War he served in the Texas Revolution, the Seminole War, and the Mexican War. Although not a zealous proponent of secession, he supported the Confederacy and commanded the Sixteenth Tennessee Regiment in the early part of the conflict. Resigning from the army when he failed to receive a promotion to Brigadier General, Savage blamed Confederate Governor Isham G. Harris for this slight and sought unsuccessfully to meet the governor in a duel. In the 1870s, Savage again began to take an active role in state politics. The reemergence of Harris as a major Democratic leader at about the same time deeply angered Savage.[24] Intensely proud of his own military record, he regarded Harris, who had served on the staffs of Confederate generals throughout the war, as a coward, a political manipulator, and a "manager of political spoils and offices," who awarded posts to his loyal followers rather than to men of ability.[25]

At odds with one of the most influential party regulars,

Savage also found little to admire in the character and career of Andrew Johnson, the state's foremost independent Democrat. Although the two men were in agreement concerning the debt and their rhetoric was loud with similar denunciations of political rings and the wealthy and appeals to the common man, Savage's dislike for Johnson's actions in the Civil War and Reconstruction precluded any chance for cooperation between the two in opposing debt payment in the early 1870s. In 1872, when Johnson ran for congressman-at-large, Savage spoke publicly against him, describing the ex-president as a man whose heart was filled with "ambition and tyranny" and who had "always trampled people and Constitution alike under his feet, when they stood in the line of his advancement."[26] Two years later, Savage condemned Johnson's senatorial aspirations. Blocked by his own antagonism from working with Johnson, he also appears never to have established an alliance with Colyar before the industrialist defected to state credit ranks.[27]

Savage rendered valuable service to the low tax cause as its chief spokesman during the height of the debt struggle. He was elected to the state house of representatives in 1876, and until 1883 the press and politicians frequently mentioned his name in connection with the governorship and a United States Senate seat. His popularity, however, was chiefly confined to his native Warren County and the area immediately surrounding, and he never won a national or statewide office after the war. State credit forces vilified him; his followers vigorously defended him. The Chattanooga *Daily Times* characterized him as an "ignorant, bumptious, conceited agrarian fraud" who was "a pigmy intellect, and totally destitute of moral sense" and a dangerous purveyor of "semi-communistic doctrines."[28] Savage represented "Denis Kearneyism," said the Memphis *Daily Avalanche,* declaring that he "misrepresented" thousands of honest people who had listened to the "sophisteries [*sic*] of dangerous demagogues."[29] In contrast, the McMinnville *New Era* in Warren County saw him as a brave man who had begun the struggle of the "people against the unjust claims of the bondholders,"[30] and the Humboldt

Argus contended that he had "done more to break up corrupt political rings than any man in the State and deserves well of the honest tax payers. All the money on Wall street can't buy him."[31]

Savage and other low tax spokesmen did not subscribe to the New South creed. With the exception of Colyar, their speeches contained none of the calls for economic diversification and the need for immigrants that were typical of those who championed business and industrial growth as the key to Tennessee's future prosperity. Acquiescence in state credit debt policies was too high a price to pay for the possibility of making the New South dream a reality. Furthermore, low tax men suspected that if the people paid heavy taxes for a state credit debt settlement and a burst of economic growth followed, the main beneficiaries would be the propertied urban capitalists, businessmen, and lawyers, not average Tennesseans. Many would pay for the benefit of a few. They rejected the argument that equated repudiation with economic disaster and payment with prosperity, and used as examples foreign countries and states such as Virginia and Massachusetts, which had not paid the full face value of their debts and yet had not suffered economic collapse from the stigma of repudiation.[32] It took "brazen impudence," Democratic state legislator R. E. Thompson said, for the state credit men to proclaim that burdening Tennessee with millions in debt would "cause immigration and make us prosperous and rich." Prosperity would come with the debt removed and the currency supply adequate.[33] On the question of attracting new residents, Savage held the opinion that he and his fellow Tennesseans "must work out [their] own salvation" and warned that, if the newcomer "has more money, muscle and brains than Tennesseans, the effect of immigration will be that Tennesseans must emigrate." He would treat the new arrival fairly if he came, but he would not "beg him" to come.[34]

Low tax Democrats displayed a marked lack of respect for the established party leadership. They charged that the ruling state credit ring or clique manipulated the party to keep themselves in office. Johnson, Colyar, and Savage, who were

ambitious for office, resented the attempts of high tax
leaders to control the governorship and the United States
Senate seats.[35] Savage insisted that these men had no right to
call themselves Democrats because "they believe[d] in pack-
ing conventions, and [sought] to rule by the corrupt use of
money and ring combinations for mutual 'aid and comfort' at
the expense of the masses."[36] At times low tax men became
bitterly personal in their denunciations and characterized
James E. Bailey, James D. Porter, and other state credit leaders as tools of bondholders and speculators.[37] In 1880 the
editor of the McMinnville *New Era* acknowledged that the
high tax leaders were better known that those in the low tax
ranks but argued that they had achieved this recognition by
being successful "note shavers, and grinders of the faces of
the poor."[38] The people, he declared, would not allow their
destiny to be controlled by "a few chronic officeholders and
office seekers and the so-called 'wealth' and 'intelligence' of
the State."[39]

One of the most telling arguments of the low tax leaders
was that the debt must be scaled because portions of it had
been illegally and fraudulently contracted; the Brownlow debt
policy provided plenty of ammunition.[40] It was, J. T. Smith
wrote to Governor Porter, the Republican "party of freed
negroes, dirt Eaters, Tar heals [*sic*], and Scalawags, [that]
got Tennessee into the fix she now finds herself [in] . . . ."[41]
Low tax men repeatedly reminded Tennesseans about the evidence of fraud connected with the Brownlow debt and associated it with other controversial acts of the Republican party
in Reconstruction. The people's liberties were "bound hand
and foot" when the Radicals issued bonds after the Civil War,
said Democratic legislator W. A. Milliken in a debate in the
General Assembly in 1877.[42] Another opponent of the state
credit position believed that Tennessee emitted tainted securities during Reconstruction when "tax payers were disfranchised" and were regarded as "merely beasts of burden, ruled
by glittering bayonets at the ballot box as well as in the halls
of justice."[43] The belief that these bonds were improperly
issued was widely held among Democrats, a fact that tar-

nished the image of the whole debt in the eyes of many. A
perceptive state credit correspondent wrote to Governor Porter in 1877 that most of his neighbors were well aware that
"a large majority of the outstanding indebtedness are Brownlow bonds."[44]

As the controversy developed, the low tax forces expanded
their charge that part of the debt was illegally created to include those amounts not contracted during Reconstruction.
Opponents of state credit policy claimed that fraud surrounded the debt contracted from 1852 to 1860 and that recipients of these securities had illegally sold them at below
par value. In 1880, S. F. Wilson asserted that evidence of impropriety extended as far back as 1834 and that the state
should pay only a small fraction of its debt. Savage went even
further: he argued that the legislature had no authority to
issue bonds of any sort. The state constitution, he said, authorized the General Assembly only to tax the people: it did not
allow the Assembly to burden the people with such a debt.[45]
In a public address in 1875, West Tennessee planter and industrialist Enoch Ensley expressed a similar sentiment, but
one held by few men of his type, when he said that the very
"nature of all free people's governments" forbade a state
from issuing bonds to mortgage "property of the citizens for
years to come, and legally or morally bind their successors to
abide and carry out this action."[46]

Low tax advocates also based their demands for debt scaling on an interpretation of that obligation which differed
from the high tax perspective. They maintained that the Civil
War had drastically changed the nature of debts contracted
earlier. The war had caused tremendous damage to the state,
had impoverished the people, and had destroyed the property
and prosperity on which the original antebellum debt had
been based.[47] Bondholders should share in that loss. According to Savage, the loss of slave property, "the earnings of the
Southern people for two hundred years," was an important
reason for scaling the debt.[48] "The State of Tennessee," a
correspondent wrote to the Memphis *Daily Avalanche*, "does
not morally owe the full amount of her present nominal

debt, because the [slave] property in part on which it was
based . . . has been as property destroyed and relieved from
taxation."[49] Representative D. J. Nobblitt of Lincoln County
said that high taxers who spoke of the state's honor were
those who had kept a "safe distance from blood" in the war
and "washed their banner's [sic] in women's tears."[50] In a
similar fashion, the poverty and decline of property values
since the war were grounds for the followers of Johnson and
Savage to demand that the bondholder take a loss on his investment.[51]

   Johnson, Savage, and their allies lacked the state credit
faction's admiration for the creditors, most of whom were
Northerners. Some saw the bondholder as partially responsible for the destruction of the Civil War and the economic
hardships of the succeeding years.[52] Convinced that Tennessee's creditors had treated the state unfairly, Savage put this
rhetorical question: "Suppose I borrow of you $1,000 to
build a house and give you a morgage [sic], and you come
along with an army, reinforced by foreigners and Dutch and
white folks and black folks, and you burn it down. Don't you
think you'd be a long time getting your morgage [sic]?"[53] A
correspondent in the Memphis *Daily Avalanche* asserted in
1876 that the state's Northern creditors were partly to blame
for the economic conditions of the decade because they had
supported federal policies that had "continued to impovrish
[sic] and almost utterly destroy the recuperative energy [of
Tennessee] granted by nature to her soil and climate."[54]

   At times, low taxers depicted the creditors as a greedy con-
spiratorial class bent on enriching themselves at the expense
of Tennesseans.[55] If the creditors had worked to help the
people by encouraging economic growth, a state legislator
pointed out in 1877, they would have already received payment for their securities; instead, "insatiable avarice" had
seized them, and they had tried to "absorb the whole wealth
of the indepted [sic] states."[56] A correspondent in the Sparta
Index depicted the owners of Tennessee securities as "kid-
gloved gentlemen about Wall street" whose funds had done
nothing for Tennessee.[57] A speaker at a black Handcock-
English Club meeting in Memphis in 1880 informed his audi-

ence that the creditors were Easterners whose hands were "soft as velvet" and who wanted full debt payment "because they hate you, hate your offspring and hate your country."[58] A printed announcement of a low tax convention described creditors as persons who would "sacrifice your home and everything that is dear to you to gratify their avaricious demands."[59]

Most of the low tax spokesmen professed a sympathy for the common man that was not often present in the rhetoric of their state credit rivals. Speaking, they said, for the average taxpayer, they attacked the high tax forces in terms reminiscent of the antebellum Democracy of Andrew Jackson. In contrast to the state credit spokesmen's concept of a classless or seamless society, they tended to see it as composed of conflicting classes and interest groups. Andrew Johnson, a former tailor, had throughout his political career appealed to the average citizen and expressed a dislike for the wealthy.[60] John J. Boon, a West Tennessee farmer, legislator, and granger who favored debt scaling, believed that the "producing classes" were the victims of a conspiracy. "Though we make everything, yet we see the smallest part of the profits of our labors," he wrote when he served in the General Assembly. "I see here every day before my eyes the want of a thorough organization & concert of action, for truly all other classes are combining their forces to rule us[,] the working and producing classes."[61] S. F. Wilson asserted that state bonds contributed to the flow of most of the nation's wealth from the control of the "laboring classes" to the "non-producing classes."[62] To Savage, the high tax forces were the "enemies of the people" who subscribed to the theory that the "wealthy or so-called better classes would make the laws and fill the offices of honor and profit, and that the great mass of men have neither the virtue nor intelligence to make laws or rule themselves wisely."[63] Nor were such arguments anathema to at least one man of wealth, for Colyar charged that a conspiracy of rich national bankers and owners of federal and state bonds was behind the currency shortage of the 1870s.[64]

Time and again low tax spokesmen stressed that the hard

times of the 1870s made it impossible for Tennessee to honor its debt.[65] Colyar believed that Tennesseans could not carry the tax burden. "We are absolutely without money," he said in May 1876; "every industry is utterly paralized [*sic*], and when the holders of our bonds demand the payment of heavy taxes *in money,* they demand something we have not and cannot give."[66] An angry correspondent in the Nashville *Republican Banner* predicted that higher taxes would turn thousands out of their homes "all for the sake of the bondholder, when one-half of our mechanics are without employment and our farmers are barely able to feed and clothe their families, having no labor that can be relied on."[67] The stagnant economy generated demands for delay of debt payment and for scaling the debt. Johnson and Colyar proposed such policies very early. Colyar called on the state to *"go and hunt up* our creditors and lay the *facts* before them, and ask for a compromise."[68] Calls for less than dollar-for-dollar payment began with a few voices and increased rapidly after the onset of the depression in the winter of 1873-74. Three years later, state credit Democrats, acknowledging the reality of fast-growing low tax sentiment and the existence of real economic hardship, began to speak of the need for an honorable compromise with the creditors at less than 100 cents on the dollar.

While low taxers were fairly unified in their opposition to full payment, they were not in total agreement as to how much of the debt should be honored. Colyar was often vague about how much scaling he favored. Savage, despite his contention that the state had no right to issue any bonds, sought to scale 66 2/3 percent of all the debt contracted since 1851 for railroads and turnpikes and to pay the remainder of the debt in full. In 1879 and 1880, at the height of the controversy over this question, many low taxers wanted Tennessee to repudiate all of the securities issued from 1852 through Reconstruction for transportation projects and to scale and pay the small additional amount of bonded debt. Because of their conviction that state credit Democrats and Republicans would commit the state to a funding policy without regard for the wishes of the average citizen, low tax men insisted on a referendum regarding any solution devised by the governor and the legislature. Most adamant in their demands between 1876 and 1880, when times were hard and their movement was strongest, low taxers became more agreeable to compromise after 1880.[69]

Opponents of the state credit position generally ignored the Negro voter. Unlike the debt-scaling Readjuster party in Virginia in this period and the Populist party in various parts of the South in the 1890s, Tennessee's low tax forces made almost no attempt to court the votes of blacks. In 1880 a low tax Democrat did try to convince his listeners at a black political rally in Memphis that they should support the low tax candidate for governor. He warned that a Republican victory would mean a funding program that would necessitate high taxes which would drive up the price of everything Negroes bought or rented. Negro property owners might have liked the idea of scaling the debt to keep taxes low, but nothing else in the platform of the dissident Democrats would have altered significantly the status of the vast majority of blacks. While low tax spokesmen did not express aggressively anti-Negro feelings in public, Savage, for one, had a strong personal antipathy for blacks and showed no desire to seek their support. Low taxers usually referred to blacks as lost slave property. Only in 1882, when low taxers were back in the regular party fold, did they work with state credit Democrats in Shelby County to convince discontented Negro Republicans in Memphis that they should bolt their party and support Democrat William B. Bate for governor.[70]

This lack of interest in the black vote is but one of the significant differences between the Tennessee low tax movement and the Readjuster revolt in neighboring Virginia. In 1879, Virginia Democrats opposed to debt payment founded the Readjuster party. Led by the dynamic ex-Confederate General William Mahone, the Readjusters swept to power, sent Mahone to the United States Senate in 1879, controlled the state legislature from 1879 to 1883, elected their candidate governor in 1881, and passed legislation significantly

scaling the state's debt. Their success was made possible by
the organizational skill of Mahone, the party's fusion with
Virginia Republicans, and the backing of the Republican administration in Washington; black support was also a crucial
element.[71] The Tennessee low tax movement had none of
these ingredients for success. Blacks were not wanted, and
neither Savage nor any of his associates displayed the ability
of a Mahone to form a cohesive political party. Although low
tax legislators did urge Republicans to support their cause in
a public statement drawn up in 1879, they made no concerted effort to ally with this party. In addition, there is no
evidence that pressure from Washington was exerted on Tennessee Republicans to cooperate with the low taxers.

The record of the Virginia Readjusters poses a provocative
question regarding what might have been if the low taxers
had ever come to power in Tennessee. Once in office, Readjusters supported measures that went far beyond their early
emphasis on debt scaling, lower taxes, and aid for public
schools. They repealed the poll tax, reformed the tax system,
appropriated record sums for education and eleemosynary institutions, and expanded social services. They inspected ferti-
lizers for quality, set standards for out-of-state insurance companies operating in the state, and pushed for railroad regulation. In addition, they encouraged economic diversification,
even to the point of backing a program of tariff protection
for Virginia products.[72] Tennessee debt scalers never showed
much interest in such a variety of reforms. Their platform of
debt reduction, an easing of the tax burden on landowners,
and support of public schools resembled that of the early Readjusters, and had they won control of state government,
Tennessee low taxers might very well have followed the pattern of the Virginians in such areas as tax reform, financing
of public education, and business regulation. But a low tax
state administration probably would not have possessed the
breadth of concerns and vitality displayed by the Virginia
Readjusters, largely because the movement in Tennessee
rested on a narrower base and was not allied with blacks or
Republicans.

CHAPTER VI

Two Democratic Attempts at Compromise

The gubernatorial race of 1876 offered a forum for the airing of low tax and state credit views and set the stage for the first major attempt at debt settlement since the passage of the funding act of 1873. In the spring and summer of 1876, newspapers debated the debt issue, and prominent politicians discussed it in preparation for the party conventions scheduled for August. The Memphis *Daily Avalanche* demanded that the next legislature repeal the funding act and announced that it would support no candidate for governor unless he endorsed a tax reduction. The editor said that, if all of the personal property in the state were to be sold at current prices, the amount obtained would not be enough to pay off the debt.[1]

Colyar and state Senator James E. Bailey added their voices to the discussion. Speaking in Nashville and Memphis, Colyar called for reduction in taxes and scaling of the debt.[2] His Nashville address caused the Memphis *Daily Appeal,* which favored state credit, to remark acidly that Colyar's stand on the debt question was erroneously based on his "attributing to the noble people of Tennessee no higher motives than those which give direction to his vile and grovelling nature."[3] Bailey, a prewar Whig from Clarksville who had actively supported state aid to internal improvements in the 1850s, took to the stump to rebut Colyar's views. This business-minded lawyer, a former director of the defunct Bank of Tennessee, used the whole battery of state credit arguments to defend debt payment. Tennessee had legally contracted the

debt, and considerations of justice, honor, and its own economic future bound the state to pay its obligation.[4] In Clarksville in May he denounced repudiation as a blow at property
rights and warned darkly that "the spirit of agrarianism once
encouraged by the state [would] grow in strength until from
every quarter [would] be heard the ominous cries of communism."[5]

By the end of July it was apparent that taxes and debt
payment were major campaign issues. Former state legislator
Dorsey B. Thomas challenged Colyar for support from low
tax Democrats. Thomas, an antebellum Whig and Conservative opponent of the Brownlow administration, publicly
called for halving the tax rate and delaying further payment
of the debt. Rumor spread that Thomas would run for the
governorship independently if the Democratic platform did
not embrace his views.[6] This led the Chattanooga *Daily
Times* to cite a "limit to party allegiance" and to announce
that it could not back Thomas and his platform of repudiation, no matter who nominated him.[7] The influential Nashville *Daily American* and several other papers urged the Democrats to unify the party by reaffirming the planks of their
1874 platform calling for the preservation of state credit and
no tax increase.[8]

The Democrats who assembled in Nashville on August 10
unanimously nominated Governor Porter for a second term.
While the platform denounced repudiation and pledged payment of the state's obligations, it added that "prostration of
all industries and impovrishment [*sic*] of our people" had
made Tennessee "unable to endure" an increase.[9] A minority
report from several delegates called for a tax rate just high
enough to pay current operating expenses as well as the debt
interest on the school fund and bonds owned by educational
institutions, and it recommended that the next legislature
seek a debt compromise from the state's creditors. Bailey
spoke against the minority report, which the delegates rejected by a vote of 737 to 275. The Chattanooga *Daily Times*
and the Memphis *Daily Appeal* quickly endorsed the action
of the convention, but the Memphis *Daily Avalanche* disap-

proved of the platform and promised to inform the public of the convention's mistake.[10]

Rebuffed by the Democratic convention, Thomas decided to run independently for governor. Porter's administration inadvertently boosted Thomas's cause soon after the convention adjourned. The state had defaulted on all its debt interest payments since January 1874, and in the spring of 1876 the comptroller had expressed the opinion that there was little hope of resuming payments until the 1877 legislature considered the matter. The New York *Commercial and Financial Chronicle* informed its readers on July 1, 1876, however, of an existing rumor that Tennessee would resume interest payments. The Nashville *Daily American,* the Memphis *Daily Avalanche,* and the Knoxville *Tribune* also cited reports that the state would, indeed, pay overdue interest. The comptroller substantiated these reports when he inexplicably announced on August 24 that after September 15 Tennessee would accept for payment past-due bond coupons still outstanding for July 1874 and January and July 1875.[11]

Reaction to this attempt to pay back interest was immediate. The Memphis *Daily Avalanche* argued that the people would not forgive Porter for paying interest on a fraudulent debt and endorsed Thomas for governor.[12] Echoing its crosstown rival, the Memphis *Ledger* asserted that Porter would not have been renominated if the public had known he planned to pay the interest: "He has taken on a big load for the rest of the canvass and we do not propose to help him carry it."[13] The Memphis *Daily Appeal* disapproved of the governor's actions but denied that interest payment was sufficient grounds for withholding party support. The Nashville *Daily American,* though unhappy with the governor's decision, defended his character and insisted he had a right to order the payment of back interest.[14] Porter justified his own action by citing his obligation to pay overdue debt interest when treasury funds accumulated. The *Daily American* published correspondence between the governor and his attorney general which revealed the attorney general's marked lack of enthusiasm for Porter's action; the letter informed the gover-

nor only that there was no specific legal bar to this use of
state monies. Although the chief executive's decision received
the firm support of the Chattanooga *Daily Times,* the Gallatin
Examiner, the Paris *Weekly Intelligencer,* and the Jackson
Tribune and Sun, Thomas continued to condemn interest
payment, and the issue lingered. In a campaign speech in
Memphis as late as mid-October, Porter felt compelled to
justify his attempt to retire overdue coupons.[15]

The Republicans also held their state convention in August.
In an obvious attempt to enhance the independent candidacy
of Thomas, the delegates decided against nominating anyone
for the governorship, and a majority rejected a motion to de-
clare their party's opposition to repudiation in the platform.
But some Republican unhappiness with the decision not to
field a candidate developed within the party after the convention had adjourned. In September two Republicans entered
the race: William F. Yardley, a black lawyer and justice of the
peace in Knoxville, and former Confederate General George
B. Maney, a railroad official.[16]

In the ensuing campaign the candidates discussed a broad
range of issues. For example, Governor Porter defended his
administration's fiscal record, charged that Maney had been a
mediocre Confederate general and an inefficient railroad executive, and dismissed Yardley as being unqualified for the
post he sought. The governor maintained that Thomas was a
late convert to the cause of lower taxes since he had demonstrated no interest in the matter when he had served in the
state legislature in 1869 and 1870. Meantime, Yardley spoke
in favor of a mechanics' lien law giving laborers a claim on
the property of their employers to ensure payment of wages,
while Maney called for sectional reconciliation. But the debt
was the major issue. Porter defended his support of the funding act of 1873 but held out the hope that the state's creditors might be more willing to compromise now that they had
seen, by the attempts to meet past-due interest payments, that
Tennessee desired to pay all it could. The two Republican
hopefuls agreed that Tennessee's credit must be preserved, but
Maney tempered his stand by asserting that interest should

not be paid if public opinion opposed it. Only Thomas came
out for tax relief and against funding the debt. He attacked
the validity of the railroad bonds, denied that the people
were obligated to honor them, and called for cutting to 20
cents the current property tax rate of 40 cents per $100.[17]

The real race was between the two Democrats. Republican
county organizations generally backed Thomas, and General
Maney withdrew his candidacy shortly before election day.
Porter easily won reelection with 123,740 votes. Thomas
reaped the vast majority of Republican votes, receiving 73,695
to 10,436 for Maney and 2,165 for Yardley. He ran well in
Republican East Tennessee and in several counties in his home
region of West Tennessee. A combination of independents
and Republicans supported him in Shelby County where he
won by more than 2,700 votes. The Democrats' margin of
victory was considerable, but the willingness of the majority
of the Republican rank and file to cooperate with an independent who stressed the debt as a major campaign theme indicated to state credit Democrats the need for a resolution of
the problem.[18]

Soon after the election, Governor Porter called for a compromise debt settlement. In his address to the legislature in
January 1877, he recommended that the state attempt to
negotiate a debt solution with its creditors. In response to a
request from several of the leading holders of Tennessee securities, the governor urged the legislature to appoint a commission to go to New York in an attempt to reach an equitable
settlement with creditors in the New York area and with
agents for bondholders. After a lengthy discussion, the senate
passed a resolution calling for the nomination of a four-man
commission by the governor.[19] House members also debated
at length the wisdom of sending a commission and finally
adopted a resolution, later accepted by the senate, asking the
governor to communicate with the bondholders and to send
to the legislature "any proposition or propositions of adjustment and compromise they desire."[20]

Porter's recommendation for negotiating with the creditors
was the first call for a compromise solution of the debt by a

Democratic chief executive. It signified Porter's recognition
of the growing opposition to the party's debt policy of the
early 1870s and of the emptiness of the state treasury. In addition, the bondholders' request for talks might have been an
attempt to counter sentiment for total or nearly complete repudiation of the outstanding bonds. They might have hoped
that a demonstration of their willingness to renounce their
claims to the full value of the debt would improve their image in Tennessee and increase their chances of realizing a substantial return on their investment.

The concept of bargaining with the bondholders received
renewed impetus when Porter notified the General Assembly
on February 22 that a group of New York creditors had organized an arbitration committee and wanted to negotiate
with a legislative committee from Tennessee. Porter urged
compliance with this request and told the lawmakers that the
debt issue was a matter of "more gravity and of greater importance" than any entrusted to the General Assembly since
the "foundation of state government."[21] Prodded by the governor, both houses now approved formation of a legislative
commission. Even John H. Savage accepted the idea, although
he tried unsuccessfully to gain approval of a resolution favoring no settlement that would take longer than twelve years to
discharge.[22]

On March 2 the house selected its representatives to the
commission. The day after their election, the members—three
from the house and two from the senate—met and chose Savage as their chairman and another Democrat, Lewis Shepherd
of East Tennessee, their secretary. The Tennesseans, four
Democrats and one independent, met in New York with five
presidents of New York, Baltimore, and Philadelphia banking
institutions whom financiers in the New York area had asked
to serve as an arbitration committee to develop compromises
between debt-ridden Southern states and their creditors. The
arbitrators planned to negotiate first with Tennessee, Virginia,
and North Carolina.[23]

The five-day meeting began on March 7, 1877. The bankers' committee, led by George S. Coe, president of the Ameri-

can Exchange National Bank of New York, met with the Tennesseans and proposed funding the matured debt and all past-due interest at 100 cents on the dollar in new fifty-year bonds. The bonds would bear interest at 3 percent for the first five years, 4 percent for the second, 5 percent for the third, and 6 percent for the remaining thirty-five years. The legislators objected; therefore, after consultation with some of the bondholders, the Coe committee proposed financing the debt and interest at sixty cents on the dollar in thirty-year bonds which would carry 6 percent interest, with the state accepting the matured coupons in payment for state taxes.[24] The bankers proposed this debt reduction in consideration of the "social derangement and general impoverishment" in Tennessee caused by the war and the current depression.[25]

Reactions to the second proposal were varied. George Coe regarded the offer as "good work" that was "auspiciously begun" and needed only legislative acceptance to be successfully completed.[26] But Savage informed the Eastern bankers before he left New York that he would not "sustain it or recommend its acceptance."[27] His fellow committeeman, Democratic state Senator George W. Martin, was also unhappy with the offer. He and other members of the committee had told the Coe committee that a 50 percent scaling plan might have a better chance of passing the legislature, but the bankers had refused to approve this idea. According to Martin, several letters from native Tennessee bondholders to Coe and his associates telling them that the state was fully able to pay its debt had undermined chances for persuading the bankers to accept a 50 percent scaling of the debt.[28]

On March 19 the legislative committee reported the results of their negotiations to the General Assembly without recommending either acceptance or rejection. Only eight days remained in the session. Many lawmakers assumed that the governor would call an extra session to deal with the offer.[29] Some, like Savage, who regarded the plan as unacceptable, undoubtedly were in no hurry to debate it; they may have agreed with a West Tennessee Democrat who expressed what he thought would be the best tactic: "Just simply let it alone until they offer us a better [plan] than that."[30] At least two lawmakers tried unsuccessfully to spur their colleagues to act on the Coe plan, but the legislature adjourned without debating it.[31]

In the spring and summer of 1877, however, the press aired the views of editors, correspondents, politicians, and others on the merits of the plan. At a public meeting in April, Stewart County citizens called for acceptance, and a month later a similar gathering in Overton County passed resolutions that characterized the settlement as "liberal, fair and honorable," and "most earnestly" requested the legislature to accept the New York offer.[32] In contrast, a May meeting of Robertson County citizens passed a resolution favoring payment of only the market value of the bonds, which had fluctuated between 10 7/8 and 45 on the New York Stock Exchange that month. A Wilson County meeting approved a similar proposal. In Memphis the *Daily Appeal* urged acceptance of the sixty-cent plan, while the rival *Daily Avalanche* insisted that a settlement of fifty cents on the dollar was the only just solution.[33]

The wisdom of calling an extra session of the legislature was also discussed in the press, as well as in letters to the governor and the comptroller. Republican Representative W. E. Kendrick of Roane County urged Porter to call one if there was a chance to obtain a settlement.[34] Democratic legislator J. R. Goodpasture, however, believed that the General Assembly was bent on repudiation; he predicted that an extra session would "destroy the only opportunity ever presented whereby the people might find an honorable relief for their heavy burden."[35] He favored letting the question of settlement become an issue in the 1878 legislative races, but Comptroller James L. Gaines feared this would increase sentiment for further scaling.[36] The editor of the Jackson *Tribune and Sun* agreed with Gaines and warned that, if the "matter [were to go] over in its present shape until another election, the patriots in the general assembly [might] take to themselves the credit of organizing the defeat of the Democracy."[37]

Speculation ended in early November when the governor announced that an extra session would consider the plan of the New York committee. Meantime, Porter had worked to strengthen the forces favoring the settlement. Several Democratic members of the state's congressional delegation, as well as United States Postmaster General David M. Key, publicly endorsed the Coe proposal in October, and the governor pressed Coe to rally creditor support behind the plan. On November 3 the banker informed Porter that he believed that most and perhaps all of the bondholders would accept the committee plan if the legislature adopted it. When the General Assembly convened in December, the governor sent to the members copies of letters from bondholders endorsing the arbitrators' proposition in order to assure the lawmakers that the creditors would accept the bankers' plan.[38]

Low tax forces in the legislature had no intention of co-operating with the governor. In the lower house, S. F. Wilson, a low tax Democrat from Sumner County, offered a resolution instructing the Judiciary Committee to determine whether the governor's message calling an extra session restricted the house to a consideration of the Coe plan only and, if so, to decide whether this infringed on the liberties of the people. This action provoked discussion which did not dissipate when the majority of the Judiciary Committee reported that the governor's call did indeed bind the lawmakers to consider only the New York plan. By December 11 the house had not acted on the Coe proposal, and there seemed little likelihood that it would do so in the immediate future. The senate also failed to act; it, too, devoted a great deal of time to the question of whether the legislature could deliberate settlements other than the bankers' offer.[39]

On the afternoon of December 11 the governor informed the legislature that he had received new assurances from "creditors of the state" that they would agree to making "the basis of compromise *fifty cents on the dollar.*"[40] He asked the lawmakers to adjourn immediately so that he might call a second extra session that would have the authority to consider a fifty-cent plan. The legislators complied, and on the following day both houses assembled under the new call. In this session, by a vote of 13 to 12 the upper house passed a bill which would have authorized funding the debt at 50 cents on the dollar. In the house of representatives, low tax sentiment was strong, but opponents of the governor's proposal were not united on any alternative. Some objected to the coupons-for-taxes feature of the bill; others argued to delay settlement. Savage wanted to pay 33 1/3 cents on the dollar, and Colyar pressed for a settlement at 40 cents with 4 percent interest. On December 27 the house rejected the governor's proposal 27 to 46.[41]

Porter's efforts miscarried for several reasons. His opponents utilized delaying tactics that consumed valuable time. A sizable portion of the legislature, these men could have been defeated only by a concerted effort, but state credit Democrats were not united. Some felt that the state should accept only the offer of 50 cents per dollar at 6 percent interest; others were willing to push for a lower rate. This division was especially noticeable in the house of representatives. On the key votes concerning the passage of the senate-approved fifty-cent plan, the low taxers' opposition was strengthened by the votes of state credit men who disapproved of the bill because it did not provide for the 6 percent interest rate the creditors desired and did not permit the acceptance of matured interest coupons by the state for all taxes and fees. In contrast to the Democrats' disarray, the small Republican minority gave nearly all of its support to Porter's proposal.[42]

The governor, Democratic Representative Campbell Brown from Middle Tennessee, and Republican Senator Henry G. Smith of Shelby County were also convinced that the lobbying activities of John J. MacKinnon, attorney for the Funding Association of the United States of America, Limited, had weakened legislative support for a debt settlement. The Funding Association, formed in New York in the fall of 1877, proposed, for a fee, to serve as the official financial agent of debt-burdened Southern states, assisting them to reduce their obligations with the consent of their creditors. On November

11, MacKinnon arrived in Nashville to press for the adoption of a debt compromise plan sponsored by his company. He first sought the support of Porter, but the governor rejected his proposal.[43] According to the Nashville *Daily American,* Porter thought the offer was an "impertinent and unwarranted interference" in Tennessee affairs.[44] Undaunted, MacKinnon turned his attention to the legislature.

MacKinnon presented his views to various members of the General Assembly during both extra sessions. Although initially he proposed a sixty-cent plan at 6 percent interest, later, while the governor still hoped to secure the adoption of the Coe award, he offered to obtain a settlement at a lower rate. In the second session, this lobbyist presented a plan to pay at fifty cents with a graduated interest scale, in contrast to the straight 6 percent that Porter and many state credit men desired. Desperately trying to promote his company, he intimated to a lawmaker that the governor opposed this idea in order to line his own pockets by administering any funding plan adopted by Tennessee. Although the legislature did not approve the Funding Association's proposals, its agent's offers and activities were much discussed on the floor of the General Assembly, and Porter was convinced that the lobbyist had undermined his efforts to secure a settlement. While it is difficult to assess the precise effects of MacKinnon's activities, doubtless they did divert the attention of the legislature from the governor's proposals, and certainly they consumed a significant proportion of the lawmakers' time.[45]

Porter resolved to make no other attempt at debt settlement before the gubernatorial election of 1878. That June he released a long public letter in which he reviewed the history of the debt and defended its legality.[46] He had called the extra sessions, he said, because he had "every reasonable assurance" that the legislators could reach a solution to the debt problem, and he regretted their failure to act. He was convinced that the debt controversy was stifling Tennessee's growth. "It has destroyed State and municipal and seriously affected individual credit abroad," he declared, and "has broken down all confidence at home." He closed his letter by ad-

monishing the public that any settlement finally agreed on
would obviously require money "from the pockets of the
tax-payers of the State."[47]

By the time Porter issued his pessimistic statement, Democrats had already begun to speculate about who would suc-
ceed him. The newspapers mentioned numerous Democrats
as possible candidates for the nomination. Among those discussed were Savage, Colyar, John C. Burch, William B. Bate,
Chancellor Albert S. Marks of Franklin, David M. Key, and
newspaperman John M. Fleming of Knoxville. Colyar, the
perennial aspirant, was especially active as an announced candidate for the nomination. He called for a compromise on the
debt issue without specifying what he regarded as a satisfactory settlement, but he recommended delaying action until
Tennessee recovered its prosperity.[48]

Assembling in Nashville on August 15, the Democrats first
considered their platform. The party's stand on the debt reflected the impact of increasing low tax sentiment. It declared anew Democratic opposition to repudiation but went
on to say that the economy was such that "none are prosperous save corporations, interest takers and money lenders."[49]
Because of economic conditions, the delegates said, they
favored a compromise. They revealed their distrust of the actions of the legislature on the debt matter when they called
for "submission to the people for ratification or rejection"
any settlement worked out by the General Assembly. In addition, they amended the platform by recommending a change
in the state constitution to prohibit Tennessee from borrowing and issuing bonds in the future except to settle the current difficulties. Even a routine motion to endorse the record
of the outgoing Porter administration ran into scattered opposition, mainly from Savage's Warren County delegation and
men from surrounding Middle Tennessee counties.[50]

The platform had a strong agrarian flavor, marked by formal endorsement of debt scaling and calls for the abolition
of national banks, expansion of the amount of greenbacks in
circulation, repeal of the Specie Resumption Act, and free
coinage of silver. These stands placed the Tennessee party in

opposition to the Eastern conservatives on these questions. Historian C. Vann Woodward argues that Southern Democrats faced a forked road in the late 1870s. One branch, the "left fork," led to an alliance with the agrarian radicalism of the West; the "right fork" led to a union with Eastern conservatism. Woodward contends that in 1878 Southern Democrats embraced Western ideas in currency, banks, public credit, and monopolies.[51] The Tennessee Democratic platform would certainly seem to fit this description. No debates took place among party leaders as to which section the party should support or accept as an ally. The choice was instinctive; delegates took the "left fork" without realizing that they were even choosing.

After nearly two dozen ballots, none of the front runners— Savage, Colyar, John M. Fleming, John A. Garner of Weakley County, and Alfred Caldwell of Knox County—could secure enough votes to win the nomination. A dark-horse candidate, Chancellor Albert S. Marks, a former Confederate colonel who had lost his foot in the Battle of Stones River in December 1862, was finally selected. Unlike Brown and Porter, Marks had not been a prewar Whig. He had supported John C. Breckinridge in the 1860 election but had initially opposed secession. He was closely identified with Colyar, having been his law partner before and after the war. Marks, the author of the 1878 platform, received the nomination largely because he was closely associated with neither wing of the party on the debt issue. He would soon become the first antebellum Democrat to be elected governor after the war.[52]

Later in August the Republicans convened in Nashville. Reflecting the displeasure of many members at their party's decision to exploit low tax sentiment in the 1876 race, their platform denounced repudiation "of any kind or by any means" and called for full payment of the debt unless "the creditors may voluntarily concede more favorable terms." It declared that the Democratic legislature's recent failure to settle the debt proved these men "unworthy [of] the office of legislators" and "unfit representatives of an honest people."[53] The Republicans nominated West Tennessean

Emerson Etheridge for governor, but he later declined. On
September 11 the executive committee named Dr. E. M.
Wright of Chattanooga, a former mayor of that city and a
member of the state board of health, as the party's nominee.
A third candidate entered the field when R. M. Edwards, a
lawyer and former Union Army colonel from Cleveland, accepted the nomination of the small Greenback party.[54]

The campaign for governor in 1878 was probably the most
lackluster of the decade. The Republican nominee abandoned
active campaigning to assist in combating a yellow fever epi-
demic that broke out in Chattanooga. This dread disease also
hit West Tennessee, especially Memphis, where, as a conse-
quence, political activity and interest was understandably below that of previous years. In his speeches, Marks endorsed
the negotiation of a debt compromise with the bondholders
and supported the platform stand; yet he offered no definite
ideas regarding what a debt settlement should contain. He attacked national Republican policies and blamed them for the
financial distress of the country. Wright called for improvement of the public schools, encouragement of immigration,
and acceptance of whatever terms the creditors offered. Edwards denounced the system of leasing convicts to private
businesses, condemned the policies of the Republican party
in Washington, and attacked Marks for being vague as to just
what sort of debt compromise he favored. The Greenback
candidate wanted no action on the debt until economic conditions improved, at which time, he said, he would favor a
negotiated settlement.[55]

On election day, Marks received 89,958 votes to Wright's
42,284 and Edwards' 15,155. The retreat of the Democrats'
state credit leadership to acceptance of scaling had contributed to party unity which, coupled with the failure of the
Republican candidate to campaign aggressively, gave the
Democrats an easy victory. Edwards' votes represented the
most the Greenback party would ever win in Tennessee. While
Marks's general endorsement of a debt compromise had
helped to preserve Democratic harmony in the party's contest
with the Republicans and had prevented the debt question

from developing into a decisive campaign issue, the question would soon explode. State credit men in the Democratic party were on the defensive, and low tax sentiment was increasing. Marks would have to abandon his vague endorsement of a compromise settlement and recommend or endorse a specific debt proposal.[56]

To the disgust of state credit men, Marks placed himself in the ranks of the low tax forces when he delivered his first message as chief executive to the legislature on January 18, 1879. The burden of his address was the subject of the debt and its origins. He alluded to evidence of fraud in the issuance of the Brownlow-era securities and classified various parts of the debt according to their "merit." The bonds issued for the purchase of the Hermitage, for the construction of the Capitol, and for the state agricultural bureau he called the "primary debt" or "state debt proper," which would be paid before the remainder of the obligation. Tennessee should not pay postwar bonds unless they had been issued according to law. A compromise settlement, Marks said, should not allow interest coupons to be receivable for taxes as this would infringe on the state's sovereign right to collect monies for government operation. But any plan adopted should be submitted to the people for their ratification.[57]

The legislature was slow to act on the debt question. It conducted an investigation of the origins of the debt and collected evidence of fraud surrounding the distribution of bonds under the Republicans in the Reconstruction era. In February the Committee of Tennessee Bondholders, a newly formed organization of creditors in the New York area holding about $10 million of Tennessee's debt, offered the General Assembly two settlement plans. One called for funding the debt at sixty cents on the dollar at 6 percent interest; the other, for funding at par with 4 percent interest. Concerned about making the legislature fully aware of their proposals, the committee sent ex-Confederate Brigadier General Roger A. Pryor, a former resident of Virginia who became a prominent member of the New York bar after the war, to lobby for their proposals in Nashville.[58]

On the eve of adjournment in late March, the legislature passed a bill calling for funding the debt and matured interest in a series of bonds at the rate of fifty cents on the dollar, bearing 4 percent interest. The law required the bondholders' approval of the plan. If accepted, it would then be submitted to the people for ratification at the polls. The passage of the bill was a victory for state credit forces, but it fell short of the terms asked by the New York creditors. Also, a number of low tax men found unacceptable the measure's 50 percent scaling and its provision for funding railroad bonds.[59]

To go to New York as his commissioners and attempt to secure the approval of creditors in that city, the governor appointed B. A. Enloe, a Jackson newspaper editor, and Nathaniel Baxter, president of the Mechanics National Bank of Nashville. Despite the opposition of Eugene Kelly, chairman of the Committee of Tennessee Bondholders, to the debt plan, the governor's representatives were able to meet with a number of prominent bondholders and secure their endorsement of the new offer. A citizens committee also went to New York to press for acceptance of the recently passed debt proposal. This group was composed of former Governor John C. Brown, former Governor James D. Porter, former Republican Congressman R. R. Butler, former Democratic United States Senator Henry Cooper, and Nashville banker Dempsey Weaver. Upon their return to Tennessee, both the citizens committee and Marks's commissioners informed the governor on May 30 of their conviction that significant numbers of bondholders would agree to the new compromise offer.[60]

Setting August 7 as the date for a popular vote on the settlement, Marks shifted his position somewhat and supported the new proposal, even though it did not demand the rejection of fraudulent bonds. He requested that those who felt the settlement was too low and those who felt it was too generous to compromise their views and accept the proposal.[61] The provision for scaling the original debt, he said, was fair to all parties concerned. Voter acceptance of the plan would result in pulling the "vexed subject up by the roots" and putting it permanently to rest.[62] Despite the governor's call for popular endorsement, the referendum did not arouse public interest. In mid-June the Memphis *Daily Appeal* reported "great indifference in every part of the state" on the issue.[63] And a little less than a month later, a correspondent from Union City reported, "Our people need arousing on this question" and expressed the desire for more public addresses.[64]

A number of state credit men who disliked Marks because of his low tax position overcame their aversion and helped the governor work for ratification of the creditors' offer. Among those Democrats who publicly advocated that the fifty cents at 4 percent proposal be accepted were former governors Neil S. Brown and James D. Porter, United States Senator James E. Bailey, former Comptroller John C. Burch, and William B. Bate of Nashville. Joining them was former low taxer Arthur S. Colyar. Arguing that he had long favored this sort of compromise, Colyar declared that it was badly needed to move the state toward the general economic recovery that appeared to be under way in the country. Editorially, the Clarksville *Semi-Weekly Tobacco Leaf,* the Nashville *Daily American,* the Chattanooga *Daily Times,* and the Memphis *Daily Appeal* supported approval of the debt settlement. Not all state credit men favored the settlement, however. Some said that the creditors had been treated unfairly and that not enough of the bondholders had accepted the offer, while others objected to submission of the settlement to the people for their ratification.[65]

There was discussion in Republican ranks regarding the party's stand in the coming referendum. Some party members stood with those who believed that the settlement was not fair to the creditors, while others hesitated to help the Democrats resolve the issue; many Republicans, therefore, did not urge acceptance. The editor of the Cleveland *Weekly Herald* was convinced that the whole proposition was a Democratic fraud and urged all good Republicans to shun the polls.[66] Trenton attorney W. M. Hall argued that his party should vote against the proposal and thus "give the Democracy a Waterloo." If the plan were defeated, he predicted, internal disagreements over the debt would cause the Demo-

crats to "go to pieces."[67] Republican Congressman L. C.
Houk, however, expressed the views held by a majority of the
party. He said that, although the debt compromise was not
completely fair to the creditors, a more equitable one could
not be secured without a "desperate struggle of factions."
Moreover, some creditors had accepted the fifty-cent offer;
therefore he could support it.[68] The party's most important
newspaper, the Knoxville *Daily Chronicle,* called for ratification because the offer was acceptable to the creditors and approval would mean the defeat of repudiation in Tennessee.[69]

The Memphis *Daily Avalanche* was the only major urban
paper to urge rejection of the fifty-cent offer. Aware that a
group of creditors was suing several railroads in an attempt to
force them to assume responsibility for the bonds issued in
their behalf, this paper urged delay until a court decision was
rendered. Savage, R. E. Thompson of Lebanon, and a number
of other legislators who had opposed the passage of the debt
plan in the General Assembly asserted that the proposal was
too generous to the creditors.[70] The Shelbyville *Commercial*
declared that the revelations of corruption connected with
part of the debt had shocked the public; this paper disapproved of Marks's endorsement of the fifty-cent plan, stating,
"We surely had a right to expect our Executive to take a different course . . . ."[71] Opponents also contended that too
few creditors had agreed to the settlement scheme to make it
work even if the electorate were to endorse it.[72]

As the voting day neared, there were indications that the
people were not favorably inclined toward the proposal. A
correspondent of the comptroller offered the opinion that
the people did not clearly understand the debt issue and believed that "they [would] be enslaved if it should be set-
tled."[73] A letter to the editor of the Knoxville *Daily Chronicle* told him of "strong influence against the 50 4 proposition" in Jefferson County.[74] Former Governor Porter wrote
from West Tennessee, "I have not felt at liberty to leave this
part of the state," as he was working to "check the tide of
repudiation."[75] On July 24 the Nashville *Daily American*
carried a report from Gibson County in West Tennessee that

two lawyers had fought about the debt plan, using bricks and knives. It concluded, "To be candid, the people of this county seem to have taken a decided stand against the compromise; and if they do not change radically and rapidly within the next two weeks, this county will go largely against it."[76]

Election day, August 7, brought defeat for the debt settlement. The vote was 76,333 to 49,772; the plan was crushed in Middle and West Tennessee. The "50-4" proposition was approved in the four counties containing the state's major cities, with the margin of victory ranging from 2,168 votes in Knox County to 84 in Shelby County. But the vote of rural Middle and West Tennessee counties proved decisive. Only four of the twenty counties west of the Tennessee River voted affirmatively; the pattern was the same in the central portion of the state, with seven of thirty-nine counties supporting the proposal. Republican East Tennessee endorsed it by a small margin. Prominent residents may have influenced the results in several counties. Giles County, Governor Porter's home, and Montgomery, James E. Bailey's home, cast majorities for the fifty-cent offer, while John H. Savage's Warren County neighbors rejected it 1,702 to 223.[77]

Voter turnout was well below that for a gubernatorial contest. Neither the supporters nor the opponents of the debt settlement worked as hard for their cause as they would have if the issue had been bound up with an election campaign for major political offices and control of the state. The return of yellow fever to Memphis in the summer of 1879 also tended to reduce the number of voters in the western part of the state. Governor Marks failed to provide energetic leadership for the state credit forces in the campaign, and this group did not appeal effectively to the voters in the weeks preceding the referendum. High tax forces were further hampered by the refusal of some state credit men to support the plan. For example, Horace H. Harrison, Frank T. Reid, and other influential Davidson County state credit Republicans a few days before the election published a letter denouncing the debt settlement as hastily conceived and unfair to the creditors because the state could afford to pay more. These men argued, as did others, that Governor Marks had not received enough bondholder acceptances to make the settlement effective. On the other side, those who questioned the legitimacy of the debt and felt strongly that the compromise would entail burdensome taxes went to the polls in sufficient numbers on August 7 to reject the proposal.[78]

Public reaction to the vote was mixed. The outcome puzzled Madison County Democrat and farmer Robert H. Cartmell, who voted for the settlement: "I voted acceptance and thought it to the interest of the People of Tenn to accept it & believed they would do so, but it was rejected by the People by a large majority—why I cannot for the life of me understand. . . . doe[s] it mean repudiation? was it that they did not understand the question—? I dont [sic] know what—!"[79] The New York *Times* concluded the result of the voting to be proof that a Democratic administration "resting in all cases on the most ignorant and least scrupulous part of the population, has an inevitable tendency toward dishonesty."[80] The Baltimore *Sun* reasoned that the legislature should have resolved the issue and that submission of the question "to the hazards of a popular vote was mere demagogery [sic], and the outcome has been repudiation."[81] The Nashville *Daily American* was convinced that the vote was unrepresentative: many who did not vote or voted against the plan did so because they either failed to understand it or believed that it was unfair to the creditors. The coming governor's race, the paper predicted, would allow for proper discussion of the issue.[82] In contrast, the Franklin *Review and Journal* praised the result, demanding that the "politicians of this State acquiesce" in the verdict and stop attempting to settle the debt in a manner abhorrent to the people.[83]

The voters had defeated the second attempt at a settlement of the debt since the abandonment of the dollar-for-dollar program of the 1873 funding act. Initially, Governor Porter had tried to resolve the debt dilemma by negotiations through a board of bankers representing some of the state's creditors. But low tax sentiment in the legislature, coupled with the activities of a corporate lobbyist, had prevented

General Assembly action on the proposals. Albert S. Marks, who succeeded to the governor's mansion in 1878, failed to provide firm leadership on the debt question. He first seemed to ally himself with the low tax elements when he called for an investigation of the origins of the debt and expressed the belief that the state's obligation to pay varied according to which part of the debt was under consideration. Later, he supported a bill that called for settling all the debt at a uniform rate of fifty cents on the dollar. Voter apathy, less than total support by state credit men, doubts concerning the legality of the debt, and fears that settlement would mean high taxes during hard times all contributed to the defeat of the fifty-cent proposal.

For state credit Democrats the results of the referendum were alarming. They had retreated since 1873 from a stand favoring dollar-for-dollar debt payment to one calling for a 50 percent scaling and a reduction in the interest rate as well. This group felt that now the state was on the road to total or near-total repudiation. The average voter, they thought, had been confused and misled by ambitious and unscrupulous demagogues like Savage, who would destroy the good name and reputation of Tennessee for the chance to gain political office. The referendum encouraged low taxers and convinced them that their stand was in harmony with the attitude of most Democrats on this issue. But its results prompted no urge to compromise among the leaders of the two camps. Rather, each side seemed even more convinced of the legitimacy of its position. Both saw the upcoming governor's race as a crucial opportunity to test their strength within the party.

CHAPTER VII

The Republicans' Turn to Try

The debacle of the debt referendum boosted the Republicans' hopes of returning to power in the 1880 elections. Assembling in Nashville on May 5, 1880, the state convention selected Alvin Hawkins of Huntingdon in Carroll County as the Republican nominee for governor. A former Whig and a Unionist in the war years, Hawkins had served on the state supreme court during Reconstruction; he had also been president of the Nashville and Northwestern Railroad Company.[1] He would be running on a platform that declared that any attempt to "change the letter or spirit" of the original debt contract "without the voluntary consent of the bondholders" was "downright repudiation . . . and highhanded dishonesty." It went on to endorse the acceptance of any compromise voluntarily extended by the creditors and to denounce the Democrats for failing to approve the recommendations of the Coe committee.[2]

Soon after the Republicans had adjourned, the Greenback party held its convention, and the delegates again selected R. M. Edwards to carry their standard in the governor's race. Their platform, unlike that of the Republicans, asserted that the bonds emitted under the internal improvements act of 1852 and its later amending acts had been illegally issued, and it opposed any measure "looking to the payment of the same in whole or in any way whatever, principal or interest." But the delegates endorsed the payment of those parts of the bonded debt contracted prior to 1852 and those issued after 1852 for purposes other than railroad and turnpike aid. The

Greenbackers accused both major parties of supporting funding plans and compromise proposals in an effort to conceal the evidence of fraud and illegality that surrounded the railroad debt.[3]

For several months preceding the opening of the Democratic convention on August 5, newspapers were full of speculation and discussion on the debt question. The influential Nashville *Daily American* called on the Democrats to make a clear, unequivocal stand for state credit. It declared that the vague 1878 platform plank on the debt and the actions of Governor Marks had seriously weakened the party.[4] War must be made on repudiators, it asserted, for a "timid, compromise policy . . . will endanger everything, and disgust many of the best men in the party . . . ."[5] The Democrats would lose their "best elements" to the Republicans if they should compromise for the sake of harmony.[6] The Memphis *Daily Avalanche*, long a supporter of low tax views under the editorship of Andrew J. Kellar, changed hands in 1880. Its new editor agreed with the champions of state credit, and now the paper, like the Nashville *Daily American*, urged the convention to take a firm stand for credit.[7] A Clarksville editor insisted that his paper would not support the party ship if it "proposes to sail by any other compass than common honesty."[8] But the Chattanooga *Daily Times* openly opposed this approach and advised state credit men to "drop all tone of threatening" in advocating an honest settlement, and called for the convention to work for a compromise position on the debt.[9] Echoing this sentiment, the Nashville *Banner* urged Democrats to work for a debt plank that would be agreeable to all. It followed its pleas for harmony with reminders that a split in the party might give victory to the Republicans in November.[10]

Low taxers had been preparing for some time to influence the Democratic convention. In December 1879 a number of legislators from rural Middle and West Tennessee, led by John H. Savage, had laid plans to organize low tax men across the state.[11] In a resolution adopted at a December 24 meeting, they declared that most of their "friends [were] in the rural

districts, while the force of the enemy [was] chiefly in the
cities as office holders, bankers, merchants[,] railroad men,
their agents and employes." They called for the organization
of low tax county committees and a state committee with
the aim of increasing support for their position and sending
low tax delegates to the convention. Remembering the results
of the August 1879 debt referendum, they called on their followers to remain firm in their opposition to "the settlement
of the so-called State debt or any part thereof, by the Legislature without submitting [s]uch settlements to the people
for ratification or rejection."[12]

Savage and his followers lacked the editorial support of a
major city paper, but the McMinnville *New Era* from his
home town, the Shelbyville *Commercial,* and the Jackson
Whig expounded low tax views.[13] The *New Era* told the people
not to be duped by the established political leadership: "For
one, we are thoroughly disgusted with the tone of authority
[with] which these would be [*sic*] *leaders* and MASTERS
of the people speak of those who oppose their pretentions
and despise their authority, and are ready to strike hands
with all who oppose their unrighteous demands upon the
people."[14] This newspaper and the Murfreesboro *Free Press*
called on opponents of debt payment to attend county conventions and work for the selection of low tax delegates to
the convention.[15] The Shelbyville *Commercial* informed its
readers that "rings, the railroads and the great money power"
were opposed to the people on the question and urged all low
taxers to "lay up a few dollars" to pay their way to the Democratic convention in August.[16]

Discussions in the Democratic press and county conventions concerning the gubernatorial nomination revealed considerable disharmony. Although both Brown and Porter had
routinely received nominations for a second term, Marks's
handling of the debt question had pleased neither the state
credit nor the low tax forces, and the Shelbyville *Commercial*
found the governor unacceptable because he was the favorite
of the state credit men.[17] The state credit Clarksville *Semi-
Weekly Tobacco Leaf* characterized Marks as an "artful

dodger" who was lacking in "every element that goes to make the statesman" and opposed his renomination.[18] The Nashville *Daily American* denied that there was a two-term tradition in the Democratic party and contended that any political leader should have the "manliness" to "stand or fall upon his views."[19] This unpopularity forced the governor to announce that he would, if necessary, step aside for the good of the party.[20]

County Democratic conventions took various stands on the debt question. Bradley and Lawrence counties selected delegates without passing resolutions on the matter. The Coffee County convention went on record as opposing repudiation but favoring the submission of any debt settlement to the people for their approval.[21] Knox County Democrats called for the legislature to effect a "speedy, honorable and satisfactory adjustment."[22] Obion County party members wanted no settlement "in violation of the legal and just rights of her [the state's] creditors."[23] In contrast, Trousdale County Democrats desired payment of only the Capitol and Hermitage bonds, and Putnam County favored payment of just $2 million of the outstanding debt.[24]

When the Democrats assembled in Nashville in August, it became apparent that the strategy of the low taxers had failed. State credit men controlled the convention, and low tax delegates decided to rally around the proposal to submit any debt settlement to the people. State credit Democrats, with the results of the recent referendum fresh in their minds, were determined to avoid the pitfall of popular ratification. The majority report of the platform committee called for the legislature to negotiate with the state's creditors and obtain the best compromise possible. Upon adoption of the majority report and rejection of the minority report favoring popular ratification, state Representative D. L. Snodgrass of White County led approximately 100 of the estimated 1,300 delegates out of the convention hall. On the following day, August 12, the remaining delegates nominated former Confederate Colonel John V. Wright of Columbia for governor.[25] Wright, a prewar Democrat who had served three terms in the federal House of Representatives, accepted the nomination and told the cheering delegates, "I am prepared to go forth in defense of your principles."[26]

Gathering in the senate chamber in the Capitol later that day, the low tax delegates who had withdrawn from the convention met and adopted a platform that favored the "adjustment and settlement" of the antebellum bonds not issued to railroads and denied the "validity against the state" of all bonds emitted for the benefit of railways in Tennessee.[27] In addition, they declared that Tennessee should not have issued bonds during Reconstruction for overdue war interest and insisted that any proposal be submitted to the people for their approval in a special referendum. The delegates passed a resolution praising Albert S. Marks for informing the rival state credit convention that he would not be a candidate for renomination and then selected S. F. Wilson of Sumner County to carry their banner in the coming election. Wilson had enlisted in the Confederate army as a private at the age of sixteen and had served until he lost an arm at the Battle of Chickamauga. He was elected to the lower house of the legislature in 1877 and two years later to the senate. He gained recognition as a low tax leader by his service as chairman of a legislative committee that uncovered evidence of fraud and illegality while investigating the origins of the bonded debt. Before they adjourned, the low tax delegates named a state executive committee and empowered it to organize a party structure at the county level.[28]

Neither group displayed much remorse at the division of the party.[29] "The Rubicon is crossed," said the Nashville *Banner;* "our bridges are burned behind us, and it is now war to the knife. So be it."[30] The Memphis *Daily Avalanche* predicted that the "democratic party [would] be stronger by the elimination of the rule or ruin repudiation leaders."[31] Ridiculing the Wilson men, the Nashville *Daily American* said the sight of a "Liliputian [sic] ticket attempting Brobdignagian [sic] strides is too much for the gravity of the public."[32]

The four-man race began in earnest later in August with each party's platform containing resolutions dealing with other matters besides the debt. All parties called for improvement of the public education system in Tennessee. The Greenbackers favored abolition of national banks, expansion of the amount of money in circulation, and the regulation of transportation rates by federal and state governments. In contrast to their 1878 platform, the two Democratic platforms did not call for free coinage of silver, abolition of national banks, and an increase in the amount of greenback currency in circulation. But their approval of the concept of paying less than the full value of the debt and of state regulation of railroad rates indicated that neither wing of the party had taken the "right fork" and accepted the ideas of Eastern conservative Democrats. Also, the call of the Wilson faction for placing more of the tax burden on railroads, capitalists, incomes, and salaries was further evidence that this wing was philosophically closer to the Western, agrarian wing of the national party. Despite the presence of these resolutions in the party platforms, however, the debt question and its ramifications absorbed nearly all the attention of the candidates. Other issues were shunted aside.[33]

Wright dealt at length with the debt in his campaign speeches and frequently reviewed its history. Both the Whigs and the Democrats in Tennessee, he alleged, had approved aid for internal improvements before the Civil War. In fact, many Democrats had endorsed the practice of issuing bonds during the Brownlow era, a policy which had resulted in the rebuilding of the state's war-torn railroads. The roads had brought great benefits to Tennessee, Wright reminded his audiences, and the failure to resolve the debt question was stunting further economic development. He insisted that the legislature and not the people should negotiate and approve a settlement with the state's creditors.[34]

To combat public charges that the state credit Democrats were more concerned with the welfare of railroads and creditors than with that of the people, Wright contended that he was not an attorney for railroad interests but a man of modest means who had never owned a state bond. He denounced Wilson supporters when they tried to tell the public that the

poor would have to pay for a debt settlement, charging that
the low taxers were attempting to turn class against class. He
repeatedly asserted that he was the legitimate candidate of
the Democratic party and that the presence of the low tax
candidate in the race endangered party control of the state.
He warned that the bolters were opening the door to a return
of Radical Republicans by dividing the votes of the Democrats.[35] At Trenton he courted the animosity of many whites
toward blacks and Republicans when he said that Wilson men
were the allies of "black Republicans."[36]

Wilson conducted a vigorous campaign. He insisted that he
was a Democrat, a far more loyal one than his state credit
opponent. The leaders of the Democracy had subverted the
will of the people at the convention when they did not demand the popular ratification of any debt settlement. According to Wilson, the power and wealth of the governing
classes in America were threatening the liberties of the working people; the laboring classes paid the taxes, and therefore
they had to assert their right to decide the debt question. The
farmers and laborers of Tennessee should reject the efforts of
bondholders, railroad rings, city lawyers and editors, and political spokesmen for the wealthy to persuade them to
shoulder an unjust debt. Wilson often defended his past legislative record when Wright charged that he had shown favorit-
ism toward railroads and had not always supported the plan
to submit the debt question to the people.[37]

The campaign offered to Hawkins, the Republican candidate, the best chance for success that his party had enjoyed
in years. During the first portion of the race, the Democrats
concentrated their fire on each other and neglected Hawkins,
but toward the end of September, Wright abandoned a series
of speaking engagements with Wilson to focus his efforts on
Hawkins. The Republican candidate expressed views on the
debt that were similar to those of the state credit Democrats;
he defended the legality of the debt and denied that the railroad bonds were invalid. He attacked the Democrats for failing to settle the issue and urged those who wanted to obtain
an honorable solution and avoid repudiation to support the

Republican party.[38]

The state credit Democrats attacked Hawkins' past record. They sharply criticized his support, as a state supreme court justice, of the Brownlow administration's disfranchisement of ex-Confederates; they also accused him of having extorted money from former Confederates in 1865 by threatening to confiscate their property when he was United States District Attorney for West Tennessee. In contrast, the three major candidates generally ignored Edwards, the Greenback nominee. They did not regard him as a serious contender, and indeed he did seem unable to generate an appreciable amount of voter interest in his candidacy.[39]

The Wright campaign fielded an impressive list of speakers. Both of Tennessee's federal senators, as well as ex-Governor John C. Brown, former Comptroller John C. Burch, and Arthur S. Colyar, were among those who worked actively for Wright. Fearing that an attitude favoring total or near-total repudiation was spreading, Colyar now supported the state credit wing's stand for a negotiated settlement.[40] In a speech at Tullahoma in September, he revealed his new-found loyalty to the state credit cause when he announced that the Wright forces were determined to rescue Tennessee from "eternal shame" and "defend the state from dishonor" by settling the debt. With no acknowledgment of his own past independent political activities, he strongly denounced Savage as a "bolter by nature" who now had given the unfortunate habit to S. F. Wilson.[41]

The Wilson Democrats and the Republicans were unable to name such a prominent group of backers, although Savage, the best-known low tax politician in the state, worked hard for Wilson. He defended the platform of the low tax Democrats and charged that railroads, banks, and city interests controlled the state credit wing of the party. United States Postmaster General Horace Maynard, a former East Tennessee congressman, made major addresses in Athens and Nashville in October on behalf of the national and state Republican tickets. Both Savage and Maynard had strong personal reasons for participating in the campaign. United States Senator

James E. Bailey, a staunch state credit advocate who was campaigning for Wright, planned to stand for reelection in January. These two men hoped to secure Bailey's Senate seat if their respective parties won control of the legislature in November.[42]

As election day neared, many Democrats manifested increasing uneasiness about the division in their party. In mid-October the Memphis *Daily Appeal* predicted a victory for Hawkins unless the two wings of the party could unite. "If the Democracy of Tennessee has not eaten the insane root and gone stark mad," said the editor, it will "agree upon an armistice which will enable the waring [*sic*] factions to turn their guns upon the common enemy they have so long fought and which they have abundant cause for hating."[43] Several Democrats suggested that both candidates withdraw and allow a unified party to put forward a compromise nominee and platform. On October 26, however, the Memphis *Daily Avalanche* reported that state credit leaders felt this plan would only further weaken the party and that they believed Wright was daily picking up supporters from the low tax ranks.[44] The next day the Nashville *Daily American* declared that the state credit men had "never thought of entertaining such a proposition, and [had] no doubt about Wright's election.[45]

In the last weeks of the campaign, newspapers carried conflicting reports on the strengths of the three major candidates. The state credit politicians and editors claimed increased support for Wright in all parts of the state, called on Wilson backers to abandon their hopeless cause, and recalled the horrors of Republican rule that would recur if Hawkins were victorious. But the low tax state committee assured their followers that Wilson would remain in the race to the end.[46] The Knoxville *Daily Chronicle* confidently predicted a Hawkins victory, reminding its readers that Republicans could hold the balance of power in the next legislature. "Our members will say who shall be United States Senator, and in return for this some state officers must be ours."[47]

On election day, Republicans realized their hopes. Haw-

kins garnered 103,964 votes, Wright 78,783, Wilson 57,080,
and Edwards 3,459. More Tennesseans voted in this election
than in any gubernatorial contest since the Civil War. The
election was a victory for the state credit position in that
both Hawkins and Wright favored a negotiated compromise.
The combined vote of the Wright Democrats and the Republicans was well over three times as large as the vote for Wilson.
In 1879, 76,333 voters had rejected a plan that called for a
50 percent scaling of the debt, and the Wilson forces had
hoped for the support of these voters and others who agreed.
But the state credit Democrats and Republicans succeeded in
reducing this number to 57,080 in the 1880 race.[48]

The election was a disaster for the Democrats, as Wilson's
candidacy had seriously divided the party. While he carried
twenty-six of thirty-eight counties in Middle Tennessee—
eighteen of these with 50 percent or more of the vote—he did
less well in West Tennessee where the Republican party was
stronger and blacks constituted a greater proportion of the
population. More fearful of Republican strength, west state
Democrats were less willing to divide their party. The low tax
ticket carried only one county and did not garner 50 percent
of the vote in any of the western counties, while in predominantly Republican East Tennessee it carried two counties.
The state election reflected the rural-urban division of the
Democratic party, as rural voters gave Wilson proportionally
more support than Democrats in towns and cities. The split
in the Democratic party also assisted the Republicans in winning a near majority of the contests for seats in the legislature.[49]

The election results evoked varied newspaper reactions.
The Knoxville *Daily Chronicle* warned Republicans that their
victory brought with it responsibilities. Denouncing the
Democrats for having "toyed with" and "nurtured" repudiation and left state affairs in such a muddle that it was a
"stench in the nostrils of honest men," the paper called on
the Republican party to restore the state's honor by acting
decisively to secure a debt settlement.[50] The Democratic
Nashville *Banner* and the Franklin *Review and Journal* urged

Map 1. Low Tax Vote in 1880.

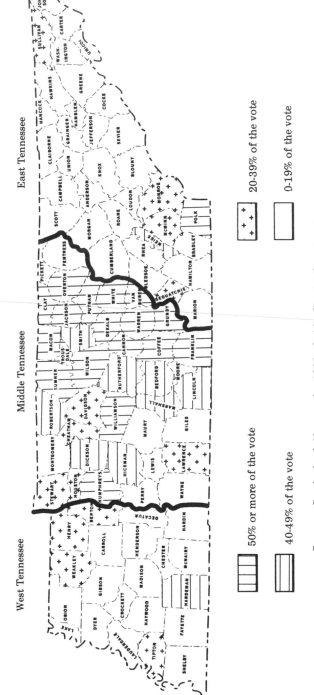

West Tennessee

Middle Tennessee

East Tennessee

50% or more of the vote

40-49% of the vote

20-39% of the vote

0-19% of the vote

Source: *Cumberland Almanac for 1882*, 8, 10. Chester County returns were included in the returns of Hardeman, McNairy, Madison, and Henderson counties; Pickett County returns were with those of Fentress and Overton counties. Vote totals for Moore and Unicoi counties are not available.

both wings of the party to cast aside past differences and work for party unity. But the Chattanooga *Daily Times* advised the party to exclude Wilson's supporters from its councils unless they were willing to abandon their heresies and strive for a proper debt settlement.[51] Taking a more embittered stand than the *Daily Times,* the editor of a Jackson newspaper held the view that the "advocates of communism, and the formenters [*sic*] of strife between different classes and callings are not Democrats. Men of that class who have gone out should stay out, and if there are any such who have not gone out let them go now and speedily."[52]

When the legislature convened in January 1881, the Republican minority hoped that the division would prevent Democratic lawmakers from working together, thus enabling Republicans to elect one of their party to the federal Senate. Indeed, the Democrats were not united behind a single candidate. Party newspapers and legislators mentioned a number of prominent men as possible choices. "In fact," one Nashville observer said, "it is hard to discover a democrat of any prominence who is not expecting that lightning my [*sic*] strike him."[53] Among those under consideration by Democrats were General William B. Bate, John H. Savage, ex-Congressman John M. Bright, former Comptroller John C. Burch, ex-Governor Albert S. Marks, and state legislator E. A. James of Chattanooga. The incumbent, James E. Bailey, desired reelection, but his ardent state credit views had earned him the animosity of low tax legislators.[54]

The leading Republican contender was Postmaster General Maynard, Tennessee's most prominent Republican politician. Some of that party's legislators favored ex-Congressman Horace H. Harrison of Davidson County, while others leaned toward Alvin Hawkins, but the majority of the forty-seven-man Republican delegation favored the postmaster general. Maynard's backers hoped to elect him by securing unanimous Republican support, by receiving the backing of the one Greenback legislator, and by picking up the votes of several Democratic lawmakers.[55]

Balloting began on January 18 and continued for more

than a week. At first, the Democrats were unable to unite
behind a single candidate. Bright, Bailey, and Democratic
Congressman R. L. Taylor received some support; Bate was
popular with both high and low tax Democrats. Republicans
tried valiantly to elect Maynard but could not get the necessary majority for him or for their other candidates. Unable to
obtain enough Democratic support or Republican backing,
Bailey withdrew from the race on January 25. On the following day, Republican legislator and former Congressman R. R.
Butler announced during the course of the thirtieth ballot
that, since it was clear that his party could not elect one of
their own, he was shifting his support to Democratic state
Representative Howell E. Jackson. Butler's announcement
caused a great deal of confusion: all of the Democrats changed
their votes to Jackson, and additional Republicans followed
Butler's lead and voted for Jackson. When the roll call was
concluded, Jackson with sixty-eight of the ninety-eight votes
cast was the victor.[56]

The selection of Jackson, a freshman representative from
Madison County in West Tennessee, was a high tax victory.
Savage and his followers were successful in ending the career
of high tax spokesman James E. Bailey, but they were not
able to elect a man of their choosing. As the ballots dragged
on, the fear of seeing the election of a Republican senator
had drawn both factions of the Democratic party closer together, but in the end twenty-three Republicans joined with
the Democrats to elect Jackson. The new senator was an old
Whig and a prominent West Tennessee lawyer and businessman, and his wife was a daughter of General William G.
Harding, master of palatial Belle Meade plantation in Davidson County. A newcomer to political office, Jackson held
strong state credit views which were responsible for his Republican support.[57] At a gathering at the Maxwell House following the election, Savage himself endorsed Jackson's selection, called for a debt settlement, and expressed the hope
that in 1882 he would see the "Democratic party stand as one
man—no low tax no high tax about it."[58] In contrast to this
display of Democratic harmony, a number of Republicans

showed dismay and anger at the results and at Butler's support of Jackson. Butler said in his own defense, "I thought it wise and best to elect a good sensible Democrat[,] a high State credit man[,] and a man of ability[.]"[59] Other Republicans charged that Maynard's own friends had crippled his chances.[60]

Once the senatorial election was over, the lawmakers turned to other matters. Governor Hawkins had discussed the debt problem in his biennial message to the legislature; he made clear his views regarding debt legitimacy when he stated, "To my mind there can be no wellfounded [*sic*] question as to the moral and legal obligation of the State for the ultimate payment of these bonds." He did acknowledge, however, that the state had not prospered since 1860 and endorsed the idea of a negotiated settlement. Such a compromise, he said, would place Tennesseans "upon a basis of restored financial integrity" and gain the "confidence of the financial world."[61] Yet he did not recommend a specific plan.[62]

By early March several bills and resolutions pertaining to the debt were before the legislature, and a number of newspapers were reporting that the governor had received a proposal for a debt compromise from a group of the state's creditors. On March 12, Governor Hawkins informed the lawmakers that the New York-based Committee of Tennessee Bondholders, which represented almost 300 American and European holders of the state's securities, desired to offer another plan for settlement of the debt. These creditors, who held a majority of the state's outstanding securities, proposed that all bonds and interest past due and maturing on July 1, 1881, be funded in a new series of bonds issued at par value but carrying only 3 percent interest. These bonds would run for ninety-nine years but could be redeemed by the state at any time after five years. To provide the creditors with some degree of assurance that Tennessee would honor these securities, the interest coupons would, after their maturity, be acceptable for taxes and debts due the state.[63]

The governor urged approval of the proposal and pointed out that the annual interest payment on the state's estimated

$27 million debt would be less than under Coe's offer in
1877. Hawkins' hopes for success hinged on the willingness
of the state credit Democrats to support the New York committee's plan. He was not disappointed: the Nashville *Daily
American,* the Nashville *Banner,* and the Chattanooga *Daily
Times* called for acceptance.[64] While admitting that it was
not "just what we had desired," the Republican Knoxville
Daily Chronicle urged all who wanted an honest settlement
to seize the "golden opportunity" presented by this proposal
and support its adoption.[65] Yet two Memphis Democratic
papers that had backed Wright in the immediately previous
campaign, the *Daily Appeal* and the *Daily Avalanche,* opposed the settlement. The *Daily Appeal* said the state should
not move to pay the full face value of the debt principal, and
the *Daily Avalanche* was especially vigorous in denouncing
the provision allowing mature interest coupons to be accepted for taxes; this would, it asserted, be an infringement
of the sovereign right of the people and the state to control
their finances.[66]

The house of representatives was the first to take up the
bondholder offer, or the 100-3 plan as it was often called. On
March 14, Republican Representative Horace H. Harrison of
Davidson County submitted a bill embodying the features of
the recent creditor communication, and three days later it
came up for its third and final reading. Opponents of the
measure raised various objections to it. Democratic Representative R. E. Thompson, a staunch low taxer, opposed it because it would mean recognition of the railroad debt, which
he considered an unjust obligation. The only Greenback
party member in the General Assembly, James Warren of
McNairy County, attempted unsuccessfully to amend the bill
to pay none of the railroad debt. Weakley County Democrat
A. W. Martin took an unusual stand for a high tax man when
he declared that, although a state credit supporter, he could
not back the bill because it contained the coupons-for-taxes
feature and lacked a requirement of acceptance by popular
referendum before taking effect.[67]

Passage of the bill was never in doubt, as some state credit

Democrats ignored past political differences and voted with the Republicans. Butler joined Harrison in defending the measure during the house debates. State credit Democratic Representative Duncan B. Cooper, a member of a prominent old-line Whig family whose constituency encompassed Maury and Williamson counties in Middle Tennessee, was also vigorous in his support.[68] Cooper, a strong defender of business interests and an investor in Mexican silver mines in the 1880s, said that representatives of his wing of the party had to choose either to side with the low tax men and "envelop this grand old Commonwealth in the shadow of deep, dark, damned repudiation" or to vote for the bill and restore the credit of the state. He "unhesitatingly" opted for the latter.[69] Other proponents of the measure spoke of the benefits the state's railroad system had brought to Tennessee and contended that the state desired and needed a debt settlement. On March 22 the 100-3 bill passed the house by a vote of 43 to 27; 31 Republicans and 12 Democrats voted for it, while 3 Republicans, 23 Democrats, and 1 Greenbacker opposed it. Most of the opponents were from rural counties in Middle and West Tennessee. The three Republicans who voted negatively were from Shelby and Fayette counties, cotton-producing areas which were economically hard pressed.[70]

Failure of the bill in the upper house may have resulted from inadequate leadership. Republican William M. Smith of Shelby County and state credit Democrat Thomas F. Perkins, representing a Middle Tennessee senatorial district, took the lead in defending the bill. Perkins asserted that he favored it because his constituents desired a settlement and because he believed low tax legislators wanted no resolution of the problem at all; but some senators opposed the coupons-for-taxes feature, and several proposed settlements at less than 100 cents on the dollar. On April 1 the bill failed to pass its third reading by a vote of 12 to 13. Just as they had in the house, Republican legislators provided most of the favorable votes: 8 Republicans and 4 Democrats voted for the bill; 2 Republicans and 11 Democrats opposed it. The bulk of the opposition consisted of Middle and West Tennessee Democrats from rural districts; both Republicans represented West Tennessee cotton constituencies. Although the exact number of high tax and low tax men in the legislature cannot be determined, it is clear that in both senate and house some state credit Democrats voted against the bill. Senators B. M. Tillman, H. F. Coleman, and representatives James M. Coulter and Alexander Bagwell, for example, were elected as state credit Democrats but opposed the debt measure. These lawmakers may have believed that the debt principal should be scaled, or perhaps they were reluctant to back a Republican-sponsored plan.[71]

This was not, however, the final senate action on the measure. On April 5 that body reconsidered its previous action, and Democratic Senator L. T. Smith from Fentress County changed his vote so that the bill passed 13 to 12.[72] Without revealing why he had not known the will of his constituents when he first voted, Smith asserted that he was now backing the bill because his district was "overwhelmingly in favor" of 100-3. He also feared, he said, that if this plan were not passed, a future settlement would require a higher interest rate than the bill contained.[73] That night low tax Democrats caucused and denounced the passage of the measure.[74] Just before the house adjourned the next day, Franklin County Democrat J. R. Beasley characterized approval of the act as "the most stupendous crime" committed in the history of Tennessee, and he vowed that its opponents would continue to resist.[75]

State credit Democratic newspapers supported the new law and defended its provisions.[76] "The settlement is final," the Nashville *Daily American* announced, adding that "it is best for the state and for all its people and for all classes of its people that it be considered final from this time."[77] The Chattanooga *Daily Times* declared that, even though the measure was not one that it had originated or proposed, it endorsed the settlement and expressed the hope that the debt issue was "eternally out of our local and State politics."[78] The Memphis *Daily Appeal,* which had opposed the measure, expressed disappointment at its approval but called on all to

accept it as final.[79] The New York *American Exchange* reported that the passage of the law had caused the price of
Tennessee securities to advance on the market and predicted
that other Southern states in default would "finally be compelled to adopt a course similar to that taken by Tennessee,
as it [became] apparent to everyone that an honest declara-
tion of an intention to pay their debts [was] essential to a
return of prosperity."[80]

Though the 100-3 statute had the support of Republicans
and most state credit Democrats, opposition remained. The
Memphis *Daily Avalanche* denounced the new law, and it
estimated in mid-April that almost a dozen papers had revealed their opposition to it. Moreover, it printed reports of
rumors that Senator Smith and others had sold their votes to
interests favoring the creditors' proposal. At a mass meeting
in Murfreesboro on May 1, John H. Savage and two legislators spoke against the measure, and those in attendance
passed resolutions charging that bribery and corruption surrounded its passage. The Hawkins administration, however,
was not deterred by these protests, and on May 9 the comptroller told a creditor that new bonds would be exchanged
for old in New York soon after June 15.[81]

Savage, however, was convinced that low tax men could
successfully challenge the debt settlement by bringing suit in
chancery court. He therefore arranged for a number of highly
respected lawyers who were not prominent low tax advocates, including former Governor Albert Marks, to argue the
suit. Marks was a valuable asset, Savage pointed out, because
he had influence with both wings of the Democratic party.
The suit took the form of a bill of complaint, filed by more
than thirty taxpayers, imploring the court to issue an injunction forbidding the comptroller, the treasurer, and the secretary of state to carry out funding under the 100-3 law. The
plaintiffs leveled a variety of charges against the debt statute.
Bonds issued to pay debt interest for the Civil War years, the
low taxers said, were emitted in violation of the common
practice in international law and trade that regarded interest
on debts owed by one belligerent to another as suspended

while hostilities existed. They alleged as well that the legislature had fraudulently and improperly issued numerous bonds in the Brownlow era. This group charged that the current General Assembly passed the new debt law without the consent of the people and that the act was the product of special interests and bondholders' influence on the lawmakers.[82]

Furthermore, the complainants asserted, the debt law was unconstitutional. Its provision for the acceptance of bond coupons for taxes for the next ninety-nine years violated the constitutional provision that limited the power of the legislature to appropriate funds for no longer than two years, or until the sitting of the next legislature. They charged that the new act amended an earlier law that described what currency would be acceptable for taxes; in so doing it violated the constitutional provision that a law that amends a previous law must contain in its caption the title of the law being altered. They also declared that, in giving the comptroller, treasurer, and secretary of state the power to determine the authenticity of bonds presented for funding, the law gave judicial powers to executive officials. Furthermore, members of government from the governor down to magistrates had to be paid if the state were to function, but the coupons-for-taxes provision gave the creditors first call on the revenue of Tennessee. This endangered the salaries of these vital officeholders and thus violated the spirit of the constitution.[83]

In late May the plaintiffs secured a preliminary injunction from district Judge J. J. Williams of Winchester, who had been an active supporter of S. F. Wilson in the 1880 governorship race. This writ ordered the state to refrain from implementing the debt law. The Hawkins administration argued its case before the chancery court of Davidson County in late June and early July 1881. On July 14, Judge A. G. Merritt ruled in favor of the state on each point of law presented by the complainants. In Merritt's opinion, the injunction had been issued on insufficient grounds, but he granted the plaintiffs' request to appeal to the state supreme court. Tennessee was thus barred from proceeding until the high court decided the matter. Declining to call a special session to hear the

100-3 case, the supreme court justices set January 17, 1882, as the date for the hearing.[84]

Rumors that the court would strike down the debt act circulated freely among politicians, lawyers, and the financial community in Nashville for several days prior to February 11, 1882, the day of the ruling. The unofficial reports were verified when, in a split decision, three of the five jurists ruled the debt settlement act unconstitutional. They upheld the plaintiffs' charge that the use of interest coupons for taxes was unconstitutional; the majority saw the coupon clause as an attempt to ensure the permanency of the debt settlement and open the door to creditor suits in federal courts if the state should ever violate the coupons-for-taxes contract. The two dissenting judges argued, on the other hand, that the law was constitutional and made no unalterable contract with the creditors.[85]

The decision created considerable consternation among state credit Democrats. The Nashville *Banner* said that the verdict placed the state "under an avalanche of gloom" and called on the "honest band of true patriots" who had fought to uphold state honor to rally and continue the struggle.[86] Although requesting public acceptance of the decision, the Nashville *Daily American* praised the opinions of the two dissenting judges as reflecting the views of "a large intelligent and conservative class of Tennesseans" on the debt question.[87] The Knoxville *Tribune* cautioned its readers to conclude that the high court was opposed not to debt payment but rather to the method of payment embodied in the now-void statute of April 1881.[88]

Low tax Democrats were delighted with the court's action. Upon receiving the news, Memphis forces held a mass meeting to celebrate the verdict. One of the speakers at the rally, Harry M. Hill, said that the decision meant the defeat of railroad interests in the state.[89] Henry J. Lynn, one of the plaintiffs in the suit, denied that he was a repudiator but told his listeners that the creditors would have to make "large concessions" to achieve an agreement.[90] The McMinnville *New Era* heralded the ruling by publishing a poem concerning the verdict entitled "Who Killed Cock Robin—100-3."[91]

The Republican Knoxville *Daily Chronicle* denounced the overthrow of the funding law, describing the supreme court's action as one that would "bring endless trouble upon the commonwealth."[92] Even though they disliked the decision, however, Republicans were aware that continuation of the debt controversy might benefit their party.[93] Concerned that Governor Hawkins was being pressed to call a special session of the legislature to settle the matter, the warden of the state penitentiary, Thomas Waters, wrote to Houk that solution of the question would mean Republican defeat. "As long as the bone of contention is left in their [the Democrats'] midst," he said, "so long will they quarrel and fight among them-selves—remove the 'bone' and they will soon settle their dif-ferences and again be the majority party." Delay of debt set-tlement for another year would greatly weaken the Demo-crats and make the state "reliably republican." The warden urged Houk to write to Hawkins if he also desired no imme-diate solution.[94]

In January, Hawkins had privately said that the "signs of the times" indicated that the Republicans' "final overthrow of the Democratic party in Tennessee" was just over the hori-zon.[95] When the court struck down the settlement plan, how-ever, he decided to step cautiously. Four days after the deci-sion the governor told Congressman Houk that he would not "commit the Republican party to any line of policy" besides that of honorable settlement until their friends had had time for "reflection and an opportunity for consultation." Al-though Hawkins gave no indication whether he favored an at-tempt to settle the debt before the fall gubernatorial election, he said that he would probably call an extra session of the legislature to deal with several other matters not resolved.[96]

Hawkins and the Republicans faced an important policy decision. The debt question and the disarray it generated in Democratic ranks had brought Republicans to power in the state after nearly a decade of wandering in the political wil-derness. Once victorious, they had been unable to capture a United States Senate seat for their party; yet, with the cooperation of state credit Democrats, they had passed a debt settlement law. Immediately following the supreme court decision a number of angry state credit Democrats had insisted that they would vote Republican in the future. If this happened on a large scale, it would make the Republicans the dominant party in the state. Hopeful but also a little skeptical, Hawkins speculated: "They are mad now. will they like the sow after awhile return to the wallow[?] some doubtless will. many I think will not."[97] On February 21, Knoxville's Republican postmaster, Oliver P. Temple, wrote to Houk on the same subject. He was "not quite sure" whether state credit Democrats would work with the Republicans; yet he did feel that many who had "heretofore acted with the Democrats," neither could nor would any longer do so. Such men could "hope for nothing from Savage, Marks & Co."[98] Nine days later, his doubts resolved, Temple informed the congressman that Republican hopes for a union with state credit Democrats were futile. "Let us not be deceived. They will desert us," he warned. Both wings of the Democratic party would unite on a compromise platform with "some moderate go between man" as their nominee for governor. "Marks & his associates will control the party, and the great body of Wright men will follow them."[99] Speculation concerning the state credit Democrats' intentions highlighted the next few months for the Republican party.

For Democrats the coming election evoked memories of the disastrous 1880 contest when their party, bitterly divided over the debt issue, had delivered victory to their traditional enemies. Dissension brought about the defeat of James E. Bailey in his bid for reelection to the federal Congress and allowed the Republicans to play a key role in naming his successor. In 1881 a group of state credit Democrats cooperated with the Republican administration to pass a funding act in April, while, for their part, low tax Democrats led by Savage engineered the successful legal challenge to 100-3. Thus, in the spring of 1882 the Democratic party, because of the long-festering debt controversy, faced an uncertain future.

CHAPTER VIII

Democratic Resurgence and Final Settlement

Convinced that positive steps were needed to end the schism in their party, Shelby County Democrats, both high and low tax, issued a plea for reconciliation. In early March 1882 they met in Memphis and endorsed a debt settlement plan that provided for funding the debt at fifty cents on the dollar, with the new bonds bearing 3 percent interest. The assembly asked the leaders of both factions to accept this recommendation as a compromise and to join in a call for a united Democratic convention to heal the breach in the party. Harmony would facilitate final settlement of the debt issue and result in the restoration of "democratic supremacy."[1] Following the Shelby County meeting, the executive committee of the state credit faction gathered in Nashville on April 4 to consider an invitation from their low tax counterparts, who proposed a joint convention aimed at restoring party unity.[2]

Some who attended the executive committee meeting displayed considerable reluctance to accept the low tax olive branch. Bailey declared that Savage's followers wanted the state credit advocates to sacrifice their principles and their organization for the sake of harmony. Several suggested separate conventions. Two speakers warned that the low taxers might use the joint meeting to disrupt the state credit ranks and win more adherents to their point of view. But the majority of the committee overrode these objections and passed a resolution instructing John W. Childress, executive committee chairman, to invite his low tax counterpart, D. F. Wallace, to join with him in a call for a single Democratic convention.[3] On April 16 the two chairmen published an announcement for a unified state Democratic convention to meet on June 20 in Nashville and expressed the hope that party members would "take such steps and precautions in selecting delegates as will secure Democratic unity and harmony."[4]

Unity efforts were threatened, however, when on April 27 Governor Hawkins called the legislature into an extraordinary session to consider a new bondholder offer. The New York-based Committee of Tennessee Bondholders had proposed that all of the bonded debt and matured interest unpaid through January 1, 1882, be funded in a new series of bonds at the rate of 60 cents on the dollar. The bonds were to mature in 30 or 40 years and bear 4 percent interest for the first 3 years, 5 percent for the next 5 years, and 6 percent thereafter until their maturity. Also on April 27, Eugene Kelly, chairman of the New York committee, wrote Hawkins that bondholders representing more than $8.5 million of the $27 million debt had agreed to accept the proposal; he was confident that all the creditors would accept it if Tennessee should pass the measure.[5]

Republicans were united behind their governor. The party's April state convention nominated Hawkins for a second term, and the platform reasserted the legality of the bonded debt and approved the new offer of debt reduction and settlement extended by the bondholders. Their platform called on "State-credit men of all parties" to cooperate in reaching a final debt solution.[6] If the compromise attracted support from state credit Democrats in the legislature, Republicans reasoned, it might also preserve the division in the Democratic party. Perceptive Democrats clearly recognized this possibility. The Nashville *Daily American,* now controlled by A. S. Colyar, branded the proposition a Republican trick to stop Democratic progress toward unity and argued that any settlement must be made by Democrats, who constituted the majority of the state's taxpayers. The McMinnville *New Era* warned that even if the new proposal passed, the people would not accept it.[7]

The bondholders' plan did, indeed, split the Democrats. The party press immediately divided on the question. The Memphis *Daily Appeal* joined the Nashville *Daily American* in condemning the offer as a Republican political trick and declaring that the majority of the people had no faith in the present legislature. But the state credit Chattanooga *Daily Times,* Nashville *Banner,* and Memphis *Daily Avalanche* backed acceptance of the plan. They rebuked the Nashville *Daily American* and the Knoxville *Tribune* for opposing what they considered a very attractive offer—as attractive as the 100-3 plan which the latter papers had earlier endorsed.[8]

In the General Assembly serious consideration of the proposition began when a committee of lawmakers was named to negotiate with Kelly. The committee reported that the creditors' organization represented a majority of the holders of state securities and that bondholders affiliated with this group owned more than half of Tennessee's outstanding bonds. The legislators persuaded the New York committee to modify the interest section of their proposition, whereupon the creditors agreed that they would accept funding bonds for 60 percent of the debt principal and overdue interest at 3 percent interest for the first two years, 4 percent for the next two years, 5 percent for the following two years, and 6 percent for the remaining years until they matured. The legislative committee recommended acceptance of this compromise.[9]

The change in the graduated interest rate schedule did not appreciably alter alignment on the debt compromise. On May 16 seven Republican senators, the majority from East and Middle Tennessee, joined with seven state credit Democrats, most of whom were from Middle Tennessee, to pass the bill fourteen to eleven. Of the ten opposing lawmakers whose party affiliation can be identified, two were Republicans from West Tennessee and eight were Democrats, the majority from Middle and West Tennessee. In the house, as had been the case in the senate, advocates presented familiar arguments for and against the measure, but the debates seemed to sway no one. The bill passed forty-two to twenty-nine. The party allegiance of thirty-nine of the representatives who favored the proposal can be identified: twenty-eight Republicans and eleven Democrats. Most of the Republicans were from their party's stronghold, East Tennessee. Twenty-six of the opponents can be identified as to party; four were Republicans, twenty-one were Democrats, and one was a Greenbacker. All of the Republicans and most of the Democrats who rejected the bill were from West Tennessee; a few of the Democrats were Middle Tennesseans. Repeating the action regarding the 100-3 bill, some state credit Democrats in both houses voted against this measure. Again, these lawmakers may have disliked the provisions of this bill, or they may have decided to oppose any Republican debt settlement. On May 24, Hawkins signed the bill into law, and a month later the New York *Mail and Express* reported that Tennessee officials were in New York, implementing the new statute.[10]

The active support that some state credit Democratic lawmakers and newspapers gave to the Republicans in enacting the new debt law jeopardized Democratic plans for reuniting the party. At least one Republican legislator was convinced that such harmony was impossible. While the house was considering the debt bill, F. D. Owings of Roane County wrote to Congressman Houk that there appeared to be "no possible chance for harmony between the two factions of the Democratic party." He added, "They are becoming more embittered every day." He believed that the low tax men would control the upcoming Democratic state convention and write their debt views into the party platform. One prominent state credit Democrat had told him that if they did not control the convention, they would bolt and "burst hell out of it." As in 1880, two Democratic candidates would run for governor along with Hawkins and the Greenback nominee. "I am fully satisfied," he asserted, "that the split will be great enough to elect Hawkins & a Republican legislature if good work is done at the proper time." Knowing that the next legislature would elect a United States senator, Owings told Houk that he would be offered the "golden opportunity of [his] life" if Republicans controlled that body.[11]

Owings' predictions were tested when the Democratic con-

vention began in Nashville on June 20. The chairmen of the
executive committees of both the low tax and state credit
factions opened the meeting. All went smoothly until the
committee on the platform reported to the delegates. The
members of that group were unable to agree on a debt plank
and presented four reports. The majority called for the repeal
of the recently passed debt law and for the adoption of a proposal to fund at 100 cents on the dollar the state debt proper,
which, they explained, consisted of antebellum bonds issued
for projects other than internal improvements under the
terms of the act of 1852 and its later amending acts. The remainder of the debt would be funded at the rate of fifty
cents on the dollar in a series of bonds which, they suggested,
should bear 3 percent interest for the first ten years and 4
percent thereafter until maturity. Two of the three minority
reports also favored overturning the recently enacted debt
compromise. One proposed funding the whole debt at 50 percent while another wanted to scale and pay only those portions incurred prior to 1852 for purposes other than transportation, to delay any action on the rest of the debt, and to
submit any proposition to the people for their ratification. A
third minority report, signed by only two of the thirty-man
committee, asked for the acceptance of the May debt law as a
"binding and complete" resolution of the issue.[12]

These proposals naturally sparked considerable debate.
James E. Bailey called on the convention to accept the law
and avoid reopening the debt question. Others sought imme-
diate payment of only the state debt proper. The delegates
amended the majority report to provide for a straight 3 percent interest on the proposed funding bonds and for the full
payment of twenty-nine bonds owned by President James K.
Polk's widow. An additional amendment stipulated that Tennessee would pay in full all securities held as of January 1,
1882, by "educational, charitable, and literary institutions."
Following the approval of these changes, the convention
adopted the majority report. Immediately after this action,
Duncan B. Cooper gained the floor. He denounced the convention's action and said that he could not support the plat-

form. Accompanied by Bailey and approximately 100 to 150 other delegates, he withdrew from the assembly.[13]

In a night session directly after Cooper and his followers bolted, the 1,400 delegates remaining turned to the business of selecting a nominee for governor. On the fifth ballot they selected former Confederate General William B. Bate. He had been a prewar Democrat, an advocate of states' rights, and a supporter of Tennessee's secession. His Confederate war record was outstanding; enlisting as a private, he rose to the rank of major general. Active in politics after the war, Bate was usually allied with the state credit wing of the party. He had not been an outspoken high tax advocate, however, and had not taken an active part in the divisive 1880 election. He was popular with members of both wings of the party, and Savage himself regarded him as an ideal compromise candidate. Upon receiving word that Bate would accept the nomination, the convention adjourned.[14]

Those state credit men who had marched out of the convention charged that the Bate Democrats desired to overturn a fair and equitable debt settlement just to gain a political victory in November. They firmly opposed the idea of discriminating between the state debt proper and the rest of the debt and announced that they would hold a convention on July 11 to select their own candidate for governor. Among the well-known public figures who participated in this convention were Bailey, F. A. James, John V. Wright, and B. F. Cheatham. One student of Tennessee history has identified twenty-five of these high tax men by occupation: sixteen lawyers, two farmers, a banker, a publisher, an editor, a realtor, a merchant, a doctor, and a railroad president. Two of the lawyers were presidents of banks and two were directors of railroad companies. The analyst concludes that these party dissidents were men of social standing, "educated, genteel professional men who lived in large towns."[15] Their platform resembled that of the Bate Democrats in nearly all its provisions except those dealing with the debt. On this question, they pronounced the May debt law "just and honorable" and stated that it "should not be disturbed or readjusted."[16] Be-

fore adjourning, the convention selected John H. Fussell of
Maury County as its standard-bearer.[17]

Fussell did not fit the pattern of the bolting Democrats.
He had followed his father's trade of carpentering for a number of years before reading law. During the Civil War he had
served under General Nathan B. Forrest's command, rising
from private to captain. Soon after the war he resumed his
law practice in Columbia; at the time of his nomination, he
was a state district attorney general. The state credit delegates
thought that a man of modest means and social standing
would have the strongest appeal to the voters. For Fussell the
nomination represented more than just the opportunity to
combat the forces of repudiation; he was a confirmed tem-
perance advocate, and he welcomed the campaign as an opportunity to strike at demon rum.[18]

Fussell's supporters were not the only Democrats unhappy
with the action of the Bate convention. The McMinnville
New Era declared that accepting the June platform would
mean abandoning all that low taxers had stood for over the
past five or six years. It charged that the state credit supporters of the 60-3-4-5-6 law had early decided to bolt but had
remained in the convention long enough to create a platform
"as offensive as possible" to the low taxers in the hope that
they would walk out. The *New Era* insisted that no settlement could be enacted that did not require prior ratification
by the people.[19] The Shelbyville *Commercial* branded as de-
serters the low taxers who accepted the Bate platform and
urged running a separate low tax candidate for governor. But
despite these complaints, there was no significant Democratic
low tax opposition to the stand of the June convention on
the debt and the Bate candidacy. There was, however, a
Greenback party candidate in the field. John R. Beasley, who
had been a low tax Democrat, rejected the regular Democratic party's debt platform and ran as the Greenback party's
candidate.[20]

In spite of the bolters, the Bate convention had achieved
nearly complete party unity. Its platform statement on the
debt represented a compromise between the factions: low tax

delegates agreed to abandon their insistence on popular acceptance of any debt adjustment and agreed to recognize the controversial railroad debt, to the extent of fifty cents on each dollar of that debt. For their part, state credit men yielded to low tax insistence on differentiation between the railroad or internal improvements debt and the rest of the debt and accepted a 50 percent scaling of the bulk of the outstanding debt. Most state credit men were eager to restore party harmony, since they were fearful that without it the low taxers might run their own candidate for governor and garner more than the 57,000 votes they had received in 1880. Low taxers, aware that continued Republican control might bring a debt solution far more favorable to the creditors than the Bate plan, regarded the June debt plank as a victory for their cause.[21] "Let Low-tax men be wise," Savage said: "to sustain Bate and the 50-3 beats Hawkins and 60-6 .... We have barely escaped 100-3, had we not better accept 50-3 for fear of something worse?"[22]

Economic trends also favored a debt settlement. The nation began to recover from the depression in 1879, and Tennessee's economy mirrored the national improvement. The assessed valuation of all property in the state increased by over $20 million between 1880 and 1882, and farmers were experiencing a rise in the price of their crops. Cotton, which had brought 8.16 cents per pound in 1878, sold for 9.12 cents in 1882, and tobacco rose from 5.4 cents per pound in 1877 to 8.5 cents in 1882. The prices of corn, wheat, and oats were also up from their depression levels. There were signs that the expansion of business and industry, so much talked about by the state credit forces, might be under way in the opening years of the decade. Production of pig iron, for example, rose from 48,000 tons in 1880 to 137,000 in 1882; and from 1880 through 1883, 411 additional miles of railroad track were laid. Memphis, which had languished in the 1870s, began to expand and prosper dramatically after 1880, and its population increased more than threefold between 1880 and 1890. These developments eased tensions between the various groups within the Democratic party. The farmers, the small-town lawyers, businessmen, and newspaper editors, and the mechanics and working men who had formed the backbone of the low tax movement were more prosperous. In turn, their improved financial condition made them more agreeable to compromise.[23]

The Fussell Democrats were unwilling to accept the compromise, however. Their ranks held some of the best-known and most socially prominent politicians in the state, but their party was small as most state credit men were in the Bate camp. The high tax bolters were among the most resolute opponents of the low taxers and could not bring themselves to join the new Bate coalition. They had struggled for years to obtain a debt settlement and had even cooperated with Republicans in the legislature to achieve this goal. They steadfastly opposed reopening the debt fight by overturning the new law of May 1882. Although their chance for victory was remote, Fussell's supporters were determined to register their protest by independent political action. These conservative, business-minded Democrats held the same views on the debt question as the Republicans, but the antipathy for Republicanism they had developed during the Civil War and Reconstruction eras precluded their merging with the Hawkins forces.[24]

Bate's decision to conduct a vigorous campaign further reduced the Fussell Democrats' slim chances for winning the governorship. When the chairman of the Republican executive committee suggested joint debates involving all of the gubernatorial candidates, John J. Vertrees, the chairman of Bate's state executive committee, rejected the proposal. He argued that such four-party discussions would only help Fussell and Beasley gain more public exposure and possibly divert support from Bate. Too much erosion of Bate's strength by the state credit and Greenback candidates would ensure a Hawkins victory. Taking Vertrees' advice, Bate did not appear with the other nominees in the course of the campaign. In his speeches, he insisted that he was the true Democratic candidate and desired party harmony to prevent the continuation of Republican rule. Fussell could not win, he assured his listeners, but every vote he received rebounded to the advantage of the Republicans. In order to rekindle the deepseated dislike of Democrats for Republicanism, Bate attacked Hawkins' past record and reminded his audiences of the horrors of the Reconstruction era.[25]

When he discussed the debt question, Bate paid little attention to the dissidents. He praised the supreme court's decision overturning the 100-3 debt law and asserted that the 50-3 plank of the June convention had the overwhelming support of the delegates. Often, he retraced the history of the origins of the debt. He defended his party's proposal to pay all of the debt not issued under the terms of the internal improvements law of 1852 and to scale the rest of the obligation.[26] In September at Chattanooga he informed a crowd that under the debt plan of Fussell and Hawkins "the tax-payers of Tennessee [would] have to pay 33-1/3 per cent. more" than they would under the solution in his platform. He went on to justify scaling of part of the debt by pointing to several European nations and other states in the Union that had followed this practice.[27]

John H. Fussell toured Tennessee and engaged in a series of debates with Hawkins and Beasley. He was careful in his speeches to arraign the policies of the national Republican administration and to insist that his cause was that of true Democrats. He, too, reviewed the history of the debt, denounced as unjust the Bate platform's division of the debt into two categories, and defended the 60-3-4-5-6 settlement as a fair and honorable one.[28] Speaking to an East Tennessee audience in September, he declared that the "very salvation of the Democratic party, as well as the honor and highest interest of the State demanded [that] the late settlement be faithfully observed."[29] At Bristol and Chattanooga he charged that the plan of the Bate forces would actually cost the state more than the compromise already in effect.[30]

The feuding Democrats somewhat overshadowed the two remaining candidates in the field, incumbent Republican Governor Alvin Hawkins and Greenbacker John R. Beasley. In his campaign addresses, the governor took the position that his party had been the most consistent defender of state credit. He characterized the recently passed debt settlement law as the fulfillment of the Republican pledge of 1880 to dispose of the problem.[31] "Ten millions of dollars in bonds have already been funded" under the law passed in May, he reminded a Chattanooga crowd, and he expressed the belief that now Tennessee would "never go back on her pledged word."[32] For his part, Beasley endorsed the payment of only those bonds not issued for transportation projects.[33]

The Fussell faction, or Sky Blue Democrats as they were sometimes called, received the editorial support of the Nashville *Banner,* the Chattanooga *Daily Times,* the Clarksville *Semi-Weekly Tobacco Leaf,* and a number of other papers across the state. Republicans hoped that these bolters would divide the Democratic vote; yet they were unable to siphon appreciable strength from the Bate camp, in part because of active support of Bate by John H. Savage and Isham G. Harris. Savage toured the state, endorsing Bate and attempting to muster backing for his own candidacy for the United States Senate.[34]

The man Savage hoped to replace, incumbent Senator Isham G. Harris, played an important role in the Bate campaign. Harris had been governor in the late 1850s and had served as Confederate chief executive during the war years. He was elected to the federal Senate in 1877, and his term was to expire in 1883. The legislature selected in November would decide his political future when it assembled in January 1883. In the past, Harris had aligned himself with the state credit forces of the party, but he had never been a vocal and unyielding advocate of their position. He had immense popularity with Democrats on both sides. Determined to assist in restoring Democratic ascendancy and aware that his own destiny depended on the election of a harmonious Democratic majority in the legislative races, Harris spoke widely in the course of the campaign. He called for unity and belittled the high tax bolters, urging all Democrats to acquiesce in the debt plan of the June platform and take control of the state from Hawkins and his party.[35] "The result must be Bate

or Hawkins," he informed a Pulaski audience, concluding
that "each must decide whether he preferred Democratic or
Republican rule."[36]

In Shelby County the Bate campaign received valuable assistance from black lawyer and politician Ed Shaw. Accusing
the Hawkins administration and white Republicans in the
Memphis area of monopolizing state and federal patronage
for the benefit of a small group and taking black support for
granted, he broke with his party and allied himself with the
Bate forces. At the Shelby County Democratic convention in
October 1882, Shaw addressed the delegates and told them
that he and his followers were opposed to the payment of
the bonds issued to railroads; for this reason they favored the
Bate platform over the Republican one.[37] "The colored
people I represent," he said, "propose to go where they receive recognition, and vote for Bate and his platform."[38] He
asked for and received two places for blacks on the Bate
Democrats' legislative ticket for the county.[39] Angry at what
it considered an unholy alliance, the Nashville *Banner,* a Fussell organ, exclaimed, "Talk about allying with Republicans,
when did ever any party in Tennessee, with one spark of
Democracy in it, take unto itself such a companion[?]"[40]

As they had in 1880, debates and discussions on the debt
question dominated candidates' speeches and newspaper
stories during the campaign. Both the Fussell and the Bate
platforms called for railroad regulation and increased support
of public education, but these concerns were generally ignored. Hawkins defended party policies on national and state
levels, while Bate, Fussell, and Beasley attacked the Republican record. Fussell did attempt, however, to broaden his base
of support by charging that the Bate camp was influenced by
liquor interests, which favored the repeal of the state "Four
Mile Law." This law was so called because it prohibited the
sale of intoxicating beverages within four miles of a chartered
institution of learning outside an incorporated town. The
Fussell platform contained a resolution calling for the preservation of this statute and praising its good influence. Bate
denied that he would support repeal, and his popularity was

not weakened by Fussell's accusation.[41]

On November 4, three days before the election, the Memphis *Daily Appeal* reported the Bate executive committee's confidence that its candidate would receive more votes than the combined total of all votes cast for his opponents. This prediction proved accurate. Bate received 120,637 votes, Hawkins 93,168, Beasley 9,660, and Fussell 4,814. Fussell did not carry a single county; in only a little more than a dozen of the state's ninety-six counties did he garner over 100 votes.[42] The Memphis *Daily Appeal* characterized Bate's victory as "complete, decisive, grand and glorious" and predicted that the next legislature would enact a final debt settlement allowing parties to "assume their normal positions" in future elections.[43] The Clarksville *Semi-Weekly Tobacco Leaf,* which had supported Fussell, acknowledged defeat with hope that the bitterness generated in the campaign would soon subside.[44] The Republican Knoxville *Daily Chronicle* expressed dismay at Hawkins' loss and predicted that the reopening of the debt issue by the next legislature would "bring with it a train of evils, from the effects of which it will be a long time before we recover."[45]

The Democratic victory was a product of the majority's strong desire for party unity, but the new-found solidarity would be put to the test when the legislature assembled in January and took up the debt question. Only a few days after the election, one of Bate's supporters in West Tennessee received word from Nashville, "Already the Bolters aided (I regret to say by some who voted for Bate) are feeling around to try to put obstacles in [the] way of carrying out our platform."[46] But on December 28 state Treasurer Marshall T. Polk, indicating that he was sure a new debt agreement would be made, announced that he did not plan to pay the coupon interest due January 1883 on the $7 million of the debt funded under the law of May 1882. He had backed Fussell, but he believed that Bate's triumph demonstrated the people's opposition to the existing funding act.[47] He would "be governed by the will of the people" on this subject and for this reason would not pay the interest due on

Map 2. Election of 1882.

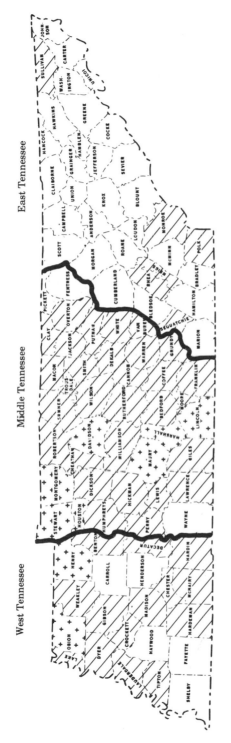

West Tennessee   Middle Tennessee   East Tennessee

◫   Carried by Bate, with less than 5% of the vote for Fussell

⊞   Carried by Bate, with 5-11% of the vote for Fussell

▢   Carried by Hawkins

Source: *The Tribune Almanac and Political Register, 1883* (New York: Tribune Association, [1882]), 72-73. Pickett County returns were included in the returns of Overton and Fentress counties.

the 60-3-4-5-6 bonds.[48]

The decision of the treasurer to defy the law angered the state comptroller and surprised a number of Tennessee political leaders. His true motive in refusing to pay the January bond interest was soon revealed, however. Shortly after the new General Assembly convened, a joint legislative committee appointed to examine the books of the comptroller and the treasurer reported to the senate that the treasurer could not be found and recommended a full investigation of Polk's office. The Nashville *Daily American* and the Memphis *Daily Appeal* estimated a shortage of as much as $400,000. On January 11, Polk was arrested in Texas on his way to Mexico; three days later he was returned under guard to Nashville and placed in jail.[49]

The treasurer's defalcation caused widespread public comment. The theft was especially shocking because of the prominence of Polk's family in Tennessee. Polk, a nephew of former President James K. Polk, was an ex-Confederate officer and a man, according to one newspaper editor, "of courtley [sic] manners well fitted to sustain the high position in society to which his family connections entitled him."[50] He had never held public office prior to his election to the treasurer's post in 1877, but he had won reelection in 1881 when the Republicans acquired the cabinet offices of secretary of state and comptroller.[51] A West Tennessean wrote that the "default of Polk fell like a boom-shell [sic] among our people here" and that the "curses of the Democracy are loud & bitter."[52] The Memphis *Daily Appeal* reported that the theft had been the main topic of conversation on the streets of Jackson.[53]

The Nashville *Daily American,* which had supported Bate, blamed a flaw in Polk's character for the incident. But the Nashville *Banner,* the Chattanooga *Daily Times*—both Fussell papers—and several out-of-state papers saw the theft as a natural product of a society that condoned debt repudiation and unjust treatment of creditors. The *Banner* observed that Polk had been an honorable man in the years before Tennessee had begun to shirk its duty in the matter of the debt, and it believed that the state's dishonest actions in this regard had debased the treasurer's character.[54] The St. Louis *Globe Democrat* asserted that Tennessee was stealing millions of the bondholders' dollars and that Polk, "following the precedent established by his superiors in the Legislature, [had] stolen from the thieving State all he could lay his hands on."[55] The New York *World* remarked that Polk was merely readjusting "the cash in the treasury into his own pocket" and asked how this could be wrong since the state had been doing this with the debt for several years.[56] Tennessean Charles W. Trousdale, whose family owned some bonds, mirrored this view when he said, "As the Cols' [Polk's] thieving fellow citizens have set the example I dont [*sic*] think they can with reason complain at his course."[57]

The Polk affair embarrassed Fussell men and weakened their image as the defenders of state honesty and fair dealing. Coupled with their dismal showing in the gubernatorial race, it underscored their political impotence. As a result of the the treasurer's activities, the Bate coalition was in an even stronger political position to enact the 50-3 scheme proposed in its campaign platform.[58]

While the Polk scandal was going on, the Democratic-controlled legislature held an election for United States senator. Unlike the 1881 election, Republican lawmakers played no decisive role in this election. Harris desired another term, and his supporters in the legislature maintained that his work in helping the Bate forces to victory entitled him to this honor. The press mentioned the names of Marks, Savage, James Palmer of Murfreesboro, and several others as possible choices, should Harris be defeated. Savage, whose enmity for Harris was well known, hoped to oust him, but the popularity of the West Tennessee senator among Democrats far exceeded that of Savage. When lawmakers cast their first ballot on January 16, Harris was an easy victor.[59] Pleased with the result, the Nashville *Daily American* saw the election as a demonstration of "the powerful hold which Senator Harris [had] on the people of Tennessee."[60] One staunch state credit observer who liked Harris but was unhappy with his

support of the Bate forces' 50-3 plan declared that he was
"glad Gov. Harris was sent back to the Senate, though the
quantity of dirt the old man had to eat must rest very heavily
on his stomach."[61] The senator's easy reelection was a mani-
festation of Democratic unity based on the debt plank
shaped at the June convention.

William B. Bate was inaugurated on January 15. The day
before, the partisan Memphis *Daily Appeal* had said that the
swearing in of Bate would be "hailed with joy" and that the
outgoing governor was a man whose "unlovable life is not redeemed by a single noble trait of character."[62] One disgusted
Republican onlooker at the Capitol ceremonies reported that
the crowd cheered every traditional Democratic sentiment,
"and poor old Hawkins was hissed." He described the event
as "the re-establishing of the Southern Confederacy alias
Bate's inauguration."[63] In his inaugural address, the new governor did not speak at length on the debt question, but he
did tell his listeners that he regarded his election as a popular
mandate in favor of the 50-3 proposal.[64]

On February 8, when Bate delivered his biennial message
to the legislature, however, the governor reviewed the history
of the debt in some detail and urged the General Assembly to
enact his party's debt plan, even though Polk had seriously
depleted the treasury. The legislature was already moving to
follow the governor's wishes. On February 26 a joint committee charged with the task of drafting a debt law reported a
bill to the house. The committee had already submitted the
measure to a series of Democratic caucuses of legislators so
that major disagreements on its provisions had been resolved
prior to formal debate in the house and senate.[65]

Both houses of the General Assembly acted on the bill in
the first half of March. Republican lawmakers were angered
at the repeal in January of the Hawkins administration's debt
act of 1882, and they disliked the provision in the new bill
for full payment of the bonds owned by Mrs. James K. Polk.
In the house few Democrats spoke against the measure, and
it passed its third and final reading on March 6 by a vote of
sixty-six to twenty-seven. Democratic unity was apparent, as

only five Democrats, representing Middle and West Tennessee, opposed it. A lone Republican voted for it. In the senate it met no effective opposition, and on March 15 it passed twenty-three to eight, with the support of all but one Democrat. The seven Republican senators unanimously opposed passage.[66] Among those Democrats voting affirmatively was Middle Tennessee state Senator R. E. Thompson, who had been an active low taxer for a number of years. In explaining his action, he said that he still questioned the validity of the debt but he voted for the measure "believing that [his] constituents want[ed] this bill to pass."[67] Five days later, on March 20, Governor Bate signed the bill into law.[68]

The new statute called for funding at full value that part of the debt contracted before the Civil War but not under the internal improvements act of 1852 and its later amending acts. This amount, the state debt proper, was to be funded at par in new thirty-year bonds bearing the same interest rates as the original securities, but with no interest for the Civil War years to be paid on this portion. Bonds held by Tennessee "educational, literary and charitable" institutions and the bonds owned by Mrs. James K. Polk were also to be paid in full.[69] In addition, these institutions and Mrs. Polk were not required to exchange their old bonds for new securities. These provisions encompassed $2,783,150 of the state's nearly $29 million indebtedness.[70]

The bulk of the debt, in excess of $26 million, was to be funded at the rate of fifty cents on the dollar of the total value of the bonds and their unpaid interest through July 1, 1883. Bonds in this category were those issued before and after the Civil War to aid railroad and turnpike companies under the guidelines of the internal improvements act of 1852. The funding bonds of 1866, 1868, 1873, and 1882 that were not issued to replace bonds of the original state debt proper would also be funded at this rate. These securities would bear 3 percent interest and, like those to be issued for the state debt proper, were to mature in thirty years but could be redeemed at any time after five years at the discretion of the state. The governor, comptroller, treasurer, and secretary of state were to carry out the process of exchanging old bonds for new ones. The comptroller was also required to report the progress of funding to the next General Assembly. The law went into effect immediately upon its passage, and by the end of May state officials had contracted for the engraving of the bonds.[71]

Passage of the measure evoked both praise and criticism from the press and bondholders. The Nashville *Daily American,* which supported the governor, declared that the lawmakers should be congratulated for accomplishing their goal. The McMinnville *New Era* held the view that the 50-3 law was the best settlement the state would ever offer to its creditors. The Memphis *Daily Avalanche,* a Fussell paper, disapproved of the law and avowed that it had destroyed Tennessee's credit.[72] The Republican Knoxville *Daily Chronicle* also expressed opposition, saying that a "disreputable conglomeration of demagogues and fanatics" had taken control of the General Assembly and passed the law.[73] An angry correspondent wrote to Governor Bate that the 50-3 settlement was "dishonest, robbing and stealing by force" and that the state's creditors would never accept its terms.[74] The governor received another letter indicating the bondholders' feeling that a minority controlled the action of the legislature. This group, Bate was told, was motivated by "hate engendered by the war—Some from an inborn wish to appropriate to their own use or the use of the State means not their own—and some from motives of pure cussedness."[75]

Bondholders disliked the 50-3 compromise intensely. A few days after Bate took office, Eugene Kelly, head of the New York organization of Tennessee creditors, had said that the proposal was "an attempt to coerce the State's creditors, and, as such, [was] repugnant to every sentiment of justice, morality and fair dealing."[76] A month later a bondholder expressed amazement that "any clear and fair minded member of the Legislature" could imagine that owners of the state's securities would accept the 50-3 offer.[77] In August a New York bondholder told Bate that he found the creditors "very bitter and severe on the State" and "full of threats that they [would] not fund."[78] An acquaintance of United States Senator Howell E. Jackson wrote to him in September that the creditors were willing to fund their bonds for the state debt proper but were reluctant to present the remainder of their holdings for scaling.[79]

At first, funding progressed slowly under the new law. Toward the end of January 1884 the governor reported that approximately $4 million in bonds had been exchanged. Many creditors hoped that political events would lead to the overturning of the law. One opponent, J. L. Hewitt, urged Jackson to run for the governorship to overthrow the debt settlement. When Jackson failed to follow this suggestion, he inquired, "Will the debt paying element of your party unite with the Republican element and carry the election for the payment of its obligations?"[80] A leading New York financial journal reported, "Most of the bondholders seem to prefer waiting, in hope of obtaining a better settlement."[81] But the creditors' hope for a change was futile. Bate was elected to a second term in 1884, and the 50-3 law remained unaltered. The following year, the United States Supreme Court rejected the suit, begun in 1879, of a group of Tennessee bondholders who sought to require the railroads which had originally received bonds to pay the owners of these securities.[82]

The 50-3 law was never repealed or superseded. Continuous Democratic control of state government until 1910 and the appearance of new political issues in the years after 1883 insured its permanence. The new statute reduced the debt from almost $29 million to $15,784,608.19. Bate announced in January 1885 that Tennessee had funded over $8 million of the debt, and in 1907 the state treasurer reported that all but approximately $600,000 of the bonds eligible for exchange had been presented by their holders under the terms of the act of 1883. Tennessee paid the interest on the new bonds promptly; in 1900 it established a sinking fund which reduced the amount of the debt principal by several million dollars. By borrowing over $10 million it retired the remaining $11,793,666 that matured in 1913. With this action, the nineteenth century bonded debt passed into history, and its

financial legacy, in the form of the large loan needed to retire
the debt, became a part of far larger financial burdens
shouldered by Tennessee in the twentieth century.[83]

Bate's victory in 1882 and the enactment of the 50-3 law
in the spring of 1883 heralded the closing of a tumultuous
chapter in Tennessee politics. After 1883 the party and the
public turned their attention to such matters as railroad regulation, prohibition, and the economic plight of farmers—concerns of the rank-and-file Democrat. These issues reflected
the influence of the low tax element on the direction and
policy of the Democrats in the years after 1883. Party rhetoric contained less of the New South business flavor and more
of a Jacksonian emphasis on the needs of the common man
in an industrializing and urbanizing America. Symbols of the
low tax bolters' strength in the reunited party were Governor
Bate's appointment of John H. Savage to a new three-man
state railroad commission in 1883, S. F. Wilson's service as a
special judge on the state supreme court from 1882 to 1884,
and the election by Bate Democrats of low tax legislator
Richard Warner to the first of two terms in congress from a
Middle Tennessee district in 1882. Factionalism within the
Democratic party did not disappear in the remaining years
of the nineteenth century, but no problem again divided this
party so bitterly and for so long as had the debt question.[84]

In 1908 state Treasurer Reau E. Folk spoke to the Tennessee Bankers Association on the history of the debt controversy. He reminded his audience that not very long before,
the debt question had "made and unmade careers" and
"severed friendships at one point and knitted new ties at another." In 1913 the last of the 50-3 debt settlement bonds
were to be redeemed, and Folk predicted that a "new era" of
prosperity would come with final debt retirement. "All over
the State," he said, like a voice from the past, "there are fer-
tile valleys and rich mineral regions which only await the
quickening touch of capital and labor to yield their untold
millions."[85]

Notes

1. Carter Goodrich, *Government Promotion of American Canals and Railroads, 1800-1890* (New York: Columbia Univ. Press, 1960), 1-16.

2. William A. Stanton, "The State Debt in Tennessee Politics" (M.A. thesis, Vanderbilt Univ., 1939), 1-4; Warren P. Grey, *The Development of Banking in Tennessee* (New Brunswick, N.J.: Rutgers Univ. Press, 1948), 6; James E. Thorogood, *A Financial History of Tennessee since 1870* (n.p. [Sewanee, 1949?]), 7-10; Memphis *Daily Appeal*, July 12, 1882; McMinnville *New Era*, Sept. 21, 1882; *A Correct Statement of the State Debt Proper and the Railroad Debt: Together with a Comparative Statement of the Amount to be Paid, according to Bate and Fussell-Hawkins Platforms* (Nashville: Robert H. Howell, 1882), 3-13, pamphlet, Joseph H. Fussell Papers, Tennessee State Library and Archives, Nashville; Stanley J. Folmsbee, *Sectionalism and Internal Improvements in Tennessee, 1796-1845* (Knoxville: East Tennessee Historical Society, 1939), 70-267 *passim*.

3. Chattanooga *Daily Times*, April 13, 1881; R. P. Porter, "State Debts and Repudiation," *International Review* 9 (Nov. 1880), 556-61, 582-83; Henry C. Adams, "The Financial Standing of the States," *Journal of Social Science* 19 (Dec. 1884), 27-28; Thorogood, *Financial History of Tennessee*, 10; Goodrich, *Government Promotion of Canals and Railroads*, 51-165.

4. Benjamin U. Ratchford, *American State Debts* (Durham: Duke Univ. Press, 1941), 122-25, 583. A description of the origin of Virginia's policy of public support for internal improvements is contained in Charles C. Pearson, *The Readjuster Movement in Virginia* (New Haven: Yale Univ. Press, 1917), 1-16.

5. A later amending act allowed the railroads to receive $100,000 in state securities for each bridge across the Tennessee, Cumberland, Clinch, Holston, and Big Hatchie rivers. Stanley J. Folmsbee, "The Radicals and the Railroads," in Philip M. Hamer, ed., *Tennessee: A History, 1673-1932* (New York: American Historical Society, 1933), II, 659-60; W. A. Scott, *Repudiation of State Debts* (New York: Crowell, 1893), 131-32; Park Marshall, *A Life of William B. Bate, Citizen, Soldier and Statesman; with Memorial Addresses by Edward W. Carmack, Charles H. Grosvenor and A. O. Stanley, and Orations by William B. Bate at Elmwood Confederate Cemetery, and Chickamauga and Chattanooga National Park* (Nashville: Park Marshall, 1908), 205. A copy of a Tennessee railroad bond of the 1850s can be found in the Nashville *Daily American*, Aug. 26, 1880.

6. "Bonds Issued to Railroad Companies before the War," Correspondence of the Secretary of State's Office of Tennessee, Tennessee State Library and Archives, Nashville; Henry V. Poor, *Poor's Manual of the Railroads of the United States for 1882* (New York: H. V. & H. W. Poor, 1882), xi; Folmsbee, "Radicals and Railroads," 660-61; John F. Stover, *The Railroads of the South, 1865-1900: A Study in Finance and Control* (Chapel Hill: Univ. of North Carolina Press, 1955), 5; Robert S. Cotterill, "Southern Railroads, 1850-1860," *Mississippi Valley Historical Review* 10 (March 1924), 398-405; James W. Holland, "The Build-

ing of the East Tennessee and Virginia Railroad," East Tennessee Historical Society's *Publications* 4 (1932), 93-96.

7. Stanton, "State Debt," 6-8, 13; Ratchford, *American State Debts*, 125-26, 133; Holland, "East Tennessee and Virginia Railroad," 95-96; R. C. McGrane, *Foreign Bondholders and American State Debts* (New York: Macmillan, 1935), 355-57; Nashville *Daily American*, Oct. 5, 1876.

8. Ratchford, *American State Debts*, 162; Allen W. Moger, *Virginia: Bourbonism to Byrd, 1870-1925* (Charlottesville: Univ. Press of Virginia, 1968), 78; Scott, *Repudiation of State Debts*, 30-31; Thorogood, *Financial History of Tennessee*, 238; "Report of G. W. Blackburn, Comptroller of the Treasury," Tennessee, *Appendix to the House Journal [of the Thirty-Fifth General Assembly of Tennessee], 1867-68*, 57-76. The titles of the volumes of appendices vary slightly from session to session of the legislature; but hereafter the appendices will be referred to as *Appendix to House (and/or Senate) Journal(s)*, followed by the year or years encompassed by the session. A county-by-county breakdown of farm property values for the period may be found in Thomas J. Pressly and William H. Schofield, eds., *Farm Real Estate Values in the United States by Counties, 1850-1959* (Seattle: Univ. of Washington Press, 1965), 52-53; United States Government, Department of the Interior, Census Office, *Census of 1880*, Vol. III, *Report on the Productions of Agriculture as Returned at the Tenth Census (June 1, 1880)* (Washington: Government Printing Office, 1883), 12-13, 16-18.

9. Verton M. Queener, "The Origin of the Republican Party in East Tennessee," East Tennessee Historical Society's *Publications* 13 (1941), 70-75, 81-83; Thomas B. Alexander, "Whiggery and Reconstruction in Tennessee," *Journal of Southern History* 16 (Aug. 1950), 291-94, and *Political Reconstruction in Tennessee* (Nashville: Vanderbilt Univ. Press, 1950), 14-31; Hamer, *Tennessee*, II, 550; Thorogood, *Financial History of Tennessee*, 6; E. Merton Coulter, *William G. Brownlow, Fighting Parson of the Southern Highlands* (Chapel Hill: Univ. of North Carolina Press, 1933; rpt. Knoxville: Univ. of Tennessee Press, 1971), 1-134 *passim*.

10. Hamer, *Tennessee*, II, 599-644; Eugene C. Feistman, "Radical Disfranchisement and the Restoration of Tennessee, 1865-1866," *Tennessee Historical Quarterly* 12 (June 1953), 131-51; Coulter, *Brownlow*, 264-364; Alexander, *Political Reconstruction*, 33-48, 79-198, and "Whiggery and Reconstruction," 295-96; Queener, "Origin of the Republican Party," 75-80, and "A Decade of East Tennessee Republicanism, 1867-1876," East Tennessee Historical Society's *Publications* 14 (1942), 59, 64-65, 76-80. Old Whigs played a prominent role in opposing Republican administrations in several Southern states. See Thomas B. Alexander, "Persistent Whiggery in the Confederate South, 1860-1877," *Journal of Southern History* 27 (Aug. 1961), 321. The law disfranchising ex-Confederates can be found in Tennessee, *Acts of the State of Tennessee, Passed at the First Session of the Thirty-Fourth General Assembly, for the Year 1865*, 32-36. The volumes of state statutes and legislative resolutions are hereafter referred to as *Acts of Tennessee*, followed by the year or years encompassed by the volume.

11. Alexander, *Political Reconstruction*, 49-68, and "Neither Peace Nor War: Conditions in Tennessee in 1865," East Tennessee Historical Society's *Publications* 21 (1949), 33-51; Bell I. Wiley, "Vicissitudes of Early Reconstruction Farming in the Lower Mississippi Valley," *Journal of Southern History* 3 (Nov. 1937), 441-52.

12. Drafts of Governor's Messages [April 1865 and Nov. 1868], William G. Brownlow Papers, Univ. of Tennessee Library, Knoxville; Coulter, *Brownlow*, 287, 374.

13. "Report of G. W. Blackburn," *Appendix to House Journal, 1867-68*, pp. 109-10.

14. McGrane, *Foreign Bondholders*, 357-58; "Report of G. W. Blackburn," *Appendix to House Journal, 1867-68*, pp. 353-68; *Acts of Tennessee, 1867-68*, p. 104; "Report of Ed. R. Pennebaker," *Appendix to House Journal, 1870-71*, p. 1034.

15. "Report of James E. Rust, Treasurer of the State of Tennessee," *Appendix to House Journal*, 1869-70, pp. 341-50.

16. Alexander, *Political Reconstruction*, 168; "Biennial Report of the Comptroller," *Appendix to House and Senate Journals*, 1883, p. 30; *Acts of Tennessee*, 1865, p. 22. This study does not purport to be an analysis of Reconstruction in Tennessee. Thomas B. Alexander, in his study of this period, contends that the spending of the Radical Republican government in the state produced no significant new social programs or services. See his *Political Reconstruction*, 241-42.

17. *Acts of Tennessee*, 1865, pp. 7-8, 10-12; Tennessee, *House Journal of the First Session of the General Assembly of the State of Tennessee, which Convened at Nashville, Monday, April 3, 1865*, 26-28. The titles of the journals of the houses of the legislature vary slightly from session to session; but hereafter the journals will be referred to as *House (and/or Senate) Journal(s)*, followed by the year or years encompassed by the session. "Report of S. W. Hatchett," *Appendix to House Journal*, 1865-66, pp. 50-51; Coulter, *Brownlow*, 374; Oliver P. Temple, *Notable Men of Tennessee from 1833 to 1875* (New York: Cosmopolitan Press, 1912), 321-22.

18. *Acts of Tennessee*, 1865-66, pp. 10-12.

19. "Annual Report of the Condition of Railroads in Tennessee," *Appendix to House Journal*, 1865-66, p. 162.

20. *Ibid.*, 161 215; Alexander, *Political Reconstruction*, 169; *Acts of Tennessee*, 1865-66, pp. 33-34. In 1880 the comptroller estimated that some $4,941,000 in new bonds were issued under the terms of the act of November 1865. James L. Gaines to A. L. Landers, Oct. 8, 1880, James L. Gaines to E. H. East, Oct. 7, 1880, Correspondence of the Comptroller's Office of Tennessee, Tennessee State Library and Archives, Nashville.

21. Folmsbee, "Radicals and Railroads," 662-63; *Acts of Tennessee*, 1868-69, pp. 10-12; *Acts of Tennessee*, 1868, pp. 15-17; "Report of G. W. Blackburn," *Appendix to House Journal*, 1868-69, p. 53; "Communication of the Comptroller of the Treasury," *Appendix to House Journal*, 1868-69, pp. 75-76; *Acts of the Legislature of the State of Tennessee Granting Charter and State Aid to the Cleveland & Ducktown Railroad, (the Road from Cleveland, Tenn., to the Copper Mines in Polk County, Tenn.)* (New York: Charles H. Clayton, 1869), 1-9, pamphlet, Robert Edward Barclay Papers, Tennessee State Library and Archives, Nashville.

22. McGrane, *Foreign Bondholders*, 357; Stanton, "State Debt," 19; D. W. C. Senter to A. J. Fletcher, Oct. 1, 1869, and Jan. 13, 1870, Correspondence of Secretary of State's Office; Folmsbee, "Radicals and Railroads," 602-70; Coulter, *Brownlow*, 379-81; Nashville *Daily American*, April 1, 1879; Knoxville *Daily Chronicle*, Jan. 24, Mar. 6, 7, 12, 1879. The exact amount of unethical and illegal activity engaged in by state officers, lawmakers, and railroad officials will probably never be known. Reliable records do not exist and in many cases never existed. The best evidence, though incomplete, can be found in the reports of the two legislative investigative committees. See *Appendix to House Journal*, 1870-71, pp. 1-255, 329-670, 721-994, and 1879, pp. 1-211.

23. Folmsbee, "Radicals and Railroads, 668, 670-71; Stanton, "State Debt," 24-29; *Acts of Tennessee*, 1868, pp. 10-11; "Governor's Message," *Appendix to House Journal*, 1868-69, pp. 4-5. See the untitled list of requirements railroads had to meet for state aid in Railroad Papers, Tennessee State Library and Archives, Nashville.

24. R. C. Morris to J. E. Raht, Aug. 21, 1868, Barclay Papers.

25. *Acts of Tennessee*, 1869-70, p. 39.

26. "Report of G. W. Blackburn," *Appendix to House Journal*, 1869-70, pp. 81-82, 85, 92. Estimates as to how large the Tennessee debt was at the time the Republicans lost control of the state range from $34 million to $42 million. See Porter, "State Debts and Repudiation," 584; Reau E. Folk, *"Tennessee's Bonded Indebtedness, Retrospective and Prospective," an Address before the Tennessee Bankers' Association* (Nashville, n.p., 1908), 6; Stanton, "State Debt," 12; Alice

H. Lynn, "Tennessee's Public Debt as an Issue in Politics, 1870-1883" (M.A. thesis, Univ. of Tennessee, 1936), 7. Poor estimates the bonded debt as of January 1869 at $34,540,807 in Poor, *Poor's Manual of Railroads for 1869-70,* 467.
27. George W. Farmer to John C. Brown, Sept. 3, 1874, Henry Warren to Gov. Porter, Feb. 12, 1877, A. W. Brockway to James D. Porter, April 13, 1877, Committee of Bondholders of the State of Tennessee to Alvin Hawkins, Mar. 4, 1881, Eugene Kelly to Alvin Hawkins, April 19, 1882, Correspondence of the Governor's Office of Tennessee, Tennessee State Library and Archives, Nashville; Dick to Jimmie [James L. Gaines], June 1, 1875, Thomas Boyd to Dear Sir [James L. Gaines], Aug. 28, 1875, W. R. Brown to James L. Gaines, Dec. 23, 1875, Lucius Frierson to Friend Jim [James L. Gaines], Feb. 22, 1877, C. M. McGhee to James L. Gaines, Jan. 10, 1880, Correspondence of Comptroller's Office; *A Correct Statement of the State Debt Proper and the Railroad Debt,* 12-13, Fussell Papers; Nashville *Daily American,* Nov. 30, 1877; "Report of the Comptroller in Relation to Tennessee State Bonds," *Appendix to House Journal,* 1865-66, p. 148.
28. Alexander, *Political Reconstruction,* 199-225; Hamer, *Tennessee,* II, 646-51; J. A. Sharp, "Downfall of the Radicals," East Tennessee Historical Society's *Publications* 5 (1933), 108-24; Charles A. Miller, *Official and Political Manual of the State of Tennessee* (Nashville: Marshall & Bruce, 1890), 170.
29. *Acts of Tennessee,* 1868-69, pp. 50-53; Thorogood, *Financial History of Tennessee,* 12; Stanton, "State Debt," 30.
30. Tennessee, *Journal of the Proceedings of the Convention of Delegates Elected by the People of Tennessee, to Amend, Revise, or Form and Make a New Constitution for the State, January 10, 1870* (Nashville: Jones, Purvis & Co., 1870), 92, 97-99, 423; Hamer, *Tennessee,* II, 654-56.
31. *Journal of the Proceedings of the Convention,* 423.
32. "Governor's Message," *Appendix to House Journal,* 1869-70, p. 16; *Acts of Tennessee,* 1870, pp. 126-28; "Report of the Commissioner in Relation to Delinquent Railroads in Tennessee," *Appendix to House Journal,* 1871, pp. 119-28; New York *Commercial and Financial Chronicle,* Sept. 24, Oct. 1, Nov. 12, Dec. 17, 1870; Margaret Butler, "The Life of John C. Brown" (M.A. thesis, Univ. of Tennessee, 1936), 93-96; C. M. McGhee to the Commissioner for the Sale of Delinquent Railroads of the State of Tennessee, Oct. 10, 1871, W. C. Kyle to the Commissioners of State of Tennessee of Deliquent Railroads, Dec. 15, 1871, Railroad Papers.

CHAPTER II. THE FUNDING ACT

1. Nashville *Union and American,* June 6, 9, Aug. 7, Sept. 3, 6, 14, 1870; Nashville *Republican Banner,* June 9, July 9, Aug. 28, 1870; Memphis *Daily Appeal,* Aug. 7, 13, 1870; Pulaski *Citizen,* Sept. 2, 1870.
2. Memphis *Daily Appeal,* Sept. 23, 1870.
3. Nashville *Republican Banner,* Oct. 7, 1870; Alexander, *Political Reconstruction,* 24-25; Joshua W. Caldwell, *Sketches of the Bench and Bar of Tennessee* (Knoxville: Ogden Brothers, 1898), 291-97; William B. Hesseltine, *Confederate Leaders in the New South* (Baton Rouge: Louisiana State Univ. Press, 1950), 119-22; Butler, "John C. Brown," 2-10, 29-30, 109-18.
4. Thomas W. Davis, "Arthur S. Colyar and the New South" (Ph.D. diss., Univ. of Missouri, 1962), 1-43.
5. Nashville *Union and American,* Oct. 2, 23, 1870; Nashville *Republican Banner,* Oct. 4, 23, 1870; Jonesboro *Herald and Tribune,* Sept. 29, 1870.
6. Nashville *Union and American,* Oct. 2, 1870.
7. Nashville *Republican Banner,* Oct. 4, 1870; Nashville *Union and American,* Oct. 4, 1870.
8. Speech of Congressman John Morgan Bright at Tullahoma, Tennessee, July 6, 1872, John Morgan Bright Papers, Southern Historical Collection, Univ. of

North Carolina, Chapel Hill; Hamer, *Tennessee,* II, 657; Miller, *Official and Political Manual,* 170. For a map of the state indicating its three grand divisions, see page 116.

9. Jonesboro *Herald and Tribune,* Feb. 15, 1872; Chattanooga *Daily Commercial,* Feb. 3, Dec. 15, 1875; Hamer, *Tennessee,* II, 675.

10. Nashville *Union and American,* May 29, June 9, 1870; John T. Moore and Austin P. Foster, *Tennessee, The Volunteer State, 1769-1923* (Chicago and Nashville: S. J. Clarke Publishing Co., 1923), II, 553-54; Lynn, "Tennessee's Public Debt," 12-15; New York *Commercial and Financial Chronicle,* Jan. 28, 1871.

11. "Report of W. Morrow, Treasurer of the State," *Appendix to House Journal,* 1870-71, p. 1035.

12. *Ibid.,* 1871, pp. 183, 187, 188.

13. Nashville *Republican Banner,* Oct. 24, 1871; New York *Commercial and Financial Chronicle,* Nov. 11, 1871; New York *Times,* Jan. 3, 1872; *Appleton's Annual Cyclopaedia and Register of Important Events* (New York: D. Appleton, 1872), XI, 718-19; John C. Brown to John C. Vaughn, Dec. 29, 1871, Correspondence of Governor's Office; *House Journal,* 1st extra sess., 1872, pp. 65-67.

14. John C. Brown to David Harlan, Jan. 25, 1872, Correspondence of Governor's Office.

15. Nashville *Union and American,* Sept. 1, Oct. 9, 1872; Nashville *Republican Banner,* Sept. 8, 18, 22, Oct. 4, 1872; Davis, "Arthur S. Colyar," 153-57; Butler, "John C. Brown," 60-62.

16. Nashville *Republican Banner,* Sept. 18, 1872.

17. Miller, *Official and Political Manual,* 170; *Appleton's Annual Cyclopaedia,* XII, 754-55; Hamer, *Tennessee,* II, 680.

18. Nashville *Union and American,* Dec. 21, 1872.

19. Nashville *Republican Banner,* Jan. 1, 1873.

20. "Message of Governor John C. Brown," *Appendix to House Journal,* 1873, p. 5.

21. *Ibid.,* 6-13, 15-23.

22. John C. Brown to Messrs. Bohn & Brother, Feb. 4, 1873, Correspondence of Governor's Office.

23. Nashville *Union and American,* Feb. 8, 1873.

24. Memphis *Daily Avalanche,* Feb. 13, 1873.

25. Nashville *Union and American,* Feb. 4, 7, 12, 1873; Knoxville *Daily Chronicle,* Feb. 20, 1873; Memphis *Daily Appeal,* Feb. 10, 11, 1873.

26. Memphis *Daily Appeal,* Feb. 15, 1873.

27. Nashville *Union and American,* Feb. 7, 14, 18, 27, Mar. 5, 6, 8, 12, 1873; Nashville *Republican Banner,* Feb. 15, 18, 26, 1873; *Senate Journal,* 1873, pp. 136, 149, 155-56, 166, 291, 292-300.

28. Nashville *Union and American,* Feb. 27, Mar. 6, 8, 1873; *Senate Journal,* 1873, pp. 252, 260-61.

29. Nashville *Union and American,* Mar. 6, 1873.

30. *Ibid.,* Mar. 6, 12, 1873; *Senate Journal,* 1873, p. 300.

31. *House Journal,* 1873, pp. 374-75; Nashville *Union and American,* Mar. 11, 1873.

32. *House Journal,* 1873, pp. 399-400.

33. *Ibid.,* 374-75, 399-400; Nashville *Union and American,* Mar. 14, 15, 18, 1873; Memphis *Daily Avalanche,* Mar. 17, April 21, 1873.

34. Nashville *Union and American,* Mar. 18, 1873.

35. Memphis *Daily Avalanche,* Mar. 17, April 21, 1873; Nashville *Union and American,* Mar. 18, 1873; *House Journal,* 1873, p. 400.

36. Memphis *Daily Avalanche,* Mar. 17, 1873.

37. Knoxville *Daily Chronicle,* Mar. 7, 11, 1873; Nashville *Union and American,* Mar. 16, 18, 19, 1873; Amos L. Gentry, "Public Career of Leonidas Campbell Houk" (M.A. thesis, Univ. of Tennessee, 1939), 30-37; *House Journal,* 1873, pp. 3-5.

38. Nashville *Union and American,* Mar. 18, 19, 1873.

39. *Ibid.*, Mar. 16, 1873.
40. *Ibid.;* Memphis *Daily Avalanche,* Mar. 18, 1873; New York *Commercial and Financial Chronicle,* Mar. 22, 1873; *House Journal,* 1873, p. 412.
41. *Acts of Tennessee,* 1873, pp. 34-38.
42. Allen S. Tate to L. C. Houk, Nov. 15, 1872, Leonidas Campbell Houk Papers, McClung Collection, Lawson McGhee Library, Knoxville; *Senate Journal,* 1873, pp. 32-33; *House Journal,* 1873, p. 22; John H. Mahoney, "Apportionments and Gerrymandering in Tennessee since 1870" (M.A. thesis, George Peabody College for Teachers, 1930), 6-19; Hamer, *Tennessee,* II, 680.
43. Nashville *Union and American,* Mar. 26, 27, 28, April 1, 3, 5, 24, May 3, 1873; Chattanooga *Daily Times,* April 4, 17, 23, 1873; Memphis *Daily Appeal,* Mar. 26, 29, April 3, 4, May 10, 1873.
44. Quoted in Nashville *Union and American,* Mar. 26, 1873.
45. Nashville *Republican Banner,* Mar. 21, 1873.
46. Quoted in Nashville *Union and American,* May 22, 1873.
47. Memphis *Daily Avalanche,* Mar. 26, 1873.
48. *Ibid.,* Mar. 18, 1873.
49. Knoxville *Daily Chronicle,* Mar. 22, 1873; Nashville *Union and American,* Mar. 21, 22, 1873.
50. *House Journal,* 1873, pp. 491-92; W. Morrow to John C. Brown, Mar. 22, 1873, Correspondence of Governor's Office.
51. *House Journal,* 1873, p. 492.
52. Nashville *Union and American,* Mar. 27, 1873.
53. *House Journal,* 1873, p. 501; Nashville *Union and American;* Mar. 27, 29, 1873; Nashville *Republican Banner,* Mar. 23, 1873; Memphis *Daily Avalanche,* Mar. 25, 1873; Jonesboro *Herald and Tribune,* Mar. 27, 1873.
54. Nashville *Union and American,* April 30, 1873.
55. *Ibid.;* Morristown *Gazette,* May 7, 1873; Draft of circular letter by John C. Brown, April 28, 1873; Correspondence of Governor's Office; New York *Commercial and Financial Chronicle,* May 10, 1873.
56. W. W. Hobbs to John C. Brown, May 1, 1873, John C. Brown to W. W. Hobbs, May 1, 1873, John C. Burch to John C. Brown, June 28, 1873, A. D. Shepard to John C. Brown, July 18 and 30, 1873, Correspondence of Governor's Office; Knoxville *Daily Chronicle,* May 4, 1873; Memphis *Daily Avalanche,* Aug. 2, 1873; Chattanooga *Daily Times,* Aug. 6, 1873; New York *Commercial and Financial Chronicle,* Aug. 23, 1873.
57. Nashville *Union and American,* Sept. 9, 1873.
58. Ben Fields to D. Weaver, Sept. 22, 1873, Dempsey Weaver Papers, Tennessee State Library and Archives, Nashville.
59. Hyde Clarke to the Governor of the State of Tennessee, Sept. 4, 1873, Correspondence of Governor's Office.
60. John C. Brown to [Hyde Clarke], Oct. 22, 1873, *ibid.*
61. John C. Brown to F. B. Snipes, Nov. 22, 1873, *ibid.*

CHAPTER III. COLLAPSE OF THE DEBT MEASURE

1. Nashville *Union and American,* Jan. 6, 1874; New York *Commercial and Financial Chronicle,* Feb. 7, 27, May 16, 1874.
2. John C. Brown to Henry Asham, Nov. 2, 1874, Correspondence of Governor's Office.
3. "Message of John C. Brown, Governor of Tennessee," *Appendix to House Journal,* 1875, pp. 10-11; New York *Times,* June 28, 1874; Edgar Jones to John C. Brown, Mar. 26, 1874, Hyde Clarke to the Governor of the State of Tennessee, Mar. 27, 1874, John C. Brown to Mr. Attorney General, June 1, 1874, Thomas N. Humes to John C. Brown, June 8, 1874, B. R. Cowen to John C. Brown, July 10, 1874, John C. Brown to B. R. Cowen, July 13, 1874, George W. Farmer to John

C. Brown, Sept. 3, 1874, Hyde Clarke to the Governor of the State of Tennessee, Dec. 15, 1874, Correspondence of Governor's Office.

 4. "Message of John C. Brown," *Appendix to House Journal,* 1875, p. 12.

 5. "Report of the Comptroller," *ibid.,* 4.

 6. Nashville *Republican Banner,* Feb. 1, Mar. 8, 11, 12, 18, April 17, May 14, 1874; Memphis *Daily Avalanche,* Mar. 7, 14, April 3, 8, 12, 1874.

 7. Nashville *Republican Banner,* Mar. 8, 1874. The effects of the depression of the 1870s are discussed at greater length in Chapter V.

 8. Memphis *Daily Avalanche,* April 8, 1874.

 9. *Ibid.,* April 3, 8, 1874; Nashville *Republican Banner,* May 14, 1874; Nashville *Union and American,* Feb. 25, 28, 1874; Memphis *Daily Appeal,* Mar. 21, April 10, May 7, 1874.

 10. Memphis *Daily Appeal,* May 7, 1874.

 11. Nashville *Union and American,* Feb. 19, 25, Mar. 17, April 5, 28, May 5, 1874; Memphis *Daily Appeal,* Mar. 21, April 10, 1874.

 12. Nashville *Republican Banner,* May 30, Aug. 6, 1871, Sept. 8, 17, Oct. 1, 12, 23, 1872; A. S. Colyar to Thomas A. R. Nelson, Oct. 15, 1872, and Oct. 24, 1872, Thomas A. R. Nelson Papers, McClung Collection, Lawson McGhee Library, Knoxville; Bible "Andrew Johnson," 11-45; Temple, *Notable Men of Tennessee from 1833 to 1875,* 448.

 13. Nashville *Union and American,* May 5, 6, 1874; Nashville *Republican Banner,* May 2, 1874; William G. Brownlow to Dear Judge [Oliver P. Temple], Feb. 23, 1874, Oliver Perry Temple Papers, University of Tennessee Library, Knoxville.

 14. Nashville *Union and American,* May 6, 1874.

 15. *Ibid.;* Davis, "Arthur S. Colyar," 162-65.

 16. Memphis *Daily Avalanche,* May 9, 1874.

 17. Chattanooga *Daily Times,* May 9, 1874.

 18. Nashville *Union and American,* May 7, 1874.

 19. *Ibid.,* May 2, 8, 9, 23, 1874.

 20. *Ibid.,* May 8, 1874.

 21. Memphis *Daily Appeal,* May 19, 1874; Chattanooga *Daily Times,* May 22, 1874; Nashville *Union and American,* May 2, 8, 10, 14, 23, 1874.

 22. Nashville *Union and American,* June 2, 10, 16, July 9, 11, Aug. 2, 18, 1874; Chattanooga *Daily Times,* June 9, 30, July 8, 30, 1874; Nashville *Republican Banner,* June 19, 30, July 11, 16, 22, Aug. 12, 19, 1874; Memphis *Daily Appeal,* June 15, 17, July 12, 1874; Jonesboro *Herald and Tribune,* July 2, 1874; New York *Commercial and Financial Chronicle,* Aug. 15, 1874.

 23. Nashville *Union and American,* Aug. 20, 1874.

 24. *Ibid.,* Aug. 20, Sept. 17, 18, 1874; Chattanooga *Daily Times,* July 2, Aug. 14, 1874; Jonesboro *Herald and Tribune,* Feb. 12, 1874; Loudon *Times,* Oct. 3, 1874.

 25. Temple, *Notable Men of Tennessee from 1833 to 1875,* 137-49; John Allison, ed. *Notable Men of Tennessee, Personal and Genealogical, with Portraits* (Atlanta: Southern Historical Association, 1905), II, 87-89; Caldwell, *Sketches of the Bench and Bar,* 265-70; Jesse C. Burt, "James D. Porter: West Tennessean and Railroad President," *West Tennessee Historical Society Papers* 5 (1951), 78-89.

 26. C. M. McGhee to John C. Brown, June 9, 1874, Correspondence of Governor's Office.

 27. Chattanooga *Daily Commercial,* Oct. 24, 1874; Nashville *Union and American,* Oct. 3, 4, 8, 15, 18, 1874; Nashville *Republican Banner,* Nov. 3, 1874; Pulaski *Citizen,* Oct. 8, 22, 1874.

 28. Nashville *Union and American,* Oct. 15, 1874.

 29. *Ibid.,* Oct. 11, 1874.

 30. *Ibid.,* Sept. 20, 1874.

 31. *Ibid.,* Oct. 7, 1874.

 32. *Ibid.*

33. *Ibid.;* Chattanooga *Daily Times,* Oct. 4, 1874.
34. Nashville *Union and American,* Sept. 20, 1874.
35. *Ibid.,* Sept. 19, 1874.
36. *Ibid.,* Oct. 7, 1874.
37. *Ibid.,* Sept. 22, Oct. 14, 27, 30, 1874; Memphis *Daily Avalanche,* Oct. 27, 31, 1874; Chattanooga *Daily Times,* Oct. 28, 1874.
38. Nashville *Union and American,* Sept. 30, 1874.
39. *Ibid.,* Sept. 22, 30, Oct. 3, 1874.
40. *Ibid.,* Sept. 30, Oct. 11, 15, 18, Nov. 3, 19, 1874; Chattanooga *Daily Commercial,* Oct. 24, 1874; Chattanooga *Daily Times,* Sept. 20, Oct. 28, 1874; Morristown *Gazette,* Nov. 11, 1874; Miller, *Official and Political Manual,* 170; Jonesboro *Herald and Tribune,* Jan. 28, 1875.
41. Nashville *Republican Banner,* Jan. 22, 1874; Memphis *Daily Avalanche,* Jan. 21, 1875; *Senate Journal,* 1875, pp. 70, 77; *House Journal,* 1875, pp. 68, 96, 114; *Acts of Tennessee,* 1875, pp. 3, 344, 384-85.
42. C. M. McGhee to John C. Brown, June 9, 1874, Correspondence of Governor's Office.
43. Nashville *Republican Banner,* May 2, 1873; Jonesboro *Herald and Tribune,* Aug. 21, 1873; Memphis *Daily Avalanche,* June 21, 1874; Nashville *Union and American,* Dec. 2, 1874; Butler, "John C. Brown," 67-68.
44. Jonesboro *Herald and Tribune,* Jan. 21, 1875; Memphis *Daily Appeal,* Jan. 13, 14, 15, 24, 1875.
45. Memphis *Daily Appeal,* Jan. 24, 1875.
46. *Ibid.*
47. *House Journal,* 1875, pp. 194-96.
48. Nashville *Union and American,* Jan. 27, 1875.
49. Committee Hearings, Jan. 15-Mar. 13, 1875, Legislative Papers, 1875, Tennessee State Library and Archives, Nashville; Memphis *Daily Appeal,* Jan. 15, 21, 1875.
50. Committee Hearings, Jan. 15, 1875.
51. *Ibid.*
52. *Ibid.,* Mar. 6, 8, 1875; Memphis *Daily Appeal,* Mar. 20, 1875.
53. Committee Hearings, Mar. 12, 1875.
54. *Ibid.,* Jan. 15, 22, Mar. 6, 8, 1875; Memphis *Daily Appeal,* Jan. 23, 1875; Gentry, "Public Career of Leonidas Campbell Houk," 38-42.
55. Committee Hearings, Jan. 22, 1875.
56. *Ibid.,* Mar. 13, 1874; Memphis *Daily Appeal,* Jan. 23, 1875.
57. *House Journal,* 1875, p. 644.
58. Memphis *Daily Avalanche,* Jan. 31, 1875; Memphis *Daily Appeal,* Jan. 15, 1875; Butler, "John C. Brown," 67-68.
59. Jonesboro *Herald and Tribune,* Jan. 7, 1875.
60. Memphis *Daily Avalanche,* Nov. 5, 1874.
61. Quoted in Nashville *Union and American,* Nov. 21, 1874.
62. Chattanooga *Daily Times,* Jan. 22, 1875.
63. *Ibid.,* Jan. 12, 13, 15, 19, 22, 1875; Mary O. Bible, "The Post Presidential Career of Andrew Johnson" (M.A. thesis, Univ. of Tennessee, 1936), 53-56; Davis, "Arthur S. Colyar," 169-70; Moore and Foster, *Tennessee, The Volunteer State,* I, 557; Hamer, *Tennessee,* II, 681.
64. Jonesboro *Herald and Tribune,* Jan. 28, 1875.
65. Davis, "Arthur S. Colyar," 169-70; Chattanooga *Daily Commercial,* Feb. 3, 1875; Morristown *Gazette,* Feb. 5, 1875; Pulaski *Citizen,* Feb. 11, 1875; Clarksville *Tobacco Leaf,* Feb. 3, 1875; Bible, "Andrew Johnson," 66.
66. "Message of John C. Brown," *Appendix to House Journal,* 1875, pp. 3-7.
67. Nashville *Union and American,* Jan. 7, 9, Feb. 5, Mar. 25, 1875; New York *Commercial and Financial Chronicle,* Feb. 13, 1875; *House Journal,* 1875, pp. 454, 586, 609, 615-17; *Acts of Tennessee,* 1875, pp. 100-5, 107-13, 122-23, 129-36.

68. Nashville *Union and American*, Nov. 19, 1874, Jan. 7, 13, Feb. 9, 25, 27, Mar. 21, 1875; Memphis *Daily Appeal*, Feb. 11, 26, 1875; Nashville *Republican Banner*, Feb. 27, 1875; *House Journal*, 1875, pp. 34-35, 65, 74, 100, 293, 312, 357, 395, 422, 429, 546, 570, 649, 663-64; *Senate Journal*, 1875, pp. 75, 79, 85, 213, 400, 668.

69. Memphis *Daily Appeal*, Feb. 13, 14, Mar. 4, 19, 1875; Nashville *Union and American*, Feb. 7, 10, 11, 19, 27, 28, Mar. 2, 4, 17, 1875; Memphis *Daily Avalanche*, Mar. 12, 1875; George M. Marsh to John C. Burch, Mar. 11, 1875, Correspondence of Governor's Office.

70. Memphis *Daily Appeal*, Mar. 19, 1875.

71. *Senate Journal*, 1875, pp. 569, 615, 678-79; Nashville *Union and American*, Feb. 19, Mar. 12, 1875; "Treasurer's Report," *Appendix to House Journal*, 1875, p. 8; Scott, *Repudiation of State Debts*, 138-39; New York *Commercial and Financial Chronicle*, May 22, Dec. 18, 1875; "Treasurer's Report," *Appendix to House Journal*, 1877, p. 237.

72. Dick to Jimmie [James L. Gaines], June 1, 1875, Correspondence of Comptroller's Office.

73. C. G. Harger to James L. Gaines, May 26, 1875, *ibid.*

74. J. R. Hills to James L. Gaines, June 21, 1875, *ibid.*

75. W. H. Kent to the Comptroller of the State of Tennessee, June 26, 1875, *ibid.*

76. The Knoxville *Daily Chronicle*'s opinion appeared in Nashville *Republican Banner*, June 15, 1875. Nashville *Union and American*, June 16, 1875.

77. New York *Commercial and Financial Chronicle*, July 3, 1875.

78. *Ibid.*, July 24, 1875; Nashville *Republican Banner*, July 17, 1875; New York *Times*, July 21, 1875; Scott, *Repudiation of State Debts*, 138-39.

79. Nashville *Republican Banner*, July 17, 1875.

80. *Ibid.*, July 8, 1875; Nashville *Union and American*, July 22, 1875.

81. Nashville *Union and American*, June 16, 1875.

82. *Ibid.*, July 31, 1875; Nashville *Republican Banner*, Aug. 11, 1875.

83. Quoted in Nashville *Union and American*, Aug. 6, 1875.

84. Horace Belden to James L. Gaines, Dec. 14, 1875, H. W. W. Elwee to J. L. Gaines, Dec. 15, 1875, James L. Gaines to D. B. Ramsey, Dec. 23, 1875, C. A. Proctor to James L. Gaines, Dec. 27, 1875, J. R. Hills to James L. Gaines, Dec. 29, 1875, James L. Gaines to C. A. Proctor, Dec. 29, 1875, James L. Gaines to J. R. Hills, Dec. 31, 1875, Correspondence of Comptroller's Office; Knoxville *Daily Chronicle*, Nov. 14, 1875; New York *Times*, Nov. 18, 1875; New York *Commercial and Financial Chronicle*, Dec. 18, 1875; Nashville *Daily American*, Dec. 16, 1875.

CHAPTER IV. THE STATE CREDIT RATIONALE

1. Nashville *Union and American*, Mar. 17, 1873, July 11, 1874; Nashville *Daily American*, Oct. 27, 1880; Jonesboro *Herald and Tribune*, May 13, 1875; Chattanooga *Daily Times*, Jan. 1, 1879; Chattanooga *Daily Commercial*, Oct. 3, 1874; Memphis *Daily Appeal*, July 12, 1874, July 11, 1876; Joseph S. Fowler to William B. Stokes, Aug. 5, 1881, William B. Stokes Papers, Tennessee State Library and Archives, Nashville; Folmsbee, *Sectionalism and Internal Improvements*, 53-55, 70-111, 116-47; Verton M. Queener, "The East Tennessee Republicans as a Minority Party, 1870-1896," East Tennessee Historical Society's *Publications* 15 (1943), 62-63.

2. Gentry, "Public Career of Leonidas Campbell Houk," 2; Stanley J. Folmsbee, Robert E. Corlew, and Enoch L. Mitchell, *Tennessee: A Short History* (Knoxville: Univ. of Tennessee Press, 1969), 209, 232; Franklin McCord, "J. E. Bailey: A Gentleman of Clarksville," *Tennessee Historical Quarterly* 23 (Sept. 1964), 246-47. For discussions of the role of former Whigs in the New South, see

C. Vann Woodward, *Origins of the New South, 1877-1913* (Baton Rouge: Louisiana State Univ. Press, 1951), 1-4, 26-28; William B. Hesseltine and David M. Smiley, *The South in American History* (Englewood Cliffs, N. J.: Prentice-Hall, 1960), 419-20; William W. Rogers, *The One-Gallused Rebellion: Agrarianism in Alabama, 1865-1896* (Baton Rouge: Louisiana State Univ. Press, 1970), 32-33; Alexander, "Whiggery and Reconstruction," 291-305, and "Persistent Whiggery," 305-29.

3. Nashville *Union and American*, Jan. 28, 1875; McMinnville *New Era*, Jan. 5, 1880; Memphis *Daily Appeal*, Aug. 13, 1882; Chattanooga *Daily Times*, Aug. 20, 1876, Jan. 16, 1881; Pulaski *Citizen*, July 9, 1874, Jan. 3, 1878; Paris *Weekly Intelligencer*, Dec. 3, 1873; Tennessee, *Biographical Directory, Tennessee General Assembly, 1796-1969 (Preliminary, No. 29): Hamilton County* (Nashville: Tennessee State Library and Archives, 1972), 40-41; "Judge Dickinson Here," scrapbook, Jacob McGavock Dickinson Papers, Tennessee State Library and Archives, Nashville; Gerald M. Capers, *The Biography of a River Town: Memphis, Its Heroic Age* (Chapel Hill: Univ. of North Carolina Press, 1939), 233; Constantine G. Belissary, "The Rise of the Industrial Spirit in Tennessee, 1865-1885" (Ph.D. diss., Vanderbilt Univ., 1949), 288-89; Hesseltine, *Confederate Leaders*, 119-22; Caldwell, *Sketches of the Bench and Bar*, 364-65; Thomas D. Clark and Albert D. Kirwan, *The South since Appomattox: A Century of Regional Change* (New York: Oxford Univ. Press, 1967), 57; Queener, "Republicans as a Minority Party," 49-50; Woodward, *Origins of the New South*, 3.

4. Allison, *Notable Men of Tennessee*, II, 30-34; Caldwell, *Sketches of the Bench and Bar*, 334-49.

5. Woodward, *Origins of the New South*, 1-22. David M. Abshire, however, in his biography of David M. Key, maintains that the Tennessee Democratic leadership of the 1870s was reactionary in its desire to turn back the clock. See his *The South Rejects a Prophet: The Life of Senator D. M. Key, 1824-1900* (New York: Praeger, 1967), 74, 213, 231. For discussions of the voluminous literature concerning the character of the Democratic leadership in the Southern states in this era, see Jacob E. Cooke, "The New South," in *Essays in American Historiography: Papers Presented in Honor of Allan Nevins*, ed. Donald H. Sheehan and Harold C. Syrett (New York: Columbia Univ. Press, 1960), 61-63; Paul M. Gaston, "The New South," in *Writing Southern History: Essays in Historiography in Honor of Fletcher M. Green*, ed. Arthur S. Link and Rembert W. Patrick (Baton Rouge: Louisiana State Univ. Press, 1965), 316-36; and Sheldon Hackney, "Origins of the New South in Retrospect," *Journal of Southern History* 38 (May 1972), 191-216.

6. Belissary, "Industrial Spirit in Tennessee," 1-237 *passim*.

7. On the local level the Nashville city council passed a law in 1875 that exempted from taxation for seven years all improvements on rolling mills and blast furnaces within its jurisdiction. *Ibid.*, 102-7, 141-45, 158-59, 163-95; Moore and Foster, *Tennessee*, II, 557-58; *Appleton's Annual Cyclopaedia*, XV, 724-26; Butler, "John C. Brown," 69; William T. Hale and Dixon L. Merritt, *A History of Tennessee and Tennesseans: The Leaders and Representative Men in Commerce, Industry and Modern Activities* (Chicago and New York: Lewis Publishing Co., 1913), II, 764. For examples of instances in which the entrenched Democratic leadership of a Southern state went beyond the efforts of state credit Democrats in Tennessee to attract business and industry and extended tax breaks to such enterprises, see James S. Ferguson, "Agrarianism in Mississippi, 1871-1900: A Study in Non-Conformity" (Ph.D. diss., Univ. of North Carolina, 1952), 330-31; and Judson C. Ward, "Georgia under the Bourbon Democrats, 1872-1890" (Ph.D. diss., Univ. of North Carolina, 1947), 521.

8. Knoxville *Daily Chronicle*, Sept. 23, 1880; Chattanooga *Daily Times*, Jan. 23, 1879, Mar. 8, 1881; Memphis *Daily Appeal*, Jan. 15, 1879; Nashville *Banner*, Mar. 16, 1881; Nashville *Union and American*, Feb. 19, 1874, Feb. 10, 1875; Nashville *Daily American*, Nov. 16, 1877, Jan. 19, 1878, July 2, 1879.

9. Memphis *Daily Appeal*, June 17, 1874.

10. Nashville *Union and American,* Feb. 10, 1875.
11. Knoxville *Daily Chronicle,* Sept. 23, 1880.
12. Chattanooga *Daily Times,* Jan. 23, 1879.
13. *Ibid.,* Jan. 23, 1879, Sept. 23, 1880, Mar. 8, April 5, 1881; Memphis *Daily Appeal,* May 7, 1874, July 6, 1879; Nashville *Union and American,* Feb. 10, 1874; Nashville *Republican Banner,* Jan. 17, 1873; Nashville *Daily American,* Nov. 16, 1877, Jan. 19, 1878, July 2, 1879; Jackson *Tribune and Sun,* May 15, 1879; Gallatin *Examiner,* Feb. 18, 1876.
14. Nashville *Daily American,* Jan. 19, 1878.
15. *Ibid.,* May 18, 1876.
16. *Ibid.,* Nov. 16, 1877.
17. *Ibid.,* June 29, 1881.
18. Memphis *Daily Appeal,* Jan. 9, July 11, 1879; Nashville *Banner,* Nov. 16, 1881; Knoxville *Daily Chronicle,* April 7, 1881; Morristown *Gazette,* Aug. 6, 1879.
19. Memphis *Daily Appeal,* Jan. 9, 1879.
20. Nashville *Banner,* Mar. 11, 1882.
21. *Ibid.,* Mar. 16, 1881.
22. Nashville *Daily American,* Mar. 15, 1881.
23. *Ibid.,* July 22, 1882.
24. Nashville *Banner,* Sept. 11, 1882; Nashville *Daily American,* Nov. 30, Dec. 9, 1877, July 7, 1878, Mar. 2, 4, 1879, Oct. 3, 1880. On September 1, 1875, the Nashville *Union and American* and the Nashville *Republican Banner* announced their consolidation as the Nashville *Daily American.* See the Nashville *Daily American,* Sept. 1, 1875. Memphis *Daily Avalanche,* Aug. 11, 1880.
25. "The State Debt: Duty and Responsibility of the Tennessee Democracy," pamphlet in scrapbook, Fussell Papers.
26. Nashville *Daily American,* Mar. 5, 1879.
27. *Ibid.,* Mar. 23, 1881.
28. Memphis *Daily Avalanche,* July 23, 1880.
29. *Ibid.,* Aug. 15, 1880; Nashville *Daily American,* Nov. 24, 30, 1877, Feb. 21, 26, 1878, Feb. 20, 1879.
30. Nashville *Daily American,* Nov. 24, 1877.
31. Memphis *Daily Avalanche,* Aug. 15, 1880.
32. *Ibid.,* Aug. 17, 1880; Memphis *Daily Appeal,* May 4, Dec. 4, 1874; Nashville *Union and American,* April 28, 1874; Knoxville *Daily Chronicle,* Dec. 1, 1878, Jan. 25, Feb. 22, 1879; Nashville *Daily American,* Nov. 24, 1877, Feb. 13, 20, 1879; Jordon Stokes, *State Debt of Tennessee: Embracing the Subjects of the Compromise Measure, the Validity of the Bonds, the Liability of the Railroads, and the Remedy of the Bondholders in the Courts* (Nashville: Tavel, Eastman & Howell, 1880), 20-23.
33. Chattanooga *Daily Times,* Sept. 26, 1880.
34. Knoxville *Daily Chronicle,* Feb. 22, 1879; Nashville *Daily American,* Nov. 16, 24, 30, 1877, Feb. 26, 1878, Feb. 20, 1880.
35. Nashville *Daily American,* Nov. 30, 1877.
36. Memphis *Daily Appeal,* May 7, 1875; Nashville *Union and American,* Feb. 28, Mar. 23, 1875; Chattanooga *Daily Times,* Jan. 18, 1878, July 21, 1880; Nashville *Union and American,* Nov. 30, 1877, Feb. 23, July 17, 23, 1879; Morristown *Gazette,* July 16, 1879; Gallatin *Examiner,* April 28, 1876.
37. Nashville *Republican Banner,* July 11, 1874.
38. Nashville *Daily American,* Nov. 16, 1877.
39. *Ibid.,* Nov. 16, 1877, Feb. 28, 1879, Aug. 13, 1880; Nashville *Republican Banner,* Feb. 14, 1882.
40. Memphis *Daily Avalanche,* July 23, 1882.
41. *Ibid.,* Aug. 6, 1882.
42. Nashville *Daily American,* Aug. 13, 1880.
43. *Ibid.,* Nov. 16, 1877.

44. Nashville *Union and American,* Dec. 1, 1874, Feb. 13, 1875; Memphis *Daily Avalanche,* July 23, 1882; Nashville *Daily American,* Jan. 3, 1880; Knoxville *Daily Chronicle,* Jan. 11, 1883.
45. Knoxville *Daily Chronicle,* Feb. 20, 1879.
46. Nashville *Daily American,* Jan. 3, 1880.
47. Knoxville *Daily Chronicle,* Jan. 11, 1883.
48. *Ibid.,* Jan. 23, 1879; Nashville *Union and American,* Mar. 18, 1873, Feb. 28, 1874; Memphis *Daily Appeal,* July 22, 1879; Memphis *Daily Avalanche,* July 9, 1879, Oct. 23, 1880; Nashville *Daily American,* Nov. 30, 1877, Feb. 26, July 19, 1878, Jan. 24, July 22, 24, 1879, Aug. 21, 1882; Gallatin *Examiner,* April 28, 1876; Pulaski *Citizen,* May 6, 1879. For an earlier defense of the railroads and their importance, see W. J. Sykes's article in the Nashville *Rural Sun,* Nov. 7, 1872.
49. Nashville *Daily American,* Nov. 30, 1877.
50. Memphis *Daily Appeal,* July 22, 1879.
51. Memphis *Daily Avalanche,* July 24, 1880.
52. Nashville *Daily American,* July 19, 1878.
53. *Ibid.,* Nov. 16, 1877, Jan. 17, July 19, 1878; Memphis *Daily Appeal,* April 10, May 7, 24, June 17, 1874, Oct. 8, 1880, April 28, July 5, 1882; Nashville *Banner,* Oct. 6, 1880; Nashville *Union and American,* June 10, 1874; Chattanooga *Daily Times,* July 21, 1880; Jonesboro *Herald and Tribune,* Dec. 3, 1874; Knoxville *Daily Chronicle,* June 10, 1879, Sept. 24, 1880, May 10, 1882.
54. Memphis *Daily Appeal,* Oct. 8, 1880.
55. Nashville *Daily American,* Nov. 16, 1877.
56. *Ibid.,* Sept. 21, Oct. 3, 30, Nov. 2, 1880; Nashville *Banner,* Oct. 5, 6, 15, 1880; Knoxville *Daily Chronicle,* Aug. 24, 1879; Jackson *Tribune and Sun,* May 29, 1879; Clarksville *Semi-Weekly Tobacco Leaf,* Sept. 3, Oct. 1, 1880.
57. Nashville *Daily American,* Sept. 21, 1880.
58. Knoxville *Daily Chronicle,* Aug. 24, 1879.
59. Nashville *Daily American,* Sept. 21, 24, 1880; Nashville *Banner,* Oct. 5, 14, 1880.
60. Nashville *Daily American,* April 23, Sept. 9, 1880, Jan. 17, 1882; Memphis *Daily Appeal,* Sept. 7, 9, 1880; Daniel M. Robison, *Bob Taylor and the Agrarian Revolt in Tennessee* (Chapel Hill: Univ. of North Carolina Press, 1935), 16. For a discussion of the use of appeals to white unity and fears of Negro rule by Democratic leadership in the South in the post-Reconstruction era, see Woodward, *Origins of the New South,* 51-52, 77-106, 254-59; Rogers, *One-Gallused Rebellion,* 46, 55; Ward, "Georgia under the Bourbon Democrats," 519-25; and Cooke, "The New South," 62-63.
61. Chattanooga *Daily Times,* Aug. 23, Oct. 22, May 19, July 26, 1882; Belissary, "Industrial Spirit in Tennessee," 34, 62-68, 70-76, 97-100, 107-10, 114-19, 123-24, 264-69.

CHAPTER V. HARD TIMES AND THE LOW TAX ARGUMENT

1. Gilbert C. Fite and Jim E. Reese, *An Economic History of the United States* (2nd ed.; Boston: Houghton, 1965), 303-5; Rendigs Fels, *American Business Cycles, 1865-1897* (Chapel Hill: Univ. of North Carolina Press, 1959), 83-112; Edward C. Kirkland, *Industry Comes of Age: Business, Labor, and Public Policy, 1860-1897* (New York: Holt), 6.
2. Pulaski *Citizen,* Aug. 31, 1876; Emery Q. Hawk, *Economic History of the South* (New York: Prentice-Hall, 1934), 445; E. Ray McCartney, "Crisis of 1873" (Ph.D. diss., Fort Hays Kansas State College, 1935), 98-101, 116; David A. Wells, *Recent Economic Changes: And Their Effect on the Production and Distribution of Wealth and the Well-Being of Society* (New York: D. Appleton, 1889), 12, 119, 167, 206; Carroll D. Wright, *The Industrial Evolution of the United States* (New

York: Russell & Russell, 1895), 226; Fred A. Shannon, *The Farmer's Last Frontier: Agriculture, 1860-1897* (New York: Holt, 1966), 294; Fels, *Business Cycles,* 62, 89-90, 97, 112-36; Kirkland, *Industry Comes of Age,* 6-8, 30; J. G. Randall and David Donald, *The Civil War and Reconstruction* (2nd ed., rev.; Lexington, Mass.: Heath, 1969), 662-63; Poor, *Poor's Manual of Railroads for 1882,* xi.

3. New York *Times,* Nov. 22, 1873; Tennessee, *Biennial Report of the Commissioner of Agriculture, Statistics and Mines, and Bureau of Immigration to the Forty-First General Assembly of the State of Tennessee* (Nashville: Printed at "The American" Steam Book and Job Office, 1879), 19-21; Belissary, "Industrial Spirit in Tennessee," 47-48, 58-63, 73, 77-80, 90, 91, 95, 110, 117, 126-60, 192-94, 256; Campbell Brown, "Why Capital Does Not Flow into the South," *Nation* 35 (Dec. 14, 1882), 501; Stover, *The Railroads of the South,* 61; Poor, *Poor's Manual of Railroads for 1882,* xi. For a discussion of the impact of the economic cycles of the latter nineteenth century on Southern railroads and their developers, see John F. Stover, "Northern Financial Interests in Southern Railroads, 1865-1900," *Georgia Historical Quarterly* 39 (Sept. 1955), 205-20.

4. Memphis *Daily Avalanche,* May 11, Sept. 19, 1876, Feb. 4, 1877; Nashville *Daily American,* May 10, Aug. 10, 1876, Feb. 9, May 11, 1877, Jan. 9, Aug. 16, 1878; Nashville *Republican Banner,* Feb. 19, 1875; "Biennial Report of the Comptroller," *Appendix to Senate & House Journals,* 1883, pp. 31-33; Thorogood, *Financial History of Tennessee,* 238.

5. Joseph B. Killebrew, *Introduction to the Resources of Tennessee* (Nashville: Tavel, Eastman & Howell, 1874), 93-104, 407; U.S. Department of Commerce, Bureau of the Census, *Historical Statistics of the United States, Colonial Times to 1957: A Statistical Abstract Supplement* (Prepared with the cooperation of the Social Science Research Council [Washington: U.S. Government Printing Office, 1960]), 297-98, 302; *Census of 1880,* Vol. III, *Report on Agriculture,* 4, 12; Tennessee, *Biennial Report of the Bureau of Agriculture, Statistics and Immigration, 1889 and 1890, B. M. Hord, Commissioner* (Nashville: Albert B. Tavel, 1891), 48-52.

6. Nashville *Daily American,* Feb. 10, Sept. 12, 1876, Feb. 26, Aug. 18, 1881; Chattanooga *Daily Times,* Nov. 18, 1874, Jan. 2, 1879; Nashville *Banner,* April 27, 1882; Nashville *Union and American,* Dec. 28, 1872, Feb. 21, 1874, Feb. 9, Mar. 26, 1875; Knoxville *Daily Chronicle,* Mar. 20, 1881; Memphis *Daily Avalanche,* Dec. 15, 1875, Feb. 6, 8, 1879, Jan. 9, 11, 12, Feb. 6, 18, 1883; William Fowler to James L. Gaines, April 16, 1875, John J. Green to Honorable Comptroller, Aug. 16, 1875, Fair Play & Justice to James L. Gaines, Aug. 10, 1875, T. H. Burden to James L. Gaines, Dec. 15, 1875, James L. Gaines to Messrs. Galloway and Keating, Mar. 31, 1876, Correspondence of Comptroller's Office; Thorogood, *Financial History of Tennessee,* 25-43, 236; Speech of William H. Jackson at Bell Buckle, Tennessee [1874?], Harding-Jackson Papers, Tennessee State Library and Archives, Nashville. These are photocopies of the original papers which are held in the Southern Historical Collection, Univ. of North Carolina, Chapel Hill. C. O. Brannen, *Taxation in Tennessee* (Louisville: Baldwin Law Book Co., 1920), 47-61; S. J. Shepherd, "Evils of the Present System of Taxation in Tennessee," *Proceedings of the Bar Association of Tennessee* 8 (July 1889), 136.

7. Memphis *Daily Avalanche,* Mar. 8, 12, April 17, 1874, Mar. 2, 1875, July 18, Aug. 22, Sept. 2, 1876; Nashville *Union and American,* May 8, 1874, Oct. 18, 1875.

8. Memphis *Daily Avalanche,* Sept. 19, 1876.

9. *Ibid.,* Sept. 2, 1876.

10. Nashville *Union and American,* May 8, 1874.

11. Quoted in Memphis *Daily Avalanche,* June 14, 1876.

12. W. A. Caruthers to James L. Gaines, Aug. 21, 1876, Correspondence of Comptroller's Office.

13. R. J. Turner to James L. Gaines, [Oct. 1876], *ibid.*

14. Nashville *Rural Sun,* Dec. 7, 1876.

15. Memphis *Daily Avalanche,* Aug. 8, 1876, Dec. 11, 1879; Chattanooga *Daily Times,* June 19, 1882; L. D. Bejack, "The Taxing District of Shelby County," West Tennessee Historical Society *Papers* 4 (1950), 5-12; John H. Ellis, "Business Leadership in Memphis Public Health Reform, 1880-1900," West Tennessee Historical Society *Papers* 19 (1965), 94-95; Capers, *River Town,* 184-85, 201-4, 207-8, 224-25.

16. Capers, *River Town,* 187-209; Ellis, "Business Leadership in Health Reform," 95-97; Bejack, "Taxing District of Shelby," 9-14.

17. Capers, *River Town,* 212; Bejack, "Taxing District of Shelby," 15-27; Memphis *Daily Avalanche,* Mar. 25, Oct. 22, 29, Nov. 11, 1874, Aug. 6, 1876, Mar. 22, 1881; Memphis *Daily Appeal,* Oct. 27, 1874, Aug. 9, 1876; Nashville *Union and American,* Oct. 24, 1874; Chattanooga *Daily Times,* June 19, 1882.

18. Memphis *Daily Appeal,* Dec. 20, 23, 1879; McMinnville *New Era,* Jan. 8, 1880. Background information on the founders of the low tax party was obtained from various volumes of the *Biographical Directory, Tennessee General Assembly.* Roger L. Hart, *Redeemers, Bourbons & Populists: Tennessee 1870-1896* (Baton Rouge: Louisiana State Univ. Press, 1975), 36-38, 44-48. In interpreting Tennessee politics, Hart stresses the role of conflicting status groups and de-emphasizes the importance of economic hardship as a stimulant to political insurgency. See pp. 224-35.

19. Nashville *Rural Sun,* Mar. 4, 11, 18, 1875; McMinnville *New Era,* Jan. 8, 1880; Nashville *Banner,* Aug. 31, Sept. 8, 1880; Nashville *Daily American,* Oct. 6, 1880, Oct. 4, 1882; John J. Boon to William McCaslin, Mar. 19, 1877, letter in possession of Professor V. Jacque Voegeli, Vanderbilt Univ., Nashville; Cartmell Diaries, Vol. IV, Aug. 7, 1879, Robert H. Cartmell Papers, Tennessee State Library and Archives, Nashville; Martha L. Weems, "The Grange in Tennessee, 1870-1908 and 1933-1966" (M.A. thesis, East Tennessee State Univ., 1969), 121; *House Journal,* 1873, p. 4; Hart, *Redeemers, Bourbons & Populists,* 44-46.

20. *Cumberland Almanac for the Year 1882* (Nashville: American Publishing Co., [1881?]), 8, 10; *Census of 1880,* Vol. III, *Report on Agriculture,* 84-89, and Vol. I, *Statistics of Population,* 79-80, 407-8.

21. *Cumberland Almanac for 1882,* 8, 10; "Biennial Report of the Comptroller of the State of Tennessee," *Appendix to House and Senate Journals,* 1883, pp. 32-37.

22. Woodward, *Origins of the New South,* 3-4; Francis B. Simkins, *A History of the South* (3rd ed.; New York: Knopf, 1963), 320; Hesseltine and Smiley, *The South in American History,* 423.

23. A. M. Shook to A. S. Colyar, Nov. 21, 1905, Arthur St. Clair Colyar Papers, Southern Historical Collection, Univ. of North Carolina, Chapel Hill; Sarah M. Howell, "The Editorials of Arthur S. Colyar, Nashville Prophet of the New South," *Tennessee Historical Quarterly* 27 (Fall 1968), 262-76. For a perceptive analysis of Colyar's role in Tennessee politics, see Davis, "Arthur S. Colyar," 162-224.

24. [John H. Savage], *The Life of John H. Savage: Citizen, Soldier, Lawyer, Congressman before the War Begun and Prosecuted by the Abolitionists of the Northern States to Reduce the Descendants of the Rebels of 1776, Who Defeated the Armies of the King of England and Gained Independence for the United States, down to the Level of the Negro Race* (Nashville: John H. Savage, 1903), 9-152; Nashville *Union and American,* Oct. 9, 1874; "Cheatham, Harris, and Savage,—War Records," in scrapbook, Fussell Papers; "Open Letter of John H. Savage," Isham G. Harris Papers, Tennessee State Library and Archives, Nashville.

25. [Savage], *Life of Savage,* 77.

26. *Ibid.,* 159.

27. *Ibid.,* 37-38, 74-76, 154-61; Nashville *Union and American,* Oct. 11, 13, 15, 17, 1874.

28. Chattanooga *Daily Times,* Sept. 30, 1880, Aug. 30, Oct. 13, 1882.

29. Memphis *Daily Avalanche,* Sept. 11, 1880.

30. McMinnville *New Era,* Dec. 7, 1882.
31. Quoted in *ibid.,* Sept. 16, 1880.
32. Nashville *Union and American,* Feb. 17, 19, 1875; Nashville *Daily American,* Dec. 1, 1877; Nashville *Republican Banner,* July 8, 1874; Memphis *Daily Appeal,* Nov. 4, 1876; Memphis *Daily Avalanche,* Feb. 15, 1881.
33. Nashville *Daily American,* Dec. 1, 1877.
34. John H. Savage to Howell E. Jackson, Nov. 24, 1884, Harding-Jackson Papers.
35. Nashville *Daily American,* June 17, Aug. 7, Sept. 9, 30, 1880; Memphis *Daily Avalanche,* May 26, Sept. 23, Oct. 1, 1876, Nov. 14, 1877; McMinnville *New Era,* June 17, 1880; Chattanooga *Daily Times,* April 6, 1878.
36. McMinnville *New Era,* May 27, 1880.
37. Memphis *Daily Avalanche,* May 26, Sept. 23, Oct. 1, 1876, Nov. 14, 1877, Sept. 30, 1880.
38. McMinnville *New Era,* June 3, 1880.
39. *Ibid.,* May 13, 1880.
40. Nashville *Union and American,* Feb. 7, 1875; Memphis *Daily Avalanche,* Nov. 1, 1876, Nov. 14, 1877; McMinnville *New Era,* Jan. 15, Mar. 25, 1880; Nashville *Daily American,* Dec. 12, 1877.
41. J. T. Smith to Hon. Governor of Tennessee, June 16, 1877, Correspondence of Governor's Office.
42. Nashville *Daily American,* Dec. 12, 1877.
43. Memphis *Daily Avalanche,* Nov. 14, 1877.
44. E. J. Taliaferro to Gov. Porter, Oct. 2, 1879, Correspondence of Governor's Office.
45. Chattanooga *Daily Times,* Aug. 7, Oct. 21, 1880; Memphis *Daily Appeal,* April 14, 1878; Nashville *Union and American,* Dec. 3, 1874, Feb. 17, 1875; McMinnville *New Era,* July 8, 1880; Nashville *Daily American,* July 29, Aug. 1, 1876, Jan. 25, 1877, Aug. 1, 1880; Belissary, "Industrial Spirit in Tennessee," 282.
46. Memphis *Daily Avalanche,* Jan. 10, 1876.
47. *Ibid.,* Dec. 30, 1874, May 11, Sept. 3, Sept. 22, 1876, Feb. 4, 1877; Nashville *Union and American,* May 20, 1876, Feb. 9, Dec. 9, 1877, Jan. 15, 1878; Knoxville *Daily Chronicle,* Sept. 8, 1880.
48. Nashville *Daily American,* Jan. 15, 1878.
49. Memphis *Daily Avalanche,* Sept. 3, 1876.
50. Nashville *Union and American,* Feb. 27, 1875.
51. *Ibid.,* Feb. 17, 18, 1875; Memphis *Daily Avalanche,* Dec. 30, 1874, May 11, Sept. 22, 1876, Feb. 4, 1877; Nashville *Daily American,* Jan. 26, 1876, Dec. 1, 9, 1877; Memphis *Daily Appeal,* Nov. 4, 1876.
52. Nashville *Republican Banner,* Mar. 2, 1875; Nashville *Daily American,* Dec. 9, 1877; Memphis *Daily Appeal,* Oct. 15, 1876; Memphis *Daily Avalanche,* Sept. 22, 1876.
53. Nashville *Daily American,* Mar. 20, 1879.
54. Memphis *Daily Avalanche,* May 23, 1876.
55. Nashville *Daily American,* Mar. 20, 1879; Aug. 1, 1880; McMinnville *New Era,* April 29, 1880; Chattanooga *Daily Times,* Feb. 16, 1882; Nashville *Republican Banner,* Mar. 2, 1875; Nashville *Union and American,* Feb. 13, 1875.
56. Nashville *Daily American,* Dec. 1, 1878.
57. Quoted in McMinnville *New Era,* Mar. 21, 1877.
58. Memphis *Daily Appeal,* Oct. 6, 1880.
59. *Ibid.,* Oct. 15, 1876.
60. Winchester *Home Journal,* Dec. 23, 1875, July 20, 1876; Nashville *Daily American,* May 20, 1876, Mar. 20, 1879, Aug. 18, 1880; Chattanooga *Daily Times,* April 6, 1878; Memphis *Daily Avalanche,* Sept. 4, 1880; McMinnville *New Era,* April 29, May 27, 1880, Mar. 16, April 27, 1882; Temple, *Notable Men of Tennessee from 1833 to 1875,* 443-45.

61. John J. Boon to William McCaslin, Feb. 24, 1877, letter in possession of V. Jacque Voegeli.
62. Nashville *Daily American,* Sept. 2, 1880.
63. McMinnville *New Era,* May 27, 1880.
64. Nashville *Daily American,* May 20, 1876.
65. *Ibid.,* Mar. 7, May 20, Aug. 10, 11, 30, 1878; Nashville *Union and American,* Feb. 6, 19, 1875; Memphis *Daily Avalanche,* Oct. 22, 1874, May 11, July 13, Sept. 30, 1876, Feb. 4, 1877, July 3, 1878; Winchester *Home Journal,* Dec. 15, 1875.
66. Nashville *Daily American,* May 20, 1876.
67. Nashville *Republican Banner,* May 14, 1874.
68. *Ibid.,* Oct. 18, 1876.
69. Chattanooga *Daily Times,* June 29, 1879; Nashville *Daily American,* Dec. 16, 1877, Oct. 26, 1878, Mar. 29, 1879, May 23, Aug. 30, 1880.
70. Memphis *Daily Appeal,* Oct. 6, 1880, April 30, July 21, Sept. 8, Oct. 1, 5, 8, 18, 22, Nov. 3, 1882; Nashville *Banner,* Oct. 13, 1882; [Savage], *Life of Savage,* 54-66; Woodward, *Origins of the New South,* 98, 101, 254-59; Moger, *Bourbonism to Byrd,* 37-38, 50, 66; Pearson, *The Readjuster Movement,* 129-31, 138, 151, 154.
71. James T. Moore, *Two Paths to the New South: The Virginia Debt Controversy, 1870-1883* (Lexington: Univ. of Kentucky Press, 1974), 56-82.
72. *Ibid.,* 82-92.

CHAPTER VI. TWO DEMOCRATIC ATTEMPTS AT COMPROMISE

1. Memphis *Daily Avalanche,* May 10, 23, June 8, 11, July 19, 1876.
2. Memphis *Daily Appeal,* May 24, June 8, 9, 1876; Nashville *Daily American,* May 19, 1876.
3. Memphis *Daily Appeal,* May 24, 1876.
4. *Ibid.,* May 5, 13, June 7, 10, 11, 1876; Nashville *Daily American,* May 19, 1876; Memphis *Daily Avalanche,* June 7, 1876; New York *Commerical and Financial Chronicle,* May 13, 1876; McCord, "J. E. Bailey," 247; Tennessee, *Biographical Directory, Tennessee General Assembly, (Preliminary, No. 17): Montgomery County,* 3-4.
5. Memphis *Daily Appeal,* May 5, 1876.
6. *Ibid.,* May 10, July 7, 10, 14, 1876; Memphis *Daily Avalanche,* July 13, 16, 21, 1876; Chattanooga *Daily Commercial,* July 9, 1876; H. Parks to James L. Gaines, July 22, 1876, John M. Luttrell to James L. Gaines, July 22, 1876, Correspondence of Comptroller's Office.
7. Quoted in Memphis *Daily Avalanche,* July 22, 1876.
8. Nashville *Daily American,* July 5, 22, 29, Aug. 8, 1876.
9. *Ibid.,* Aug. 10, 1876.
10. *Ibid.;* Memphis *Daily Appeal,* Aug. 10, 1876; Chattanooga *Daily Times,* Aug. 11, 1876; Memphis *Daily Avalanche,* Aug. 11, 1876; Winchester *Home Journal,* Aug. 17, 1876.
11. Nashville *Daily American,* Aug. 18, 31, 1876; Memphis *Daily Avalanche,* Aug. 23, 1876; New York *Commercial and Financial Chronicle,* July 1, Aug. 26, 1876; James L. Gaines to S. L. Anderson, Feb. 21, 1876, James L. Gaines to Thomas Cabine, Mar. 7, 1876, John Hillyer to James L. Gaines, Aug. 30, 1876, Correspondence of Comptroller's Office.
12. Memphis *Daily Avalanche,* Aug. 25, 26, Sept. 13, 1876.
13. Quoted in Memphis *Daily Appeal,* Sept. 2, 1876.
14. Nashville *Daily American,* Aug. 31, 1876; Memphis *Daily Appeal,* Aug. 27, 29, 31, Sept. 2, 5, 1876.
15. Nashville *Daily American,* Aug. 29, Sept. 1, Oct. 13, 1876; Chattanooga *Daily Times,* Sept. 2, 1876; Memphis *Daily Avalanche,* Sept. 5, 12, Oct. 4, 1876;

Memphis *Daily Appeal*, Sept. 6, 1876; Paris *Weekly Intelligencer*, Sept. 7, 1876; James D. Porter to J. B. Heiskell, Aug. 28, 1876, J. B. Heiskell to James D. Porter, Aug. 29, 1876, Correspondence of Governor's Office.

16. Nashville *Daily American*, Aug. 30, 1876; Memphis *Daily Appeal*, Aug. 25, Sept. 3, 1876; Pulaski *Citizen*, Sept. 7, 1876; Memphis *Daily Avalanche*, Aug. 25, Sept. 30, 1876; Folmsbee, Corlew, and Mitchell, *Tennessee*, 379-80.

17. Nashville *Daily American*, Aug. 29, Sept. 12, 17, 23, 26, 29, Oct. 5, 13, 1876; Memphis *Daily Appeal*, Oct. 10, 29, 31, 1876; Memphis *Daily Avalanche*, Sept. 2, 28, 1876.

18. Memphis *Daily Appeal*, Nov. 9, 1876; Memphis *Daily Avalanche*, Oct. 9, Nov. 14, 21, 1876; Nashville *Daily American*, Nov. 3, 1876; Miller, *Official and Political Manual*, 170; Queener, "A Decade of East Tennessee Republicanism," 76.

19. Memphis *Daily Avalanche*, Jan. 5, 26, 1877; Nashville *Daily American*, Jan. 7, 11, 12, 16, 24, 25, 26, 27, 1877; "Message of Jas. D. Porter, Governor of Tennessee," *Appendix to House Journal*, 1877, p. 5; *House Journal*, 1877, pp. 174-75, 258, 271; *Senate Journal*, 1877, pp. 69-70, 83-84, 98-99, 114, 128, 136-37, 144, 148, 247.

20. Nashville *Daily American*, Jan. 26, 1877.

21. *Senate Journal*, 1877, p. 346.

22. *Ibid.*, 344-46, 352-53, 357, 382, 390, 396; Nashville *Daily American*, Feb. 23, 24, 25, 27, 28, 29, Mar. 3, 1877; Memphis *Daily Avalanche*, Feb. 24, 1877; New York *Times*, Feb. 26, 1877; *House Journal*, 1877, pp. 502, 516-29.

23. Nashville *Daily American*, Jan. 9, Feb. 25, Mar. 3, 1877; R. S. Moral to Governor Porter, Mar. 17, 1877, George S. Coe to John H. Savage, Mar. 12, 1877, Correspondence of Governor's Office; "The Defaulting State Debts," *Banker's Magazine and Statistical Register* 31 (Jan. 1877), 587-90; George W. Green, "Repudiation," in *Cyclopedia of Political Science, Political Economy, and of the Political History of the United States, by the Best American and European Writers*, ed. John J. Lalor (New York: C. E. Merrill, 1888), II, 609.

24. Nashville *Daily American*, Jan. 9, Mar. 15, 16, 1877; New York *Times*, Mar. 15, 1877; George S. Coe to John H. Savage, Mar. 12, 1877, Correspondence of Governor's Office; "Committee on the State Debt," *Appendix to House Journal*, 1877, pp. 1-7; *Discussions Respecting the Tennessee State Debt Between the Committee of Tennessee Legislature and Committee of Arbitration, in the City of New York, March 8, 1877, and the Award of the Arbitrators: Stenographic Report* (New York: Evening Post Steam Presses, 1877), 1-49.

25. George S. Coe to John H. Savage, Mar. 12, 1877, Correspondence of Governor's Office.

26. George S. Coe to James D. Porter, Mar. 13, 1877, *ibid.*

27. "Committee on the State Debt," *Appendix to House Journal*, 1877, p. 3.

28. Nashville *Daily American*, Mar. 16, 17, 1877.

29. *Ibid.*, Mar. 28, 31, 1877; Memphis *Daily Appeal*, Mar. 27, 28, 1877; New York *Commercial and Financial Chronicle*, Mar. 31, 1877; Charles L. Smith to James D. Porter, Mar. 28, 1877, Correspondence of Governor's Office.

30. John J. Boon to William McCaslin, Mar. 19, 1877, letter in possession of V. Jacque Voegeli.

31. Memphis *Daily Avalanche*, Mar. 29, 1877; Nashville *Daily American*, Mar. 22, 23, 1877; *Senate Journal*, 1877, pp. 679-80.

32. Nashville *Daily American*, May 12, 1877.

33. *Ibid.*, April 4, 20, May 10, 12, 13, 1877; Memphis *Daily Appeal*, April 24, May 17, 1877; Memphis *Daily Avalanche*, April 7, May 1, 26, June 12, 18, July 14, 1877; New York *Commercial and Financial Chronicle*, Jan. 6, 1877.

34. Nashville *Daily American*, May 19, 1877; Memphis *Daily Appeal*, April 4, 1877; J. R. F. Remine to James D. Porter, April 4, 1877, A. C. Hawkins to Gov. Porter, April 18, 1877, W. L. Harbison to James D. Porter, Oct. 12, 1877, Correspondence of Governor's Office.

35. Nashville *Daily American,* May 1, 1877.
36. P. Geddes to James L. Gaines, Aug. 23, 1877, Correspondence of Comptroller's Office.
37. Quoted in Memphis *Daily Appeal,* April 4, 1877.
38. Nashville *Daily American,* Nov. 7, 16, 1877; Memphis *Daily Appeal,* Nov. 25, Dec. 6, 1877; New York *Commercial and Financial Chronicle,* Nov. 10, 1877; James D. Porter to George Coe, Oct. 11, 1877, George S. Coe to James D. Porter, Oct. 17, 1877, George S. Coe, J. D. Vermilye, B. B. Sherman, B. B. Comegys, and Enoch Pratt to James D. Porter, Oct. 25, 1877, George S. Coe to James D. Porter, Nov. 3, 1877, George S. Coe to J. D. Porter, Nov. 27, 1877, Correspondence of Governor's Office; "Proclamation by the Governor," Nov. 6, 1877, David McKendree Key Papers, Chattanooga Public Library, Chattanooga; "Senator Harris to Governor Porter," scrapbook, Dickinson Papers; "Message of the Governor," *House and Senate Journals,* 1st extra sess., 1877, pp. 10-12.
39. Nashville *Daily American,* Dec. 6, 7, 8, 9, 10, 11, 1877; *House and Senate Journals,* 1st extra sess., 1877, pp. 16, 19, 23-24, 144, 146.
40. Italics not author's. *House and Senate Journals,* 1st extra sess., 1877, p. 32.
41. Nashville *Daily American,* Dec. 4, 11, 13, 15, 16, 18, 19, 20, 21, 22, 23, 25, 27, 28, 29, 1877, Jan. 2, 17, 1878; Memphis *Daily Appeal,* Dec. 11, 18, 22, 1877; Memphis *Daily Avalanche,* Dec. 18, 27, 1877; *Senate and House Journals,* 1st extra sess., 1877, p. 32; *Senate and House Journals,* 2nd extra sess., 1877, pp. 38, 57, 73-74, 82-87, 90-91, 94-121, 187-93, 195, 198-210.
42. Nashville *Daily American,* Jan. 2, 12, 17, 30, 1878; *Senate and House Journals,* 2nd extra sess., 1877, pp. 107-8, 110, 120; Memphis *Daily Avalanche,* Dec. 18, 1877; Speaker of the Senate J. A. Trousdale also opposed any deviation from the terms offered by the creditors. See J. A. Trousdale to Cap [Charles W. Trousdale], Dec. 22, 1877, William Trousdale Papers, Tennessee State Library and Archives, Nashville. E. L. Godkin, editor of the *Nation,* stated that the creditors had been foolhardy to offer to take anything less than the full value of their securities. See "The First Step toward Repudiation," *Nation* 26 (Feb. 28, 1878), 144.
43. Nashville *Daily American,* Oct. 31, Nov. 1, 11, Dec. 5, 1877; E. D. Morgan to James D. Porter, Dec. 10, 1877, Correspondence of Governor's Office.
44. Nashville *Daily American,* Dec. 5, 1877.
45. *Ibid.,* Dec. 5, 9, 16, 20, 21, 22, 28, 1877; Memphis *Daily Appeal,* Dec. 15, 1877; *House and Senate Journals,* 1st extra sess., 1877, pp. 20-23; James D. Morgan to E. D. Morgan & Co., Dec. 7, 1877, E. D. Morgan & Co. to James D. Porter, Dec. 10, 1877, James D. Porter to Hugh McCulloch, Dec. 15, 1877, Hugh McCulloch to James D. Porter, Dec. 18, 1877, James D. Porter to Hugh McCulloch, Dec. 21, 1877, John J. MacKinnon to James D. Porter, Dec. 17, 1877, James D. Porter to J. J. Mackionon [*sic*], Dec. 28, 1877, John J. MacKinnon to James D. Porter, Dec. 28, 1877, James D. Porter to E. D. Morgan & Co., Jan. 17, 1878, Correspondence of Governor's Office.
46. James D. Porter to E. D. Morgan & Co., Jan. 17, 1878, Correspondence of Governor's Office; Nashville *Daily American,* June 30, 1878; New York *Times,* July 6, 1878; *Letter of Gov. James D. Porter to W. F. Harrington, Esq.: A History of the State Debt—How It Was Created—Its Present Status—How It May Be Met* (Nashville: American, Book and Job Printers, 1878), 3-14, pamphlet, Fussell Papers.
47. Nashville *Daily American,* June 30, 1878.
48. *Ibid.,* Jan. 17, 22, 1878; Memphis *Daily Appeal,* July 7, Aug. 11, 1878; Memphis *Daily Avalanche,* Jan. 27, Mar. 19, June 26, 1878; Butler P. Anderson to Dear Sir [David M. Key], Jan. 22, 1878, Key Papers; Abshire, *The South Rejects a Prophet,* 199-200.
49. Nashville *Daily American,* Aug. 16, 1878.
50. *Ibid.,* Aug. 16, 17, 1878; Memphis *Daily Appeal,* Aug. 17, 1878; Hart, *Redeemers, Bourbons & Populists,* 31-32.

51. Nashville *Daily American*, Aug. 17, 1878; Woodward, *Origins of the New South*, 47-50.
52. Nashville *Daily American*, Aug. 17, 18, 1878; Morristown *Gazette*, Aug. 24, 1878; Caldwell, *Sketches of the Bench and Bar*, 349-51; Allison, *Notable Men of Tennessee*, II, 69-71.
53. Nashville *Daily American*, Aug. 23, 1878.
54. *Ibid.*, Aug. 23, 24, Sept. 12, 1878; Cleveland *Weekly Herald*, Sept. 19, 1878, May 27, 1880; New York *Times*, Oct. 23, 1878.
55. Knoxville *Daily Chronicle*, Oct. 29, 1878; Memphis *Daily Avalanche*, Nov. 5, 1878; Memphis *Daily Appeal*, Nov. 25, 1878; Nashville *Daily American*, Sept. 26, Oct. 16, 17, 26, 1878; Cleveland *Weekly Herald*, Oct. 10, 1878; Hamer, *Tennessee*, II, 684.
56. Miller, *Official and Political Manual*, 170; Cleveland *Weekly Herald*, Dec. 12, 1878; Chattanooga *Daily Times*, Jan. 8, 1879.
57. Nashville *Daily American*, Jan. 18, 1879.
58. *Ibid.*, Jan. 17, 18, 1878, Feb. 11, 12, 1879; Memphis *Daily Appeal*, Jan. 19, Nov. 27, 1878, Feb. 19, 1879; Memphis *Daily Avalanche*, Feb. 5, 12, 1879; Loudon *Journal*, Feb. 14, 1879; Paris *Weekly Intelligencer*, Feb. 6, 1879; New York *Commercial and Financial Chronicle*, Jan. 19, 1878, Feb. 15, 1879; "Notice to Tennessee Bondholders," Jan. 19, 1878, Correspondence of Governor's Office.
59. Cleveland *Weekly Herald*, April 10, 1879; Chattanooga *Daily Times*, April 1, 1879; Knoxville *Daily Chronicle*, April 4, 12, 1879; Nashville *Daily American*, Mar. 28, 1879; New York *Commercial and Financial Chronicle*, Mar. 28, April 5, 1879.
60. Memphis *Daily Appeal*, April 1, 1879; Knoxville *Daily Chronicle*, April 16, 25, 1879; Memphis *Daily Avalanche*, April 5, 1879; Chattanooga *Daily Times*, April 4, 6, 1879; Nashville *Daily American*, April 4, 5, 9, 20, 22, 24, 25, May 1, 1879; New York *Commercial and Financial Chronicle*, April 5, 26, 1879. One group of creditors shunned talk of compromise and initiated suits against a number of railroads, claiming that these companies, as recipients of the bonds, were liable for their payment. See Chattanooga *Daily Times*, Jan. 28, 30, 1879; Knoxville *Daily Chronicle*, April 10, 1879; New York *Commercial and Financial Chronicle*, Feb. 1, June 21, 1879; Memphis *Daily Avalanche*, May 24, 1879; McMinnville *New Era*, May 6, 1880.
61. Chattanooga *Daily Times*, May 3, June 8, 1879; Nashville *Daily American*, June 8, 1879.
62. Nashville *Daily American*, May 31, 1879.
63. Memphis *Daily Appeal*, June 20, 1879.
64. Nashville *Daily American*, July 15, 1879.
65. *Ibid.*, May 20, June 26, July 10, 23, Aug. 1, 10, 13, 1879; Memphis *Daily Appeal*, May 31, June 20, July 16, Aug. 7, 1879; Chattanooga *Daily Times*, June 8, 1879; Morristown *Gazette*, July 9, 1879; Pulaski *Citizen*, July 31, 1879; Clarksville *Semi-Weekly Tobacco Leaf*, July 16, 1879.
66. Cleveland *Weekly Herald*, May 15, 1879.
67. W. M. Hall to L. C. Houk, June 5, 1879, Houk Papers.
68. L. C. Houk to B. A. Enloe & Nathaniel Baxter, April 5, 1879, *ibid.*
69. Nashville *Daily American*, July 24, Aug. 2, 1879; Knoxville *Daily Chronicle*, June 4, July 4, 13, 17, 18, 23, 26, Aug. 1, 3, 5, 6, 1879.
70. Memphis *Daily Avalanche*, June 24, July 2, 6, Aug. 6, 1879; Chattanooga *Daily Times*, June 29, 1879; Nashville *Daily American*, June 6, July 15, 1879; Knoxville *Daily Chronicle*, July 17, 19, 27, Aug. 1, 5, 1879.
71. Quoted in Memphis *Daily Avalanche*, July 2, 1879.
72. Knoxville *Daily Chronicle*, July 19, 1879; Memphis *Daily Avalanche*, July 2, 1879; Nashville *Daily American*, May 20, 1879.
73. Thomas D. Martin to James L. Gaines, July 22, 1879, Correspondence of Comptroller's Office.
74. Knoxville *Daily Chronicle*, Aug. 3, 1879.

75. James D. Porter to James L. Gaines, July 29, 1879, Correspondence of Comptroller's Office.
76. Nashville *Daily American,* July 24, 1879.
77. *Ibid.,* Aug. 9, 10, 1879; Memphis *Daily Appeal,* Aug. 8, 1879, July 28, 1882; Memphis *Daily Avalanche,* Aug. 8, 10, 1879; McMinnville *New Era,* May 13, 1880; Miller, *Official and Political Manual,* 170; Scott, *Repudiation of State Debts,* 144-45; Lynn, "Tennessee's Public Debt," 42-48; Killebrew, *Introduction to the Resources of Tennessee,* 102.
78. Nashville *Daily American,* Aug. 2, 10, 13, 1879; Knoxville *Daily Chronicle,* Aug. 13, 1879; Memphis *Daily Appeal,* Aug. 6, 1879; Pulaski *Citizen,* July 10, Aug. 21, 1879; Clarksville *Semi-Weekly Tobacco Leaf,* Aug. 12, 1879; Hart, *Redeemers, Bourbons & Populists,* 37-38.
79. Cartmell Diaries, Vol. IV, Aug. 7, 1879, Cartmell Papers.
80. New York *Times,* Aug. 20, 1879.
81. Quoted in Nashville *Daily American,* Aug. 17, 1879.
82. *Ibid.,* Aug. 13, 1879.
83. Quoted in Knoxville *Daily Chronicle,* Aug. 9, 1879.

CHAPTER VII. THE REPUBLICANS' TURN TO TRY

1. Nashville *Daily American,* May 6, 7, 1880; Allison, *Notable Men of Tennessee,* I, 92-93; John W. Green, *Lives of the Judges of the Supreme Court of Tennessee, 1796-1947* ([Knoxville: Archer and Smith], 1947), 145-48.
2. Hamer, *Tennessee,* II, 686.
3. Nashville *Daily American,* May 23, 1880.
4. *Ibid.,* April 1, 9, June 11, 19, July 7, Aug. 10, 1880.
5. *Ibid.,* July 7, 1880.
6. *Ibid.,* April 1, 1880.
7. Memphis *Daily Avalanche,* July 2, 13, 22, 1880; Grady Tollison, "Andrew J. Kellar, Memphis Republican," West Tennessee Historical Society *Papers* 16 (1962), 55.
8. Clarksville *Semi-Weekly Tobacco Leaf,* April 30, 1880.
9. Chattanooga *Daily Times,* Aug. 6, 1880.
10. Nashville *Banner,* July 5, 19, 27, 30, Aug. 9, 1880.
11. McMinnville *New Era,* Jan. 8, 1880; Memphis *Daily Appeal,* Dec. 20, 23, 25, 1879.
12. McMinnville *New Era,* Jan. 8, 1880.
13. *Ibid.,* Mar. 25, April 15, 29, May 6, 27, June 3, 17, July 8, 1880.
14. Italics not author's. *Ibid.,* June 3, 1880.
15. *Ibid.,* May 13, 27, 1880.
16. Quoted in *ibid.,* April 29, 1880.
17. Nashville *Daily American,* June 22, Aug. 6, 1880; Knoxville *Daily Chronicle,* July 8, 1880; Chattanooga *Daily Times,* Aug. 6, 1880; Memphis *Daily Avalanche,* July 16, 18, 1880; "The Recollections of My Life," I, 256-57, Joseph Buckner Killebrew Papers, Tennessee State Library and Archives, Nashville.
18. Quoted in Memphis *Daily Avalanche,* July 16, 1880.
19. Nashville *Daily American,* Aug. 6, 1880.
20. Nashville *Banner,* July 5, 1880.
21. Knoxville *Daily Chronicle,* July 17, 1880; Nashville *Daily American,* July 8, 9, 1880.
22. Knoxville *Daily Chronicle* Aug. 3, 1880.
23. Nashville *Daily American,* Aug. 6, 1880.
24. McMinnville *New Era,* April 15, 1880; Nashville *Daily American,* July 9, 1880.
25. Nashville *Daily American,* Aug. 12, 13, 1880; Memphis *Daily Appeal,* Aug. 11, 12, 13, 1880; Chattanooga *Daily Times,* Aug. 13, 14, 1880; Memphis

Daily Avalanche, Aug. 21, 1880.
   26. Nashville *Daily American,* Aug. 13, 1880.
   27. *Ibid.*
   28. *Ibid.;* "The Low Tax Platform," Harding-Jackson Papers; Allison, *Notable Men of Tennessee,* I, 72-74; Morgan Blake and Stuart Towe, *Lawmakers and Public Men of Tennessee* (Nashville: Eagle Printing Co., [1915?]), 171.
   29. Nashville *Daily American,* Aug. 13, 14, 15, 22, 1880; Chattanooga *Daily Times,* Aug. 15, 20, 1880.
   30. Nashville *Banner,* Aug. 13, 1880.
   31. Memphis *Daily Avalanche,* Aug. 14, 1880.
   32. Nashville *Daily American,* Aug. 25, 1880.
   33. *Ibid.,* May 6, 7, 23, Aug. 12, 13, 1880; Clarksville *Semi-Weekly Tobacco Leaf,* Aug. 17, 1880; Pulaski *Citizen,* Aug. 19, 1880. Woodward argues that in 1880 Southern Democrats abandoned Western agrarian ideas, took the "right fork," and meekly submitted to Eastern conservative Democratic leadership until the late 1880s. See *Origins of the New South,* 47-50.
   34. Memphis *Daily Avalanche,* Aug. 20, Sept. 14, 1880; Memphis *Daily Appeal,* Sept. 14, 1880; Chattanooga *Daily Times,* Oct. 9, 1880; Nashville *Daily American,* Sept. 2, 3, 7, 11, Oct. 7, 1880.
   35. Memphis *Daily Appeal,* Sept. 9, 1880; Memphis *Daily Avalanche,* Aug. 20, 1880; Nashville *Daily American,* Sept. 2, 3, 9, 11, Oct. 7, 1880; Chattanooga *Daily Times,* Oct. 9, 1880.
   36. Nashville *Daily American,* Sept. 9, 1880.
   37. *Ibid.,* Sept. 2, 3, 7, 10, 11, Oct. 1, 1880; Memphis *Daily Avalanche,* Aug. 19, Sept. 14, 1880; Nashville *Banner,* Sept. 23, 1880; Paris *Weekly Intelligencer,* Sept. 9, 1880; Clarksville *Semi-Weekly Tobacco Leaf,* Oct. 29, 1880; Pulaski *Citizen,* Sept. 30, 1880.
   38. Knoxville *Daily Chronicle,* Oct. 1, 1880; McMinnville *New Era,* Sept. 22, 23, 1880; Memphis *Daily Avalanche,* Aug. 20, 1880; Nashville *Daily American,* Sept. 22, 24, 25, 1880.
   39. Chattanooga *Daily Times,* Sept. 22, 1880; Memphis *Daily Appeal,* Sept. 17, 1880; Memphis *Daily Avalanche,* Sept. 14, 25, 1880; Nashville *Daily American,* Sept. 2, 25, Oct. 1, 5, 1880.
   40. Memphis *Daily Appeal,* Sept. 14, 24, Oct. 7, 1880; Memphis *Daily Avalanche,* Oct. 16, 1880; Chattanooga *Daily Times,* Sept. 12, Oct. 10, 27, 30, 1880; Nashville *Banner,* Oct. 11, 1880; Nashville *Daily American,* Sept. 1, 7, 12, 14, 22, 23, Oct. 17, 21, 1880.
   41. Nashville *Daily American,* Sept. 1, 1880.
   42. *Ibid.,* Sept. 4, 9, Oct. 16, 24, 1880; Knoxville *Daily Chronicle,* Oct. 19, 23, 1880; Nashville *Banner,* Oct. 14, 1880.
   43. Memphis *Daily Appeal,* Oct. 17, 1880.
   44. *Ibid.,* Oct. 16, 17, 20, 1880; Memphis *Daily Avalanche,* Oct. 19, 26, 1880; Nashville *Banner,* Oct. 19, 1880.
   45. Nashville *Daily American,* Oct. 27, 1880.
   46. *Ibid.,* Oct. 17, 21, 27, 1880; Nashville *Banner,* Oct. 2, 7, 14, 20, 26, 27, 29, 30, Nov. 1, 1880; Memphis *Daily Appeal,* Oct. 9, 23, 27, 28, 29, 31, 1880; Memphis *Daily Avalanche,* Oct. 27, 1880; Knoxville *Daily Chronicle,* Oct. 5, Nov. 2, 1880; Chattanooga *Daily Times,* Oct. 23, 1880.
   47. Knoxville *Daily Chronicle,* Oct. 27, 1880.
   48. Chattanooga *Daily Times,* Nov. 3, 1880; Nashville *Daily American,* Nov. 4, 5, 6, 7, 9, 1880; Memphis *Daily Appeal,* Nov. 3, 4, 5, 1880; Memphis *Daily Avalanche,* Nov. 3, 4, 1880; Election Returns for 1880, Papers of the Secretary of State of Tennessee, Tennessee State Library and Archives, Nashville; *Cumberland Almanac for 1882,* 8, 10, Miller, *Official and Political Manual,* 170; Hamer, *Tennessee,* II, 688.
   49. *Cumberland Almanac for 1882,* 8, 10; Nashville *Daily American,* Nov. 4, 1880; Knoxville *Daily Chronicle,* Nov. 6, 1880. Roger L. Hart analyzes the

1880 election returns and finds a clear tendency for rural Democratic voters to support Wilson more often than did party members living in cities and towns. See his *Redeemers, Bourbons & Populists,* 44-47.

50. Knoxville *Daily Chronicle,* Nov. 6, 1880.

51. Nashville *Banner,* Nov. 5, 1880; Chattanooga *Daily Times,* Nov. 9, 1880.

52. Jackson *Tribune and Sun,* Nov. 4, 1880.

53. Knoxville *Daily Chronicle,* Jan. 4, 1881.

54. *Ibid.,* Jan. 1, 4, 5, 6, 1881; Nashville *Banner,* Jan. 5, 7, 1881; Nashville *Daily American,* Jan. 6, 18, 1881; Clarksville *Semi-Weekly Tobacco Leaf,* Jan. 18, 1881.

55. Nashville *Daily American,* Jan. 10, Feb. 1, 8, 1881; Chattanooga *Daily Times,* Jan. 6, 1881; Memphis *Daily Appeal,* Jan. 14, 21, 1881; Memphis *Daily Avalanche,* Jan. 25, 1881; Knoxville *Daily Chronicle,* Jan. 15, 1881; M. S. T. to O. P. Temple, Nov. 29, 1880, L. C. Houk to O. P. Temple, Dec. 9, 1880, Temple Papers.

56. Knoxville *Daily Chronicle,* Jan. 20, 21, 25, 26, 1881; Memphis *Daily Appeal,* Jan. 21, 22, 25, 27, 1881; Chattanooga *Daily Times,* Jan. 25, 27, 1881; Nashville *Banner,* Jan. 24, 1881; Memphis *Daily Avalanche,* Jan. 18, 20, 21, 27, 1881; Nashville *Daily American,* Jan. 18, 26, 27, 1881; Tennessee, *Biographical Directory, Tennessee General Assembly (Preliminary No. 41): Madison County,* 20-21.

57. Knoxville *Daily Chronicle,* Jan. 26, 27, 1881; Chattanooga *Daily Times,* Jan. 27, 29, 1881; O. P. Temple to Howell E. Jackson, Jan. 29, 1881, Harding-Jackson Papers; Caldwell, *Sketches of the Bench and Bar,* 355-62.

58. Nashville *Daily American,* Jan. 27, 1881.

59. R. R. Butler to O. P. Temple, Temple Papers.

60. Chattanooga *Daily Times,* Feb. 19, 1881; Nashville *Daily American,* Feb. 1, 8, 1881.

61. *House Journal,* 1881, pp. 477-78.

62. *Ibid.,* 472-78; Knoxville *Daily Chronicle,* Feb. 27, 1881; Nashville *Daily American,* Feb. 25, 1881.

63. Nashville *Daily American,* Mar. 5, 10, 1881; Nashville *Banner,* Mar. 11, 1881; Memphis *Daily Avalanche,* Mar. 11, 12, 1881; James N. Nolan to O. F. Fitch, Mar. 7, 1881, Correspondence of Comptroller's Office; Committee of Bondholders of the State of Tennessee to Alvin Hawkins, Mar. 4, 1881, P. Geddes to Alvin Hawkins, Mar. 5, 1881, Correspondence of Governor's Office; *Appendix to House Journal,* 1881, pp. 3-6.

64. Nashville *Daily American,* Mar. 12, 15, 29, 1881; Nashville *Banner,* Mar. 17, 1881; Chattanooga *Daily Times,* Mar. 15, 1881.

65. Knoxville *Daily Chronicle,* Mar. 13, 1881.

66. Memphis *Daily Appeal,* Mar. 12, 16, 22, 27, 1881; Memphis *Daily Avalanche,* Mar. 12, 13, 15, 19, 20, 22, 23, 29, 1881.

67. New York *Times,* Mar. 15, 1881; Nashville *Daily American,* Mar. 13, 15, 17, 18, 20, 22, 23, 1881; *House Journal,* 1881, pp. 592, 608, 610-11, 650-51, 687-702.

68. William D. Smith, "The Carmack-Patterson Campaign and Its Aftermath in Tennessee Politics" (M.A. thesis, Vanderbilt Univ., 1939), 80-82; Moore and Foster, *Tennessee,* II, 103.

69. Nashville *Daily American,* Mar. 20, 1881.

70. *Ibid.,* Mar. 17, 18, 20, 22, 23, 1881; Chattanooga *Daily Times,* Mar. 23, 1881.

71. Nashville *Daily American,* Mar. 29, 30, 31, April 1, 1881; Memphis *Daily Appeal,* Nov. 3, 4, 1880, April 2, 1881; Memphis *Daily Avalanche,* April 2, 1881; Nashville *Banner,* April 2, 1881; [State Credit Democrats of the Forty-Second General Assembly] to Eugene Kelly and others, April 26, 1882, scrapbook, Fussell Papers; *Senate Journal,* 1881, pp. 547, 565, 597-98, 601, 613, 618-25.

72. Nashville *Banner,* April 6, 1881; Memphis *Daily Avalanche,* April 6, 1881;

Chattanooga *Daily Times,* April 6, 1881; Nashville *Daily American,* April 6, 1881; James L. Gaston to O. P. Temple, Nov. 21, 1881, Temple Papers; *Senate Journal,* 1881, pp. 678-79.

    73. *Senate Journal,* 1881, p. 679.

    74. Memphis *Daily Avalanche,* April 6, 1881.

    75. Nashville *Daily American,* April 8, 1881.

    76. Pulaski *Citizen,* April 7, 1881; Jackson *Tribune and Sun,* May 22, 1881; Morristown *Gazette,* April 13, 1881.

    77. Nashville *Daily American,* April 6, 1881.

    78. Chattanooga *Daily Times,* April 6, 1881.

    79. Memphis *Daily Appeal,* April 6, 1881.

    80. Quoted in Nashville *Daily American,* April 13, 1881.

    81. Memphis *Daily Avalanche,* April 6, 12, 14, 15, 17, May 16, 1881; Nashville *Banner,* April 14, 1881; James N. Nolan and Marshall T. Polk to Gov. Hawkins, April 29, 1881, R. R. Butler to Alvin Hawkins, May 3, 1881, Correspondence of Governor's Office; James N. Nolan to H. Kellog, May 9, 1881, Correspondence of Comptroller's Office.

    82. [Savage], *Life of Savage,* 168-78; Nashville *Daily American,* April 27, May 4, 25, 1881; Chattanooga *Daily Times,* April 28, 1881; New York *Times,* May 25, 1881.

    83. Nashville *Daily American,* May 25, 1881.

    84. *Ibid.,* May 4, 21, 25, July 9, 14, Aug. 12, 25, 1881; Chattanooga *Daily Times,* May 26, 1881; McMinnville *New Era,* Jan. 12, 1882.

    85. Nashville *Daily American,* Feb. 9, 12, 1882; Nashville *Banner,* Feb. 10, 1882, Knoxville *Daily Chronicle,* Feb. 10, 1882; New York *Times,* Feb. 12, 1882; J. W. Judd, "The 100-3 Case," *Proceedings of the Bar Association of Tennessee* 5 (July 4, 1882), 73-78; "Lynn v. Polk," Briefs of Tennessee State Supreme Court Cases, Tennessee State Library and Archives, Nashville; R. P. Cole to Howell E. Jackson, Feb. 11, 1882, Harding-Jackson Papers; Robert T. Shannon, *Reports of Cases Argued and Determined in the Supreme Court of Tennessee for the Eastern Division, September Term, 1881; for the Middle Division, December Term, 1881; and for the Western Division, April Term, 1882* (new ed. with citations; Nashville: Albert B. Tavel, 1882), VIII, 121-343 *passim.*

    86. Nashville *Banner,* Feb. 11, 1882.

    87. Nashville *Daily American,* Feb. 12, 1882.

    88. Nashville *Banner,* Feb. 13, 1882.

    89. Nashville *Daily American,* Feb. 12, 1882; Memphis *Daily Avalanche,* Feb. 12, 1882.

    90. Memphis *Daily Avalanche,* Feb. 12, 1882.

    91. McMinnville *New Era,* Feb. 23, 1882.

    92. Quoted in Nashville *Daily American,* Feb. 13, 1882.

    93. *Ibid.,* Feb. 21, 1882; H. F. Girscom to L. C. Houk, Feb. 12, 1882, James R. Dillin to L. C. Houk, Feb. 13, 1882, James Putman to L. C. Houk, Mar. 4, 1882, Houk Papers.

    94. Thomas Waters to L. C. Houk, Feb. 15, 1882, Houk Papers.

    95. Alvin Hawkins to L. C. Houk, Jan. 14, 1882, *ibid.*

    96. Alvin Hawkins to L. C. Houk, Feb. 15, 1882, *ibid.*

    97. *Ibid.*

    98. O. P. Temple to L. C. Houk, Feb. 21, 1882, *ibid.*

    99. O. P. Temple to L. C. Houk, Mar. 1, 1882, *ibid.*

CHAPTER VIII. DEMOCRATIC RESURGENCE AND FINAL SETTLEMENT

    1. Memphis *Daily Avalanche,* Mar. 8, 1882.

    2. John W. Childress to S. A. Champion, Mar. 15, 1882, S. A. Champion Papers, Tennessee State Library and Archives, Nashville; Nashville *Banner,* April 3,

1882; Nashville *Daily American*, April 5, 1882; Chattanooga *Daily Times*, April 6, 1882.

3. Nashville *Daily American*, April 5, 6, 1882; Chattanooga *Daily Times*, April 6, 1882.

4. Nashville *Daily American*, April 16, 1882.

5. Memphis *Daily Appeal*, April 28, 1882; New York *Times*, April 20, 1882; New York *Commercial and Financial Chronicle*, April 22, 1882; Eugene Kelly to Alvin Hawkins, April 19, 1882, Eugene Kelly to Alvin Hawkins, April 25, 1882, Eugene Kelly to Alvin Hawkins, April 27, 1882, Correspondence of Governor's Office.

6. Nashville *Daily American*, April 28, 1882.

7. *Ibid.*, April 26, 27, 28, 1882; McMinnville *New Era*, April 27, 1882; W. H. Cherry to S. A. Champion, April 21, 1882, Champion Papers; Hart, *Redeemers, Bourbons & Populists*, 59.

8. Memphis *Daily Appeal*, May 4, 5, 1882; Nashville *Daily American*, May 2, 3, 4, 13, 23, 28, 1882; Memphis *Daily Avalanche*, May 17, 1882; Nashville *Banner*, May 10, 19, 28, 1882; Chattanooga *Daily Times*, May 9, 11, 25, 27, 1882.

9. Nashville *Daily American*, May 11, 1882; Memphis *Daily Avalanche*, May 10, 1882; New York *Times*, May 7, 1882; Chattanooga *Daily Times*, May 11, 1882; *House Journal*, 3rd extra sess., 1882, pp. 40-46.

10. Nashville *Daily American*, May 11, 13, 14, 15, 16, 18, 19, June 25, 1882; Memphis *Daily Avalanche*, May 16, 1882; New York *Times*, May 16, 20, 25, 1882; [State Credit Democrats of the Forty-Second General Assembly] to Eugene Kelly and others, April 26, 1882, Eugene Kelly to D. D. Bell, B. M. Tillman, R. P. Cole, George W. Martin, and others, n.d. [1882], scrapbook, Fussell Papers; *Senate Journal*, 3rd extra sess., 1882, pp. 33, 38, 43-49, 50-61; *House Journal*, 3rd extra sess., 1882, pp. 92-97, 106-15.

11. F. D. Owings to L. C. Houk, May 22, 1882, Correspondence of Governor's Office.

12. Nashville *Daily American*, June 21, 22, 1882.

13. *Ibid.*, June 22, 1882; Morristown *Gazette*, June 28, 1882; "Cooper on Credit," scrapbook, Fussell Papers.

14. Nashville *Daily American*, June 22, 1882; Pulaski *Citizen*, June 21, 29, 1882; George R. Farnum, "William B. Bate, Soldier of Dixie, Lawyer, and Statesman of the Union," *American Bar Association Journal* 30 (Feb. 1944), 104-5; Allison, *Notable Men of Tennessee*, II, 30-34; [Savage], *Life of Savage*, 190-91.

15. Hart, *Redeemers, Bourbons & Populists*, 62-63.

16. Nashville *Daily American*, July 12, 1882.

17. *Ibid.*, Nashville *Banner*, June 27, July 12, 1882; Chattanooga *Daily Times*, June 23, 24, 1882; Memphis *Daily Avalanche*, June 23, 1882; "The State-Credit Wing," scrapbook, Dickinson Papers; W. A. Collier to Howell E. Jackson, July 14, 1882, Harding-Jackson Papers.

18. "Joseph H. Fussell" and "Captain Joseph H. Fussell, Great Southerner, Passes Away," scrapbook, Fussell Papers; Allison, *Notable Men of Tennessee*, II, 177-80.

19. Quoted in Nashville *Banner*, July 1, 1882.

20. Nashville *Daily American*, July 19, 1882; McMinnville *New Era*, Oct. 26, 1882; W. H. Cherry to S. A. Champion, July 3, 1882, Champion Papers.

21. Nashville *Daily American*, June 21, 22, July 9, 1882; *Extracts from the Speeches of the Hon. John H. Savage, Delivered in the Canvass of 1882* (Nashville: Marshall & Bruce, 1882), 5-8, pamphlet in the possession of Walter Womack, Warren County Historian, McMinnville, Tennessee.

22. *Extracts from the Speeches of Savage*, 8.

23. Poor, *Poor's Manual of Railroads for 1882*, 489, and *Poor's Manual of Railroads for 1884*, xiv; Belissary, "Industrial Spirit in Tennessee," 256-91; Thorogood, *Financial History of Tennessee*, 238; Capers, *River Town*, 216-25.

24. Chattanooga *Daily Times*, Aug. 30, 1882; Hart, *Redeemers, Bourbons & Populists*, 62-66.

25. Memphis *Daily Appeal*, July 28, Aug. 12, Sept. 1, Oct. 24, 1882; Memphis *Daily Avalanche*, Aug. 15, Oct. 24, 1882; Nashville *Daily American*, Aug. 13, 18, Oct. 12, 14, 24, 31, Nov. 7, 1882; McMinnville *New Era*, Sept. 28, 1882; Chattanooga *Daily Times*, Aug. 25, Sept. 10, 1882.

26. Chattanooga *Daily Times*, Sept. 10, 1882; Nashville *Daily American*, Oct. 11, 12, 1882; Memphis *Daily Appeal*, Sept. 1, Oct. 24, 1882.

27. Chattanooga *Daily Times*, Sept. 10, 1882.

28. *Ibid.*, Sept. 12, 1882; Memphis *Daily Avalanche*, Aug. 20, Sept. 3, Oct. 3, 1882; Memphis *Daily Appeal*, Aug. 1, 31, Sept. 6, 7, 8, Oct. 12, 1882; Nashville *Daily American*, Aug. 21, 1882; Nashville *Banner*, Oct. 13, 31, Nov. 3, 1882.

29. Chattanooga *Daily Times*, Sept. 12, 1882.

30. *Ibid.*; Nashville *Daily American*, Aug. 29, 1882.

31. Nashville *Daily American*, Aug. 19, 1882; Chattanooga *Daily Times*, Sept. 12, 1882; Memphis *Daily Appeal*, Oct. 12, 1882.

32. Chattanooga *Daily Times*, Sept. 12, 1882.

33. *Ibid.*; Memphis *Daily Appeal*, Oct. 12, 1882; McMinnville *New Era*, Oct. 26, 1882; Nashville *Daily American*, Aug. 29, 1882; "Greenback Platform," and "To the People of Tennessee," scrapbook, Fussell Papers.

34. Nashville *Daily American*, Aug. 13, 22, Sept. 5, 13, 19, 22, 27, Oct. 6, 9, 1882; Nashville *Banner*, Oct. 17, 1882; McMinnville *New Era*, Sept. 28, 1882; Chattanooga *Daily Times*, Sept. 2, Oct. 8, 15, 1882; Memphis *Daily Appeal*, July 18, Aug. 9, 20, Oct. 13, 25, 1882; Memphis *Daily Avalanche*, July 2, 22, Aug. 15, 1882; Clarksville *Semi-Weekly Tobacco Leaf*, Aug. 8, Oct. 17, 1882; "State Credit Democracy," Dickinson Papers; William R. Moore to Joseph Sands, June 26, 188[2], Houk Papers.

35. Nashville *Daily American*, July 1, Aug. 30, Sept. 6, 12, 1882; Nashville *Banner*, Sept. 4, 6, Oct. 24, 1882; Memphis *Daily Appeal*, Sept. 7, 1882; Chattanooga *Daily Times*, Sept. 6, 1882; Morristown *Gazette*, Nov. 1, 1882; Caldwell, *Sketches of the Bench and Bar*, 334-49; Cartmell Diaries, Vol. XXIX, Jan. 26, 1911, Cartmell Papers; Doak Autobiography, 53-54, Henry M. Doak Papers, Tennessee State Library and Archives, Nashville.

36. Nashville *Daily American*, Sept. 28, 1882.

37. *Ibid.*, April 28, 1882; Memphis *Daily Appeal*, April 30, July 1, Sept. 8, Oct. 1, 1882; Memphis *Daily Avalanche*, Mar. 22, 1881, July 4, Aug. 17, 1882.

38. Memphis *Daily Avalanche*, Oct. 5, 1882.

39. *Ibid.*, Oct. 5, 6, 26, 1882; Nashville *Banner*, Oct. 13, 1882; Chattanooga *Daily Times*, Oct. 16, 1882; Memphis *Daily Appeal*, Oct. 5, 8, 18, 22, Nov. 3, 1882.

40. Nashville *Banner*, Oct. 13, 1882.

41. *Ibid.*, July 15, Oct. 17, 31, 1882; Memphis *Daily Avalanche*, Aug. 20, Sept. 10, 14, Oct. 3, 25, 1882; Knoxville *Daily Chronicle*, Aug. 30, Sept. 2, 1882; Nashville *Daily American*, Oct. 11, 14, 31, 1882; Chattanooga *Daily Times*, Sept. 12, 1882; Memphis *Daily Appeal*, Sept. 6, Oct. 17, Nov. 2, 1882; J. B. Warren to Dear Bro. [Joseph H. Fussell], July 13, 1882, Fussell Papers; Almira E. Jewell, "The Prohibition Movement in Tennessee" (M.A. thesis, Univ. of Virginia, 1930), 31; Paul E. Isaac, *Prohibition and Politics: Turbulent Decades in Tennessee, 1885-1920* (Knoxville: Univ. of Tennessee Press, 1965), 10-11, 14-15, 142.

42. Memphis *Daily Appeal*, Nov. 4, 8, 1882; Nashville *Daily American*, Nov. 8, 9, 10, 11, 1882; Miller, *Official and Political Manual*, 170.

43. Memphis *Daily Appeal*, Nov. 8, 1882.

44. Clarksville *Semi-Weekly Tobacco Leaf*, Nov. 10, 1882. Two well-known Democrats continued their feuding in print over the merits of the Bate, Fussell, and Hawkins debt settlement plans. See James Phelan's "Communication," *American* 5 (Dec. 9, 1882), 142, and "Communication: The Tennessee Repudiation Again," *American* 5 (Dec. 30, 1882), 191; and J. E. McGowan, "Tennessee's State Debt," *American* 5 (Dec. 16, 1882), 153-54.

45. Knoxville *Daily Chronicle*, Nov. 9, 1882.

46. W. H. Cherry to S. A. Champion, Nov. 16, 1882, Champion Papers.

47. Memphis *Daily Avalanche,* Dec. 29, 1882; New York *Commercial and Financial Chronicle,* Dec. 30, 1882; M. T. Polk to H. E. Jackson, July 16, 1882, Harding-Jackson Papers.

48. Memphis *Daily Avalanche,* Dec. 29, 1882.

49. Nashville *Daily American,* Jan. 6, 7, 8, 9, 10, 11, 14, 1883; Memphis *Daily Appeal,* Jan. 4, 6, 7, 1883; Knoxville *Daily Chronicle,* Jan. 2, 1883; Cleveland *Weekly Herald,* Jan. 5, Feb. 8, 15, 1883; Morristown *Gazette,* Jan. 10, 17, 1883.

50. Nashville *Daily American,* Jan. 6, 1883.

51. Nashville *Banner,* Feb. 2, 1881.

52. A. G. Travistree to S. A. Champion, Jan. 9, 1883, Champion Papers.

53. Memphis *Daily Appeal,* Jan. 14, 1883.

54. Nashville *Daily American,* Jan. 8, 9, 1883; Knoxville *Daily Chronicle,* Jan. 10, 12, 1883; B. F. Allen to Charles W. Trousdale, Jan. 21, 1884, Trousdale Papers; "Tennessee's Unreasonable Indignation," *Banker's Magazine and Statistical Register* 37 (Feb. 1883), 564-65; John F. Hume, "Responsibility for State Roguery," *North American Review* 139 (Dec. 1884), 569-70.

55. Quoted in Knoxville *Daily Chronicle,* Jan. 12, 1883.

56. Quoted in *ibid.*

57. Charles W. Trousdale to Mr. Allen, Jan. 23, 1883, Trousdale Papers.

58. Knoxville *Daily Chronicle,* Mar. 6, 1883; Nashville *Daily American,* Mar. 3, 1883; "The Recollections of My Life," II, 14-15, Killebrew Papers; *Senate Journal,* 1883, pp. 167-73, 585-89.

59. Nashville *Daily American,* Jan. 17, 18, 1883; Knoxville *Daily Chronicle,* Jan. 7, 13, 17, 19, 1883; Memphis *Daily Avalanche,* Jan. 2, 3, 7, 16, 17, 1883; Memphis *Daily Appeal,* Jan. 10, 16, 17, 1883; New York *Times,* Dec. 30, 1882; James W. Hayward to L. C. Houk, April 27, 1882, J. R. Dillin to L. C. Houk, June 3, 1882, W. H. D. Bryant to L. C. Houk, July 3, 1882, R. M. Chapman to L. C. Houk, Jan. 17, 1883, J. H. Agee to L. C. Houk, Jan. 18, 1883, Houk Papers.

60. Nashville *Daily American,* Jan. 17, 1883.

61. C. W. Trousdale to Dear Junius [J. A. Trousdale], Feb. 9, 1883, Trousdale Papers.

62. Memphis *Daily Appeal,* Jan. 14, 1883.

63. A. M. Hughes to Dear Judge [L. C. Houk], Jan. 15, 1883, Houk Papers.

64. Memphis *Daily Appeal,* Jan. 17, 1883; *Senate Journal,* 1883, pp. 180-84.

65. Nashville *Daily American,* Jan. 4, 6, Feb. 12, 13, 14, 15, 17, 27, 1883; Memphis *Daily Avalanche,* Jan. 17, Feb. 28, 1883; Memphis *Daily Appeal,* Feb. 28, 1883; *House Journal,* 1883, pp. 311-331; *Acts of Tennessee,* 1883, pp. 6, 410-11.

66. Nashville *Daily American,* Mar. 7, 12, 1883; McMinnville *New Era,* Mar. 22, 1883; *House Journal,* 1883, pp. 3-5, 504-5, 601-7, 911-12; *Senate Journal,* 1883, pp. 3-7, 527-28, 571-78.

67. *Senate Journal,* 1883, p. 578.

68. *Acts of Tennessee,* 1883, pp. 76-84.

69. Nashville *Daily American,* Mar. 23, 1883.

70. *Ibid.; Acts of Tennessee,* 1883, pp. 78-82; Stanton, "State Debt," 86-87; McGrane, *Foreign Bondholders,* 363-64.

71. *Acts of Tennessee,* 1883, pp. 80-84; McMinnville *New Era,* May 31, 1883.

72. Nashville *Daily American,* Mar. 31, 1883; McMinnville *New Era,* Mar. 22, 1883; Memphis *Daily Avalanche,* April 22, 1883.

73. Knoxville *Daily Chronicle,* April 1, 1883.

74. L. E. Schnieder to W. B. Bate, Mar. 16, 1883, Correspondence of Governor's Office.

75. J. L. Hewitt to W. B. Bate, Mar. 29, 1883, *ibid.*

76. Eugene Kelly to William B. Bate, Jan. 20, 1883, *ibid.*

77. S. B. Chittenden to Judge Cooper [William F. Cooper], Feb. 16, 1883, Cooper Family Papers, Tennessee State Library and Archives, Nashville.

78. J. M. Win to W. B. Bate, Aug. 18, 1883, Correspondence of Governor's Office.

79. J. L. Hewitt to H. E. Jackson, Sept. 20, 1883, Harding-Jackson Papers.

80. J. L. Hewitt to H. E. Jackson, April 8, 1884, *ibid.*

81. New York *Commercial and Financial Chronicle,* Mar. 8, 1884.

82. *Ibid.,* Sept. 8, 1883, Mar. 4, 1884; New York *Times,* Sept. 1, 1883; J. M. Win to W. B. Bate, Aug. 18, 1883, Correspondence of Governor's Office; J. L. Hewitt to H. E. Jackson, Oct. 30, 1883, J. L. Hewitt to H. E. Jackson, April 18, 1884, Harding-Jackson Papers; Stanton, "State Debt," 88.

83. "Message of Governor William B. Bate," *Appendix to House Journal,* 1885, p. 5; Folk, *"Tennessee's Bonded Indebtedness,"* 4-15; Thorogood, *Financial History of Tennessee,* 215-33; McGrane, *Foreign Bondholders,* 364; Lynn, "Tennessee's Public Debt," 88-89.

84. Robison, *Bob Taylor,* 23-218 *passim;* Hamer, *Tennessee,* II, 673-701; Hart, *Redeemers, Bourbons & Populists,* 71-223 *passim.*

85. Folk, *"Tennessee's Bonded Indebtedness,"* 2, 15.

Works Cited

I. MANUSCRIPTS

Robert Edward Barclay Papers. Tennessee State Library and Archives, Nashville.

John J. Boon to William McCaslin, Feb. 24, 1877, John J. Boon to William McCaslin, Mar. 19, 1877. These letters are in the possession of Professor V. Jacque Voegeli, Vanderbilt University, Nashville.

John Morgan Bright Papers. Southern Historical Collection, University of North Carolina, Chapel Hill.

William G. Brownlow Papers. University of Tennessee Library, Knoxville.

Robert H. Cartmell Papers. Tennessee State Library and Archives, Nashville.

S. A. Champion Papers. Tennessee State Library and Archives, Nashville.

Arthur St. Clair Colyar Papers. Southern Historical Collection, University of North Carolina, Chapel Hill.

Correspondence of the Comptroller's Office of Tennessee. Tennessee State Library and Archives, Nashville.

Cooper Family Papers. Tennessee State Library and Archives, Nashville.

Jacob McGavock Dickinson Papers. Tennessee State Library and Archives, Nashville.

Henry M. Doak Papers. Tennessee State Library and Archives, Nashville.

Joseph H. Fussell Papers. Tennessee State Library and Archives, Nashville.

Correspondence of the Governor's Office of Tennessee. Tennessee State Library and Archives, Nashville.

Harding-Jackson Papers. Tennessee State Library and Archives, Nashville. These are photocopies of the original papers which are held in the Southern Historical Collection, University of North Carolina, Chapel Hill.

Isham G. Harris Papers. Tennessee State Library and Archives, Nashville.

Leonidas Campbell Houk Papers. McClung Collection, Lawson McGhee Library, Knoxville.

David McKendree Key Papers. Chattanooga Public Library, Chattanooga.

Joseph Buckner Killebrew Papers. Tennessee State Library and Archives, Nashville.

Committee Hearings, Legislative Papers, 1875. Tennessee State Library and Archives, Nashville.

Thomas A. R. Nelson Papers. McClung Collection, Lawson McGhee Library, Knoxville.

Railroad Papers. Tennessee State Library and Archives, Nashville.

Correspondence of the Secretary of State's Office of Tennessee. Tennessee State Library and Archives, Nashville.

Election Returns for 1880, Papers of the Secretary of State of Tennessee. Tennessee State Library and Archives, Nashville.

William B. Stokes Papers. Tennessee State Library and Archives, Nashville.

Briefs of Tennessee State Supreme Court Cases. Tennessee State Library and Archives, Nashville.

Oliver Perry Temple Papers. University of Tennessee Library, Knoxville.

William Trousdale Papers. Tennessee State Library and Archives, Nashville.

Dempsey Weaver Papers. Tennessee State Library and Archives, Nashville.

II. PUBLISHED OFFICIAL DOCUMENTS

Killebrew, Joseph B. *Introduction to the Resources of Tennessee.* Nashville: Tavel, Eastman & Howell, 1874.

Tennessee. *Acts of Tennessee* (1865-1883).

_____. *Appendix to the House Journal* (1865-1883).

_____. *Appendix to the Senate Journal* (1865-1883).

_____. *Biennial Report of the Bureau of Agriculture, Statistics and Immigration, 1889 and 1890, B. M. Hord, Commissioner.* Nashville: Albert B. Tavel, 1891.

_____. *Biennial Report of the Commissioner of Agriculture, Statistics and Mines, and Bureau of Immigration to the Forty-First General Assembly of the State of Tennessee.* Nashville: Printed at "The American" Steam Book and Job Office, 1879.

_____. *Biographical Directory, Tennessee General Assembly, 1796-1969.* Preliminary Nos. 1-46. Nashville: Tennessee State Library and Archives, 1969-74.

_____. *Journal of the House* (1865-1883).

_____. *Journal of the Proceedings of the Convention of Delegates Elected by the People of Tennessee, to Amend, Revise, or Form and Make a New Constitution for the State, January 10, 1870.* Nashville: Jones, Purvis & Co., 1870.

_____. *Journal of the Senate* (1865-1883).

U.S. Department of Commerce. Bureau of the Census. *Historical Statistics of the United States, Colonial Times to 1957: A Statistical Ab-*

stract Supplement. Prepared with the cooperation of the Social
Science Research Council. [Washington: U.S. Government Printing
Office, 1960.]

U.S. Department of the Interior. Census Office. *Census of 1880.* Vol. I.
*Statistics of the Population of the United States at the Tenth Census
(June 1, 1880).* Vol. III. *Report on the Productions of Agriculture as
Returned in the Tenth Census (June 1, 1880).* Washington: Govern-
ment Printing Office, 1883.

III. COMPILATIONS AND YEARBOOKS

Appleton's Annual Cyclopaedia and Register of Important Events.
    Vols. I-XLII (1861-1902). New York: D. Appleton, 1862-1903.
Cumberland Almanac for the Year 1882. Nashville: American Publish-
    ing Co., [1881?].
Miller, Charles A. *Official and Political Manual of the State of Tennes-
    see.* Nashville: Marshall & Bruce, 1890.
Poor, Henry V. *Poor's Manual of Railroads.* [1st]-57th, 1868/69-1924.
    New York: H. V. & H. W. Poor, 1868-1924.
The Tribune Almanac and Political Register, 1883. New York: Tribune
    Association, [1882].

IV. NEWSPAPERS

Chattanooga *Daily Commercial.* 1873-1876.
Chattanooga *Daily Times.* 1873-1883.
Clarksville *Tobacco Leaf* [after Feb. 1879 the *Semi-Weekly Tobacco
    Leaf*]. 1875-1882.
Cleveland *Weekly Herald.* 1878-1883.
Gallatin *Examiner.* 1876.
Jackson *Tribune and Sun.* 1879-1881.
Jonesboro *Herald and Tribune.* 1870-1883.
Knoxville *Daily Chronicle.* 1870-1883.
Loudon *Journal.* 1879.
Loudon *Times.* 1874.
McMinnville *New Era.* 1872-1883.
Memphis *Daily Appeal.* 1870-1883.
Memphis *Daily Avalanche.* 1873-1883.
Morristown *Gazette.* 1873-1883.
Nashville *Banner.* 1880-1883.
Nashville *Daily American.* 1875-1883.
Nashville *Republican Banner.* 1870-1875.
Nashville *Rural Sun.* 1872-1879.
Nashville *Union and American.* 1870-1875.
New York *Commercial and Financial Chronicle.* 1870-1883.
New York *Times.* 1870-1883.

Paris *Weekly Intelligencer*. 1872-1880.
Pulaski *Citizen*. 1870-1882.
Winchester *Home Journal*. 1875-1878.

V. UNPUBLISHED MATERIAL

Belissary, Constantine G. "The Rise of the Industrial Spirit in Tennessee, 1865-1885." Ph.D. diss., Vanderbilt Univ., 1949.
Bible, Mary O. "The Post Presidential Career of Andrew Johnson." M.A. thesis, Univ. of Tennessee, 1936.
Butler, Margaret. "The Life of John C. Brown." M.A. thesis, Univ. of Tennessee, 1936.
Davis, Thomas W. "Arthur S. Colyar and the New South." Ph.D. diss., Univ. of Missouri, 1962.
Ferguson, James S. "Agrarianism in Mississippi, 1871-1900: A Study in Non-Conformity." Ph.D. diss., Univ. of North Carolina, 1952.
Gentry, Amos L. "Public Career of Leonidas Campbell Houk." M.A. thesis, Univ. of Tennessee, 1939.
Jewell, Almira E. "The Prohibition Movement in Tennessee." M.A. thesis, Univ. of Virginia, 1930.
Lynn, Alice H. "Tennessee's Public Debt as an Issue in Politics, 1870-1883." M.A. thesis, Univ. of Tennessee, 1936.
Mahoney, John H. "Apportionments and Gerrymandering in Tennessee since 1870." M.A. thesis, George Peabody College for Teachers, 1930.
McCartney, F. Ray "Crisis of 1873." Ph.D. diss., Fort Hayes Kansas State College, 1935.
Smith, William D. "The Carmack-Patterson Campaign and Its Aftermath in Tennessee Politics." M.A. thesis, Vanderbilt Univ., 1939.
Stanton, William A. "The State Debt in Tennessee Politics." M.A. thesis, Vanderbilt Univ., 1939.
Ward, Judson C. "Georgia under the Bourbon Democrats, 1872 1890." Ph.D. diss., Univ. of North Carolina, 1947.
Weems, Martha L. "The Grange in Tennessee, 1870-1908 and 1933-1966." M.A. thesis, East Tennessee State Univ., 1969.

VI. BOOKS AND PAMPHLETS

Abshire, David M. *The South Rejects a Prophet: The Life of Senator D. M. Key, 1824-1900.* New York: Praeger, 1967.
Alexander, Thomas B. *Political Reconstruction in Tennessee.* Nashville: Vanderbilt Univ. Press, 1950.
Allison, John, ed. *Notable Men of Tennessee, Personal and Genealogical, with Portraits.* 2 vols. Atlanta: Southern Historical Association, 1905.
Blake, Morgan, and Stuart Towe. *Lawmakers and Public Men of Ten-*

nessee. Nashville: Eagle Printing Co., [1915?].

Brannen, C. O. *Taxation in Tennessee.* Louisville: Baldwin Law Book Co., 1920.

Caldwell, Joshua W. *Sketches of the Bench and Bar of Tennessee.* Knoxville: Ogden Brothers, 1898.

Capers, Gerald M., Jr. *The Biography of a River Town: Memphis, Its Heroic Age.* Chapel Hill: Univ. of North Carolina Press, 1939.

Clark, Thomas D., and Albert D. Kirwan. *The South since Appomattox: A Century of Regional Change.* New York: Oxford Univ. Press, 1967.

Cooke, Jacob E. "The New South." *Essays in American Historiography: Papers Presented in Honor of Allan Nevins.* Ed. Donald H. Sheehan and Harold C. Syrett. New York: Columbia Univ. Press, 1960.

Coulter, E. Merton. *William G. Brownlow, Fighting Parson of the Southern Highlands.* Chapel Hill: Univ. of North Carolina Press, 1933; rpt. Knoxville: Univ. of Tennessee Press, 1971.

Discussions Respecting the Tennessee State Debt Between the Committee of Tennessee Legislature and Committee of Arbitration, in the City of New York, March 8, 1877, and the Award of the Arbitrators: Stenographic Report. New York: Evening Post Steam Presses, 1877.

Extracts from the Speeches of the Hon. John H. Savage, Delivered in the Canvass of 1882. Nashville: Marshall & Bruce, 1882. Pamphlet in the possession of Walter Womack, Warren County Historian, Mc-Minnville, Tenn.

Fels, Rendigs. *American Business Cycles, 1865-1897.* Chapel Hill: Univ. of North Carolina Press, 1959.

Fite, Gilbert C., and Jim E. Reece. *An Economic History of the United States.* 2nd ed. Boston: Houghton, 1965.

Folk, Reau E. *"Tennessee's Bonded Indebtedness, Retrospective and Prospective," an Address before the Tennessee Bankers' Association.* Nashville: n.p., 1908.

Folmsbee, Stanley J. "The Radicals and the Railroads." *Tennessee: A History, 1673-1932.* Ed. Philip M. Hamer. Vol. II. New York: American Historical Society, 1933.

————. *Sectionalism and Internal Improvements in Tennessee, 1796-1845.* Knoxville: East Tennessee Historical Society, 1939.

————, Robert E. Corlew, and Enoch L. Mitchell. *Tennessee, A Short History.* Knoxville: Univ. of Tennessee Press, 1969.

Gaston, Paul M. "The New South." *Writing Southern History: Essays in Historiography in Honor of Fletcher M. Green.* Ed. Arthur S. Link and Rembert W. Patrick. Baton Rouge: Louisiana State Univ. Press, 1965.

Goodrich, Carter. *Government Promotion of American Canals and Railroads, 1800-1890.* New York: Columbia Univ. Press, 1960.

Green, George W. "Repudiation." *Cyclopedia of Political Science, Polit-*

ical Economy, and of the Political History of the United States, by the Best American and European Writers. Ed. John J. Lalor. Vol. II. New York: Merrill, 1888.

Green, John W. *Lives of the Judges of the Supreme Court of Tennessee, 1796-1947.* [Knoxville: Archer and Smith], 1947.

Grey, Warren P. *The Development of Banking in Tennessee.* New Brunswick, N. J.: Rutgers Univ., 1948.

Hale, William Thomas and Dixon L. Merritt. *A History of Tennessee and Tennesseans: The Leaders and Representative Men in Commerce, Industry and Modern Activities.* 8 vols. Chicago and New York: Lewis Publishing Co., 1913.

Hamer, Philip M., ed. *Tennessee: A History, 1673-1932.* 4 vols. New York: American Historical Society, 1933.

Hart, Roger L. *Redeemers, Bourbons & Populists: Tennessee, 1870-1896.* Baton Rouge: Louisiana State Univ. Press, 1975.

Hawk, Emory Q. *Economic History of the South.* New York: Prentice-Hall, 1934.

Hesseltine, William B. *Confederate Leaders in the New South.* Baton Rouge: Louisiana State Univ. Press, 1950.

————, and David M. Smiley. *The South in American History.* Englewood Cliffs, N. J.: Prentice-Hall, 1960.

Isaac, Paul E. *Prohibition and Politics: Turbulent Decades in Tennessee, 1885-1920.* Knoxville: Univ. of Tennessee Press, 1965.

Kirkland, Edward C. *Industry Comes of Age: Business, Labor, and Public Policy, 1860-1897.* New York: Holt, 1961.

Marshall, Park. *A Life of William B. Bate, Citizen, Soldier and Statesman; with Memorial Addresses by Edward W. Carmack, Charles H. Grosvenor and A. O. Stanley, and Orations by William B. Bate at Elmwood Confederate Cemetery, and Chickamauga and Chattanooga National Park.* Nashville: Park Marshall, 1908.

McGrane, R. C. *Foreign Bondholders and American State Debts.* New York: Macmillan, 1935.

Moger, Allen W. *Virginia: Bourbonism to Byrd, 1870-1925.* Charlottesville: Univ. Press of Virginia, 1968.

Moore, James T. *Two Paths to the New South: The Virginia Debt Controversy, 1870-1883.* Lexington: Univ. of Kentucky Press, 1974.

Moore, John Trotwood, and Austin P. Foster. *Tennessee, The Volunteer State, 1769-1923.* 4 vols. Chicago and Nashville: S. J. Clarke Publishing Co., 1923.

Pearson, Charles C. *The Readjuster Movement in Virginia.* New Haven: Yale Univ. Press, 1917.

Pressly, Thomas J., and William H. Scofield, eds. *Farm Real Estate Values in the United States by Counties, 1850-1959.* Seattle: Univ. of Washington Press, 1965.

Randall, J. G., and David Donald. *The Civil War and Reconstruction.*

2nd ed., rev. Lexington, Mass.: Heath, 1969.

Ratchford, Benjamin U. *American State Debts.* Durham: Duke Univ. Press, 1941.

Robison, Daniel M. *Bob Taylor and the Agrarian Revolt in Tennessee.* Chapel Hill: Univ. of North Carolina Press, 1935.

Rogers, William W. *The One-Gallused Rebellion: Agrarianism in Alabama, 1865-1896.* Baton Rouge: Louisiana State Univ. Press, 1970.

[Savage, John H.] *The Life of John H. Savage: Citizen, Soldier, Lawyer, Congressman before the War Begun and Prosecuted by the Abolitionists of the Northern States to Reduce the Descendants of the Rebels of 1776, Who Defeated the Armies of the King of England and Gained Independence for the United States, down to the Level of the Negro Race.* Nashville: John H. Savage, 1903.

Scott, W. A. *Repudiation of State Debts.* New York: Crowell, 1893.

Shannon, Fred A. *The Farmer's Last Frontier: Agriculture, 1860-1897.* New York: Holt, 1966.

Shannon, Robert T. *Reports of Cases Argued and Determined in the Supreme Court of Tennessee for the Eastern Division, September Term, 1881; for the Middle Division, December Term, 1881; and for the Western Division, April Term, 1882.* Vol. VIII, a new ed. with citations. Nashville: Albert B. Tavel, 1882.

Simkins, Francis B. *A History of the South.* 3rd ed. New York: Knopf, 1963.

Stokes, Jordan. *State Debt of Tennessee: Embracing the Subjects of the Compromise Measure, the Validity of the Bonds, the Liability of the Railroads, and the Remedy of the Bondholders in the Courts.* Nashville: Tavel, Eastman & Howell, 1880.

Stover, John F. *The Railroads of the South, 1865-1900: A Study in Finance and Control.* Chapel Hill: Univ. of North Carolina Press, 1955.

Temple, Oliver P. *Notable Men of Tennessee from 1833 to 1875.* New York: Cosmopolitan Press, 1912.

Thorogood, James E. *A Financial History of Tennessee since 1870.* n.p. [Sewanee, 1949?].

Wells, David A. *Recent Economic Changes: And Their Effect on the Production and Distribution of Wealth and the Well-Being of Society.* New York: D. Appleton, 1889.

Woodward, C. Vann. *Origins of the New South, 1877-1913.* Baton Rouge: Louisiana State Univ. Press, 1951.

Wright, Carroll D. *The Industrial Evolution of the United States.* New York: Russell & Russell, 1895.

VII. ARTICLES

Adams, Henry C. "The Financial Standing of States." *Journal of Social Science* 19 (Dec. 1884), 27-46.

Alexander, Thomas B. "Neither Peace nor War: Conditions in Tennessee in 1865." *East Tennessee Historical Society Publications* 21 (1949), 33-51.

——. "Persistent Whiggery in the Confederate South, 1860-1877." *Journal of Southern History* 27 (Aug. 1961), 305-29.

——. "Whiggery and Reconstruction in Tennessee." *Journal of Southern History* 16 (Aug. 1950), 291-305.

Bejack, L. D. "The Taxing District of Shelby County." West Tennessee Historical Society *Papers* 4 (1950), 5-27.

Brown, Campbell. "Why Capital Does Not Flow into the South." *Nation* 35 (Dec. 14, 1882), 501.

Burt, Jesse C. "James D. Porter: West Tennessean and Railroad President." West Tennessee Historical Society *Papers* 5 (1951), 79-89.

Cotterill, Robert S. "Southern Railroads, 1850-1860." *Mississippi Valley Historical Review* 10 (Mar. 1924), 396-405.

"The Defaulting State Debts." *Banker's Magazine and Statistical Register* 31 (Jan. 1877), 587-90.

Ellis, John H. "Business Leadership in Memphis Public Health Reform, 1880-1900." West Tennessee Historical Society *Papers* 19 (1965), 94-104.

Farnum, George R. "William B. Bate, Soldier of Dixie, Lawyer, and Statesman of the Union." *American Bar Association Journal* 30 (Feb. 1944), 104-5.

Feistman, Eugene G. "Radical Disfranchisement and the Restoration of Tennessee, 1865-1866." *Tennessee Historical Quarterly* 12 (June 1953), 135-51.

Godkin, E. L. "The First Step toward Repudiation." *Nation* 26 (Feb. 28, 1878), 144-45.

Hackney, Sheldon. "Origins of the New South in Retrospect." *Journal of Southern History* 38 (May 1972), 191-216.

Holland, James W. "The Building of the East Tennessee and Virginia Railroad." *East Tennessee Historical Society's Publications* 4 (1932), 83-101.

Howell, Sarah M. "The Editorials of Arthur S. Colyar, Nashville Prophet of the New South." *Tennessee Historical Quarterly* 27 (Fall, 1968), 262-76.

Hume, John F. "Responsibility for State Roguery." *North American Review* 139 (Dec. 1884), 563-79.

Judd, J. W. "The 100-3 Case." *Proceedings of the Bar Association of Tennessee* 5 (July 4, 1882), 73-78.

McCord, Franklin. "J. E. Bailey: A Gentleman of Clarksville." *Tennessee Historical Quarterly* 23 (Sept. 1964), 246-68.

McGowan, J. E. "Tennessee's State Debt." *American* 5 (Dec. 16, 1882), 153-54.

Phelan, James. "Communication." *American* 5 (Dec. 9, 1882), 142.

——. "Communication: The Tennessee Repudiation Again."

American 5 (Dec. 30, 1882), 191.

Porter, R. P. "State Debts and Repudiation." *International Review* 9 (Nov. 1880), 556-92.

Queener, Verton M. "A Decade of East Tennessee Republicanism, 1867-1876." *East Tennessee Historical Society's Publications* 14 (1942), 59-85.

————. "The East Tennessee Republicans as a Minority Party, 1870-1896." *East Tennessee Historical Society's Publications* 15 (1943), 49-73.

————. "The Origin of the Republican Party in East Tennessee." *East Tennessee Historical Society's Publications* 13 (1941), 66-90.

Sharp, J. A. "Downfall of the Radicals." *East Tennessee Historical Society's Publications* 5 (1933), 105-24.

Shepherd, S. J. "Evils of the Present System of Taxation in Tennessee." *Proceedings of the Bar Association of Tennessee* 8 (July 1889), 130-36.

Stover, John F. "Northern Financial Interests in Southern Railroads, 1865-1900." *Georgia Historical Quarterly* 39 (Sept. 1955), 205-20.

"Tennessee's Unreasonable Indignation." *Banker's Magazine and Statistical Register* 37 (Feb. 1883), 564-65.

Tollison, Grady. "Andrew J. Kellar, Memphis Republican." *West Tennessee Historical Society Papers* 16 (1962), 29-55.

Wiley, Bell I. "Vicissitudes of Early Reconstruction Farming in the Lower Mississippi Valley." *Journal of Southern History* 3 (Nov. 1937), 441-52.

Index